CRITICAL A
FOR *TRAVELE1*

D0824031

"The *Travelers' Tales* series is altogether re
> —Jan Morris, author of *Journeys*, *Locations*, and
> *Trieste and the Meaning of Nowhere*

"For the thoughtful traveler, these books are an invaluable resource.
There's nothing like them on the market."
> —Pico Iyer, author of *The Global Soul*

"This is the stuff memories can be duplicated from."
> —*Foreign Service Journal*

"I can't think of a better way to get comfortable with a destination
than by delving into *Travelers' Tales*…before reading a guidebook, before
seeing a travel agent.
> —Paul Glassman, Society of American Travel Writers

"*Travelers' Tales* is a valuable addition to any predeparture reading list."
> —Tony Wheeler, founder, Lonely Planet Publications

"*Travelers' Tales* delivers something most guidebooks only promise: a real
sense of what a country is all about.…"
> —*Hartford Courant*

"The *Travelers' Tales* series should become required reading for anyone
visiting a foreign country who wants to truly step off the tourist track
and experience another culture, another place, firsthand."
> —*St. Petersburg Times*

"If there's one thing traditional guidebooks lack, it's the really juicy travel
information, the personal stories about back alleys and brief encounters.
The *Travelers' Tales* series fills this gap with an approach that's all anecdotes,
no directions."
> —*Diversion*

Travelers' Tales Books

Country and Regional Guides
America, Australia, Brazil, Central America, Cuba, France, Greece,
India, Ireland, Italy, Japan, Mexico, Nepal, Spain, Thailand, Tibet,
Turkey; American Southwest, Grand Canyon, Hawai'i,
Hong Kong, Paris, Provence, San Francisco, Tuscany

Women's Travel
Her Fork in the Road, A Woman's Path, A Woman's
Passion for Travel, A Woman's World, Women in the Wild,
A Mother's World, Safety and Security for Women
Who Travel, Gutsy Women, Gutsy Mamas

Body & Soul
The Spiritual Gifts of Travel, The Road Within,
Love & Romance, Food, The Fearless Diner, The Adventure
of Food, The Ultimate Journey, Pilgrimage

Special Interest
Not So Funny When It Happened,
The Gift of Rivers, Shitting Pretty, Testosterone Planet,
Danger!, The Fearless Shopper, The Penny Pincher's
Passport to Luxury Travel, The Gift of Birds, Family Travel,
A Dog's World, There's No Toilet Paper on the Road
Less Traveled, The Gift of Travel, 365 Travel,
Adventures in Wine, Sand in My Bra and Other Misadventures

Footsteps
Kite Strings of the Southern Cross, The Sword of Heaven,
Storm, Take Me With You, Last Trout in Venice, The Way of
the Wanderer, One Year Off, The Fire Never Dies

Classics
The Royal Road to Romance,
Unbeaten Tracks in Japan, The Rivers Ran East,
Coast to Coast, Trader Horn

PROVENCE
and the South of France

TRUE STORIES

PROVENCE
and the South of France

TRUE STORIES

Edited by

JAMES O'REILLY AND
TARA AUSTEN WEAVER

TRAVELERS' TALES
SAN FRANCISCO

Copyright © 2003 Travelers' Tales, Inc. All rights reserved.
Introduction copyright © 2003 Richard Goodman

Travelers' Tales and *Travelers' Tales Guides* are trademarks of Travelers' Tales, Inc.

Credits and copyright notices for the individual articles in this collection are given starting on page 259.

We have made every effort to trace the ownership of all copyrighted material and to secure permission from copyright holders. In the event of any question arising as to the ownership of any material, we will be pleased to make the necessary correction in future printings. Contact Travelers' Tales, Inc., 330 Townsend Street Suite 208, San Francisco, California 94107. www.travelerstales.com

Art Direction: Michele Wetherbee
Interior design: Kathryn Heflin and Susan Bailey
Cover photograph: © Travel Pix/Taxi. Lavender fields at Senaque Abbey, Gordes, France.
Page layout: Patty Holden using the fonts Bembo and Boulevard

Distributed by: Publishers Group West, 1700 Fourth Street, Berkeley, California 94710.

Library of Congress Cataloguing-in-Publication Data

Travelers' tales Provence and the south of France: true stories / edited by
    James O'Reilly and Tara Austen Weaver.—1st ed.
        p. cm. — (Travelers' Tales guides)
    ISBN 1-885211-87-2 (pbk.)
    1. Provence (France)—Description and travel. 2. Provence (France)—Social life
and customs. I. O'Reilly, James, 1953– II. Weaver, Tara Austen. III Series.
DC611.P958 T66 2003
914.4'9504—dc21

                        2003009771

                     First Edition
               Printed in the United States
               10 9 8 7 6 5 4 3 2

...For me, upon the sea of history,
Thou wast, Provence, a pure symbol
A mirage of glory and victory,
That in the dusky flight of centuries,
Grants us a gleam of the Beautiful.

— FRÉDÉRIC MISTRAL (1830–1914)

Table of Contents

Part Two
SOME THINGS TO DO

Part Three
GOING YOUR OWN WAY

Provence: An Introduction

by Richard Goodman

It was a stone house that was big and old with many rooms and walls as thick as a fortress. We lived there for a year in a small village in a corner of Provence about an hour from Avignon. It was a lovely way to live, in a house that had been built 200 years ago, hewn out of stone found not in quarries but in the fields. It wasn't easy at first, though. The village life seemed as durable and unchanging as the house, and as mute. It was a while before the woman I loved and I could begin to fathom the rhythm of its ways. Why didn't the villagers respond to our greetings, except for the briefest answers? Why weren't they the least bit interested in us? Why didn't they accept us with open arms?

A village in Provence can be exquisite and maddening. It took time for us to see that our sojourn was merely a blink in the villagers' unwavering eyes. We did, at last, and it was the land that led us. As she and I woke up day after day to a sun-flooded room, our casement windows open to the new morning, we began to become part of Provence. We couldn't look out onto the softly undulating hills, with their legions of precisely-lined vine plants, without giving away our hearts. We couldn't smell the subtle morning air, a perfume of everything that grew there, without becoming a little more lost in love. We couldn't have our vision enhanced by the marvel of the light without wanting never to leave.

The gap between their ways and ours lessened, and that was in part due to the power of the place. We were under its sway, and so many of the things that were important to the villagers became important to us. We walked the rough little hills above the village and saw wild thyme growing. The plant is like a dwarf version of a stunted tundra tree, all twisted and leaning. It's a tough thing, difficult to cut. I began using it in my cooking. I soon found the taste is not the same as domesticated thyme. Like many wild versions of a plant or spice we know, its flavor is more subtle and quieter, and more interesting. It's a good metaphor for some of the villagers we met. They were wild thyme. Their tastes weren't revealed just by a single encounter.

No, we'd never be *paysans*—as the villagers unhesitatingly called themselves. Not farmers, peasants. They were people rooted to the land. Eventually, most everything in Provence comes back to the land. It is as basic and rooted as the thyme that grew above the village. *Pays*, the root word of *paysan*, means "country." Before you leave Provence, walk in the *maquis* or the *garrigue*, the scrub hills, full of dry wonders and simplicity. Let yourself become part of this remarkable land. Day by day, we surrendered to its spirit.

In surrender, Provence simplified our lives. That's what the place will do. Simplicity will come over anyone who stays there for even more than a few days. "Only in this sun-steeped country," Colette writes, "can a heavy table, a wicker chair, an earthenware jar crowned with flowers, and a dish whose thick enameling has run over the edge, make a complete furnishing." And we began to understand, like everyone else who has become attached to Provence, that there is no place on earth like it. No one can possibly prepare you for this consistently ethereal level of beauty. Not any book, movie, or essay. Not these words. No painting. Nowhere else do you find such a confluence of pellucid air, fierce sun, ravishing smells and tastes, and grace.

It may not be your country, but it is not altogether foreign to you, either. As M.F.K. Fisher said of her first visit to Aix-en-Provence, "I was once more in my own place, an invader of what was already mine." It may be singular, but you can become its citizen. You may feel as if you were born there, and perhaps you were.

We had a used car we had bought, scruffy and prone to seizures, but on the whole reliable. In it, we ventured near and far in the South of France and came to see much more of the land beyond our village during that year. We went to nearby Avignon first. What a shock it was to go from our little hamlet, with its stubbornly self-important ways, to a city that has had such a prominent role on the world stage! We—at least I—felt Avignon is a sad place. Even though it's on the lyrical Rhône, that magnificent water, the city has a melancholy air. Cities have lived lives, too, and when you walk them, you begin to see exactly who they have become. I think of Avignon as not at peace with itself. For that very reason, it's impossible to forget.

We drove to Aix, that exquisite town, then on to palm-lined Nice and to Menton. We went to the Gorges du Verdon in Haute Provence, Colorado in France, except that Colorado is far too young to have the ancient sense those small, high villages possess. Haute Provence, walking realm of Provence's greatest writer, Jean Giono, whose rare, dignified sensibility reflects the land and the people he loved. We drove to Apt and to old Gordes, and wound our way to its top as so many others have, rapt. We drove to Arles and to les Baux and to the Camargue, and to the moving village of Aigues Mortes, and to the gypsy enclave at St.-Marie.

We went to St.-Rémy in search of van Gogh's ghost, and then walked the sun-scorched hills nearby, the Alpilles, which he painted. We drove to Marseilles, a city as unjustly feared as New York, and that's a pity, because Marseilles is so sharply flavored and so alive. M.F.K. Fisher described the Marseilles she loved as "mysterious, unknowable," and it will haunt you and draw you back as it did her. We went to Nîmes and walked into its amphitheater and felt dread and awe at the Roman Empire. We drove to L'Isle-sur-la-Sorgue and watched trout swimming in the cool little stream and stayed in that pretty place until dusk at a table outdoors. We saw all these wonders and many more, and we continued to make forays into the heart of the heart of Provence all year.

Travelers' Tales Provence mirrors this diversity in its own wide-ranging and eclectic choice of stories. These stories waft the air of Provence your way, introducing you to just a few of the myriad characters who inhabit Provence, taking you from coast to mountain, vineyard to city, just as our own journeys did.

But no matter how far we went, we always came home to our village. To the well-wrought house that now was our home. To the simplicity and timelessness of a life that unfolded before us. We met everyone in the place, and we began to piece together their lives. We were even luckier to find work in the fields, so we experienced Provence's light and air and scents throughout the long days. The wine tasted better in our dirt-caked hands, and so did the *daube* I cooked for us when the day was through. They paid us, too, in francs, by God!

It was a privilege to go to sleep weary in our village, and to wake up with that slight feeling of regret physical labor bestows on you every morning. We had the gift of responsibility in Provence, and how much luckier can two people get? You cannot steal idle moments when everything is given to you. We were not used to the hard work, to the bending, pulling, digging and planting. We were old people for an hour every morning, but nothing in the world would have induced us to quit. We went home to lunch midday as the villagers did. We spooned our soup and devoured our bread happily with the morning's cool still hovering over us. Sundays became as precious to us as long-waited vacations. Nothing that year was sweeter than buying villagers we liked a *pastis* with money we earned working their land. If you can work in Provence, even for a single day, you should do it.

Despite the fact that we were frugal and that we worked, we could see our money dwindling. This alarmed us, and saddened us. We didn't want to leave. We wanted to stay forever. We had brought a dog with us to Provence, and in our desperation to stay longer, we hatched a plan. We decided to teach her to hunt for truffles. Dogs as well as pigs hunt for truffles in Provence, and if we could turn our Brooklyn-born stray into a truffle-finder, we'd be flush. We heard that a man had a dog in a village not far from us who could find truffles, but we never found him. We bought a jar of cheap truffles in our local supermarket—perhaps they were from Bulgaria—and made her sniff these oily black things six or seven times a day for a week. Then one day we drove her to the woods where the villagers said if there were truffles, they had to be there. We whispered in our dog's ear, "Go find truffles! Find truffles!" and let her go. She ran about, delighted. She paused at a spot near the foot of a small oak tree. Hadn't she? Perfect! We brought our shovels and began to dig.

Five holes later, truffleless, and drenched in sweat, we drove home.

So, we had to leave. We had to say goodbye to Provence, and to the village we had grown to love and that had taken root in our souls. We all have to say goodbye to Provence sooner or later, and when we come home we all spend the next months or years dreaming of the place. We dote on our memories like political exiles that long to return to the mother country. We'll talk to anyone who will listen to us about its marvels. Sooner or later, we'll come back, we know. It's just a matter of when. It might be ten years, or twelve, but we'll come back. So far,

Provence is stronger than anything we have brought to it, or done to it. Pray that never changes.

Colette's words I quoted are from her book, *Break of Day*. If you love Provence, or you are going to Provence for the first time, you must read it. The prose is as potent and sensual as those Dionysian scents distilled from Provençal flowers in Grasse. Colette had a house in St.-Tropez, and she began staying there before that fishing village was anointed by Parisians to become famous. *Break of Day* was published in 1928, but not an observation is obsolete. Her house was above the village, and she writes about gardening, the movements of the day, her animals, and the people who come and go, and the delicious sensual tastes of the place. Here, Mother Nature doesn't wear a silky dress, she walks naked. Colette writes with a pen dipped in sun, oil, sweat and salt.

"What a country!" she exclaims. "The invader endows it with villas and garages, with motorcars and dance-halls built to look like *Mas*. But during the course of the centuries how many ravishers have not fallen in love with such a captive? They arrive plotting to ruin her, stop suddenly and listen to her breathing in her sleep, and then, turning silent and respectful, they softly shut the gate in the fence. Submissive to your wishes, Provence...they have no other desire, Beauty, than to serve you and enjoy it."

Go. Submit. Surrender.

Richard Goodman is the author of French Dirt: The Story of a Garden in the South of France. *He has written on a variety of subjects for many publications, including* Saveur, The New York Times, Garden Design, Creative Nonfiction, Commonweal, Vanity Fair, Grand Tour, salon.com, *and* The Michigan Quarterly Review. *He has twice been the recipient of a MacDowell Colony residency. His work also appears in* Travelers' Tales France, Food: A Taste of the Road, *and* The Road Within.

PART ONE

ESSENCE OF PROVENCE

* * *

Aix-en-Provence

Welcome to a place that has stirred many lives.

So here is the town, founded more than two thousand years ago by the brash Roman invaders, on much older ruins which still stick up their stones and artifacts. I was as brash a newcomer to it, and yet when I first felt the rhythm of its streets and smelled its ancient smells, and listened at night to the music of its many fountains, I said, "Of course," for I was once more in my own place, an invader of what was already mine.

Depending upon one's vocabulary, it is facile enough to speak of karma or atavism or even extrasensory memory. For me, there was no need to draw on this well of casual semantics, to recognize Aix from my own invisible map of it. I already knew where I was.

I had been conditioned to this acceptance by a stay in another old town on the northward Roman road, when I was younger and perhaps more vulnerable. I lived for some time in Dijon in my twenties, and compulsively I return to it when I can, never with real gratification. And I dream occasionally of it, and while the dream-streets are not quite the same as in

waking life (the Rue de la Liberté swings to the right toward
the railroad yards instead of going fairly straight to the Place
d'Armes and the Ducal Palace, for instance, but I always know
exactly where I am going), still *I* am a remote but easy visitor,
happier as such than as a visible one.

I do not, in my imagination, feel as easy there as in Aix. I
have long since made my own map of Dijon, and it is intrin-
sic to my being, but the
one of Aix is better, a
refuge from any sounds but
its own, a harbor from any
streets but its own: great
upheavals and riots and pil-
lages and invasions and lib-
erations and all the ageless
turmoil of an old place.

I feel somewhat like a
cobweb there. I do not
bother anyone. I do not
even wisp myself across a
face, or catch in the hair of
a passerby, because I have
been there before, and will
be again, on my own map.

I can walk the same
streets, and make my own
history from them, as I
once did in a lesser but still structural way in Dijon, my first
return to the past, forever present to me.

Aix-en-Provence was very
clean; but so hot, and so
intensely light, that when I
walked out at noon it was like
coming suddenly from the
darkened room into crisp
blue fire. The air was so very
clear, that distant hills and
rocky points appeared within
an hour's walk; while the
town immediately at hand—
with a kind of blue wind
between me and it—seemed
to be white hot, and to be
throwing off a fiery air from
the surface.

—Charles Dickens (1846)

The town was put on its feet by a Roman whose elegant
bathing place still splutters out waters, tepid to hot and slightly
stinking, for a ceaseless genteel flow of ancient countesses and

their consorts and a quiet dogged procession of arthritic postal clerks and Swiss bankers and English spinsters suffering from indefinable malaises usually attributed to either their native climates or their equally native diets. This spa, more ancient than anyone who could possibly stay in it except perhaps I myself, is at the edge of the Old Town, at the head of the Cours Sextius, and more than one good writer has generated his own acid to etch its strange watery attraction.

Countless poems have been written too, in wine rather than acid and countless pictures have been painted, about the healing waters and the ever-flowing fountains of the place. They will continue as long as does man, and the delicate iron balconies will cling to the rose-yellow walls, and if anyone else, from 200 B.C. to now, ever marked the same places on the map, in acid or wine or even tears, his reasons would not be mine. That is why Aix is what it is.

Mary Francis Kennedy (M.F.K.) Fisher was widely regarded in the middle of the twentieth century as the finest writer of prose in America. She said that her chief responsibility as a writer was "to write the good and pleasing sentence." Of her many works, some of her better known are: Long Ago in France; Consider the Oyster; The Gastronomical Me; An Alphabet for Gourmets; *and* Serve Forth. *This story was excerpted from her book,* Two Towns in Provence. *She died in 1992.*

✦ ✦ ✦

The Dangers of Provence

The author offers a warning label for the good life.

NONE OF US THESE DAYS CAN ESCAPE THOSE SMALL, BRIGHTLY colored and infinitely alluring scraps of propaganda that our more fortunate friends send us when they're on vacation and we're not. Nothing provokes envy and Monday morning gloom faster than a postcard. And when that postcard is from Provence, slightly wine-stained, redolent with heat and sunlight and tranquility, it is probably enough to make you kick the cat as you leave to go to the office.

All, however, is not what it seems. Beneath that implausibly blue sky, a number of surprises—never even hinted at in the photograph of the picturesque village or the genial lavender-cutter—lie in wait for the innocent visitor. I believe I've experienced most of them, and these words of caution are the result of personal and occasionally painful research. Be warned. If you venture to Provence, you will encounter some, if not all, of the following local specialties.

Provence has been accurately described as a cold country with more than its fair share of sunshine, and the climate can't seem to make up its mind whether to imitate Alaska or the Sahara. There were days during our first winter when the temperature fell to 15 degrees Fahrenheit; in summer, it can stay at 85-plus for week after rainless week. The local zephyr is the mistral, which has been known to blow at 110 miles an hour, taking hats, spectacles, roof tiles, open shutters, old ladies, and small unsecured animals with it. And there are storms of quite spectacular violence. It is the meteorological equivalent of a meal consisting of curry and ice cream.

Your first few hours on the roads of Provence will not be dull. The Provençal motorist, brimming with élan, impatience, and sometimes, it must be said, with half a liter of good red wine, regards driving in much the same way that a matador looks on his encounters with a bull—that is, as a challenge to come as close to catastrophe as possible without incurring physical damage. And so you will find, to your alarm, that cars appear to be glued to your exhaust pipe until a sufficiently perilous moment to overtake you presents itself. This will be achieved with centimeters to spare on a blind bend, while the driver conducts a spirited conversation with his passenger that requires at least one hand being off the wheel. (Conversation in Provence cannot take place without manual assistance.) The mistake made by most visitors is to give in to natural impulses and close the eyes as certain disaster looms. If you can resist that, you will probably survive.

The Provençal attitude toward time is that there is plenty of it. If by chance you should run out of it today, more will be available tomorrow. Or the day after. Or next week.

This admirably relaxed state of mind is, of course, at odds with the curious habit that many visitors bring with them from Paris or London or New York: the exotic concept of punctuality. It's not that this is ignored. Indeed, the important matter of the next rendezvous is often discussed seriously and at great length over two or three drinks. But somehow the arrangement is never quite as precise as you might expect. A day—let's say Tuesday—will be agreed upon with much emphatic nodding. This encourages you to suggest that a time on Tuesday should be fixed, and here you begin to sense a certain amiable but firm disinclination to pin down the rendezvous to anything more exact than a tentative commitment to either the morning or the afternoon. As it turns out, even this is optimistic, since nobody comes until Friday. Excuses are performed by the shoulders. Elsewhere in the world, patience is a virtue. In Provence, it's a necessity.

There have been many occasions when a five-minute chat with a Provençal friend has left me feeling as though I've undergone a course of brisk exploratory surgery. Apart from the obligatory mangling handshake—or, with the opposite sex, the double or triple kiss—there is the vigorous kneading of the shoulder, the attack on the breastbone by the tapping of an iron index finger, the friendly clap around the kidneys, the odd glancing blow from the knuckles of a gesticulating hand, and the tweak administered to the cheek by way of a fond farewell.

In other words, conversation is more than a mere exchange of words. It is a bruising physical encounter with a human windmill. One is invited and expected to drink. Provence is awash with locally produced wine, from the modest *ordinaire* to the grand and heady vintages of Chateauneuf-du-Pape, and it would be impolite and unadventurous not to try as many of them as your liver can stand. There are, however, two alcoholic booby traps that should be approached with extreme caution.

The first is *vin rosé*. It may be a pale, smoky pink, or a deeper tint not unlike the blush of a grog-blossom nose, and it looks light, frivolous, and harmless. It tastes delicious, crisp and chilled, the perfect drink for a blinding hot day. You reach for another glass (or another bottle, as the first one slipped down so pleasantly) and congratulate yourself on avoiding anything too heavy. This is a mistake, since many rosés contain as much as 13 percent alcohol. This, combined with an hour or two in the after-lunch sun, can produce a truly epic hangover.

And then there is pastis, by far the most popular aperitif in Provence. The taste is clean and sharp and refreshing, exactly what one needs to settle the dust and stimulate the palate after a hectic morning in the market. There is no immediate jolt, as the alcohol is masked by the other ingredients, and it is insidiously easy to drink. Only later, when you try unsuccessfully to walk to lunch in a straight line, do you feel the effects of this delightful Provençal invention.

A house in Provence, whether you own it or rent it, is a magnet. No sooner are you installed, in what you hoped would be a blissful seclusion, than the

> The Provençal is all alive, and feels his nerves agitated in a supreme degree by accidents and objects that would scarce move a muscle or a feature in the phlegmatic natives of more northern climes; his spirits are flurried by the slightest sensations of pleasure or of pain, and seem always on the watch to seize the transient impressions of either; but to balance this destructive propensity, nature has wisely rendered it difficult for those impressions to sink into their souls; they easily receive, but as easily discard and forget, thus daily offering a surface smoothed afresh for new pains and pleasures to trace their light affections upon.
>
> —Henry Swinburne
> (1752–1803)

phone calls begin. They are from friends, or friends of friends, who are concerned that you might be lonely or bored. By chance, they find themselves free to come down, cheer you up, and entertain you.

What a noble sacrifice! They have made the journey from some distant rain-sodden paradise in the north just to be with you, to share the discomforts of your bucolic existence—the sun, the pool, the endless racket of corks coming out of bottles, the siestas. And their stamina is quite extraordinary. Despite third-degree sunburn, gastric disorders (always blamed on the local water, never the local wine), lack of television, mercilessly long meals, and all the other shortcomings of the simple life, they bravely soldier on. And on. And on. A weekend visit stretches to a week, and then ten days, or longer. One hero arrived in October and was still with us on New Year's Eve, only leaving when the builders came to knock down his bedroom wall.

And still they come, from Easter until Christmas, willing to endure anything that man and nature can throw at them in Provence. I suppose that, like me, they're gluttons for punishment.

Former British ad man Peter Mayle has made a career out of living in the South of France and writing books about it, including the bestseller A Year in Provence. *His eighth book, from which this story was excerpted, is* French Lessons: Adventures with Knife, Fork, and Corkscrew. *Mayle lives with his wife and their two dogs. His hobbies include walking, reading, writing, and lunch.*

FRANCESCA RHEANNON

The Shepherd's Mantra

He didn't mean to be a teacher, but he was.

I HESITATED TO SAY IT BEFORE—THINKING THAT PERHAPS I was being deceived by a late January winter thaw—but, no, spring has arrived. I have been ensconced in this corner of Provence since September, not the gentle, sybaritic Provence of the Côte d'Azur and Avignon, but Haute Provence, a rude and wild country, where the dark alpine hills stream like a school of humpback whales toward the distant shores of the Mediterranean and sheep and lavender share the land. The wind is fierce, the people few, the soil stony. I was quickly snared by the region's stark enchantment.

For the past week, the weather has been glorious. Warm, sunny—even when the mistral blows it has lost its winter bite. Today the sky is hazed over with a thin film of white so I decide to take advantage of the weather before it changes. I start off in the direction of Lardiers, with ambitious plans to hike the three miles to that neighboring commune. But, five minutes into my walk, I get waylaid. I hear the bells of sheep, a seductive sound, archaic and wistful, and immediately a net

11

of tranquility settles over me. I look across the narrow valley and there, splayed out over the hillside, undulates an intricate pattern of wooly shapes, a school of sheep-fish grazing in the deeps of the meadow. The colors of their barrel-like bodies mimic the duns of their winter forage: tans, yellows, and browns, offset by the lighter stick legs flickering underneath as they munch and move.

The shepherd reclines on the earth, propped on one elbow, facing away from me. I steal up behind him to get a closer look and then remain standing some one hundred meters away, watching, for perhaps thirty minutes. I have been puzzling over the shepherds around here for some time. They spend all day, every day, out with their sheep and their dogs, wandering the hills and dales of the region. When I pass them on my hikes, they respond to my "*bonjour*" with a warm glance of greeting flashing from their eyes, but no word passes their lips. Perhaps they have lost the knack of human speech, I wonder, fallen into disuse during the days and years of solitary roaming. (Later, my friend Génia tells me that for many years she walked the hills with an old Andalusian shepherd who joked to her that he only spoke "Sheep.")

What do they do to keep from getting bored, I have wondered, out there with their charges? They don't have earphones peeking out from under their caps, no radios that I can see or hear. I never see them carrying any books or magazines. They are always just there with their crooks and their dogs and the sheep. Now, observing my subject as he goes about his business, I see what shepherds do to keep themselves from getting bored: they watch sheep. Intently. With the same one-pointed absorption as his dog, the shepherd is attuned to every shift and shudder in the massed animals before him. There is a force field out there, palpable, that is composed of man–dog–sheep; it is not only the herd that acts as one organism, but the whole triad.

The shepherd calls out something. At first, I think he is talking to his sheep, and they seem to be answering him with a chorus of bleats. One group strikes up the tune, then another on the other side of the herd, then another, as a wave of *ba-a-as* sweeps through them. The shepherd mimics them playfully. He *ba-a-as*; they *ba-a-a* back. Then he laughs.

A stream of sheep begins to pour into the adjacent meadow, and I notice the swift black shape of the dog glancing along the edges of the herd. The troop swirls in a muttonish ballet. The shepherd calls out another command as one small group of rebels begins to move in the opposite direction. The dog streaks to the left, neatening up the borders of the herd as he goes. But, caught up in the excitement of the game, he gets a bit over-zealous. The sheep, pressed, start to become agitated. It only lasts a second, for the shepherd sings out a warning to the dog, who drops back immediately. Then "*à droit!*" and the dog streaks to the right where the front flank of the herd is beginning to spread out raggedly toward a lavender field. "*Arrête!*" And the dog drops to the ground like a stone between two wintry rows of lavender bushes. Then man and dog go back to a watchful stillness.

The minutes stretch out as I stand, transfixed, waiting. It occurs to me that while it looks like nothing is happening, something is going on all the time: observation and action are

The Provençal language… is a most disagreeable jargon, as unintelligible even to those who understand French as to those who do not, and delighting in intonations of the voice, which always reminded me of a crying child.

—Charles Lewis Meryon,
Travels with Lady Hester Stanhope (1846)

seamless. The shepherd spends his days in meditation; sheep are his mantra.

As I move off finally, I notice a pile of dead lavender wood lying at the edges of the adjacent field. It contains a resin that makes for excellent tinder, so, my hike forgotten, I return home to snatch a bag to carry my find back to the wood stove. As I walk, I ponder the life of a shepherd, my thoughts tinged with envy and admiration. Its timelessness and tranquility lure me, although I know that I am irrevocably time-bound in the modern world. "He lived a life of husbandry and liberty, inhabitant and hermit, half sage, half sorcerer, always poet…" Is it merely coincidence when the next day I pick up a book about Provence in the home of a friend and find this description of a shepherd?

A few weeks later, I take a walk in the high hills above Banon with a friend who is a visiting nurse. She tells me the story of an old shepherd who lived all alone in an ancient stone hut on the top of a mountain until well into his eighties. There, without electricity or running water, heating his little home with an old wood stove, he lived in utter contentment. One day, on one of her appointed nursely rounds to see the old man, she asked him if he ever missed having a television. "If they would show sheep on the TV, I would buy one," he answered. Then she asked him what was the happiest moment of his life. "It was night, there was the moon, and I was with my sheep," was his reply.

When I return to the lavender field, I see that the sheep are swarming homeward, a seemingly endless line stretching along the contours of the landscape, bells tinkling in the deepening afternoon light. The black silhouette of the dog stands sentinel alongside in the dip of a narrow valley. I look for the shepherd, but he seems to have vanished. Then, out of the bushes, I see him moving toward me, staff in hand, his sun- and wind-brown face visible now under his broad-brimmed hat, his jacket slung around his shoulders like a cape. It is a figure out of the Middle Ages, or older, ancient and beautiful. With a nod of acknowledgment, we move off, each to our own direction.

Francesca Rheannon is a teacher and writer. She is an avid randonneur *(hiker), which recently took her to the remote Alps of Haute Provence for nine months. A few weeks after September 11, 2001, she embarked on this long-scheduled trip to France to write a book. Too much in shock from the terrible events of that day, she found herself unable to work on her original book. So she began a memoir of her sojourn in Provence.* "The Shepherd's Mantra" *is an excerpt from that journal. She lives in Massachusetts.*

⁎

Provençal Dawn

Get out of bed and get ahead!

THE BEST WAY TO STRIKE UP AN ACQUAINTANCE WITH Provençal towns is to arrive around daybreak, preferably on a market day when the place is full of sleepy vendors unloading their vans and trucks of everything you can imagine, from pigeons and hams to olives and plums. The whole town seems to be stretching and yawning and waiting for the sunrise to warm it up. Only the early morning bistros are open but there is many a lesson to be learned, for the market people are specialists in the early morning nip—a swift stab of some neat alcohol to set the wheels of commerce turning. In the smoking bistro you will observe certain elderly traders who greet the dawn with a classic glass of marc or cherry brandy or port or a *canon* of red wine. Perhaps others will only settle for a caressing dose of Armagnac or pepper vodka…. In my own case I recall a visit with Jérôme which was made memorable by the discovery of a singular drink called Arquebuse, which he claimed was harmless yet agreeable. I was given a full wine glass of this product which looked like vodka or gin. The morning was a trifle cool. I somewhat imprudently drained the glass. When I picked myself up off the floor I asked politely if I might examine the bottle in which this prodigious fire-water was delivered to the world. The letterpress which accompanied the drink was highly suggestive. It informed me that what I had just tasted was not an alcohol but, strictly speaking, a "vulnerary," which had been invented in the Middle Ages for use on the battle-fields. The recent invention of the Arquebuse had had a marked effect on warfare, causing a new type of flesh wound, more grievous than the arrow wounds known in the past. The doctors of the day welcomed the invention of this stanching and cleansing "vulnerary." But at some point (the bottle does not say when or how) somebody must have sucked his bandage, and

> If one closed one's eyes and only smelled, Provence seemed heavenly and entirely one's own in spite of its celebrity or pilgrimage status as a gourmet and cultural mecca. The senses are redeemed in Provence and Provence is saved from both hype and cliché by the senses.
>
> —Joan Haladay,
> "The Perfect Meal"

from then on there was no looking back; Arquebuse found its place among the more powerful firewaters available to man, ordinary man, and indeed a comfort to all humanity. It appears to be a specific for everything except receding hair, and I know a number of people who swear by it, and always keep a bottle in the larder in order to save lives when need be. This is the kind of information one gathers if one gets up early enough and arrives with the first dawn light in a Provençal town.

Another occasion, which I found somewhat unexpected and disconcerting, but which seemed rather typical of meridional procedures, turns upon the enigmatic behaviors of an introspective-looking individual sitting alone in a secluded corner of a popular bistro. The waiter began a prolonged handout of free doses of Armagnac to all and sundry—a most welcome act of generosity on a chilly morning. Moreover, no sooner was one glass emptied than another appeared in its place and it was clear that if we were not careful we would be in for a prolonged binge. I had, of course, read all about meridional hospitality to strangers, and dutifully toasted my host by raising my glass before draining it. But when the second glass appeared and it became clear that there would be more to follow, I became intrigued enough to wonder what he could be celebrating in such exemplary fashion. (I adore Armagnac, but I was also at the wheel of the car that day.) I could not resist asking the waiter who the gentleman in the corner was, and what he was celebrating. "Has he won the lottery or broken the bank at the casino?" The waiter shook his head and said, "Much better than that. He has been a martyr for years to a most persistent tapeworm. He has tried everything without avail. But today the head came away and he passed it. *Ça se fête, n'est-ce pas?*"

Lawrence Durrell was one of the greatest novelists of the twentieth century. Born in India, Durrell lived in and celebrated the Mediterranean world, not only as a novelist but also as an acclaimed poet, travel writer, essayist, dramatist, and humorist. Among his many and varied works are the novel The Revolt of Aphrodite *and those of* The Alexandria Quartet, *as well as the travel books* Prospero's Cell, Bitter Lemons, *and* Provence, *from which this story was excerpted. Lawrence Durrell died in 1990.*

* * *

The Baker

He has a loaf waiting just for you.

"SO WHAT'S THE BOULDER FOR?" THE ROLE OF THE BIG ROCK on the floor near the wood-fired oven had so far puzzled me. In Georges's country bakery on the Luberon plain, everything looked as though it had been handmade by gnomes in the seventeenth century, and had been bashed about by demented Provençal bakers ever since. Why would you need a rock the size of your head in a bakery?

"*Eh bien, regardes*," he advised me with a wink, so I remained attentive as he stood there in his flapping shorts and frayed tank top, leaning against the counter shelf in front of the black iron door to the hot oven, keeping one sly eye on my companions, the other on the lumps of dough he'd just deftly slit, dusted with flour, and slid into the huge domed oven for transformation. The sight of him periodically holding the scoring razor between his bare lips while he worked had silently raised a few eyebrows and possibly a *frisson* or two.

I'd brought him a small group of fellow American food enthusiasts, or foodies, arriving before dawn to witness the

ancient ritual of flour, water, and yeast becoming bread, the
staff of life. It was strictly a happy coincidence for Georges that
there were a couple of comely gals among us. Georges still did
his baking the old way, kept very odd hours, sweating alone in
his brief costume in the bakery behind his house in the valley
below Bonnieux. I'd first met him at the weekly village market,
at his stand, selling beautiful brown loaves, wearing a hat over
his smooth head to shade his laughing eyes, enjoying the girls
in their clingy summer dresses pass by in the blazing sunlight.
Whenever I was in Provence, I'd stop to chat with him, buy a
loaf or two of his glorious wares for my habitual afternoon
picnic, and one day when I saw him behind his market stall, I
summoned the courage to ask if we could visit some time to
see him work. Who will you bring, he wondered aloud, his
eyes undistracted from the sight of the derrière of his neighbor's young wife as she bent over to set out another crate of
tomatoes. Oh, some Americans, I replied. Fine, he said, how
about tomorrow? It was a deal.

The first thing caught in our headlights when I pulled the
van up to the little compound of house, bakery, and tool shed,
still in the pre-dawn darkness, was the huge pile of black
uprooted vine stocks, all twisted and gnarled like a Van Gogh
nightmare, stacked as high as a barn. He later explained that he
has a standing request to be telephoned whenever a vintner is
ripping out old vines. Georges then summons a band of buddies, their assorted trucks, vans, and battered *camionettes* to
make the run out to the vineyard in question and pick up as
many dead vines as were available, convoy back to the bakery
and, primed with strong coffee and pastis, fling them onto the
pile behind the oven building, and *voilà*, fuel for the fires
Georges builds in his oven, every day of the week, nine
months of the year.

We skittered in the cold dark from the van to the one light

we saw, over the entrance to the bakery. It was warm inside, even hot after a while. We were soon peeling off sweatshirts, scarves, and jackets. Georges had begun sizing up his visitors the instant we came in, trying to determine who spoke a few words of French, who could follow his drift, who didn't wear a pesky wedding ring, who looked frisky and fun.

To him, he conceded, the words of my companions sounded romantic, musical, appealing—but always completely unintelligible. Georges doesn't know one word that isn't French. But he is ever attentive to body language, and I feared I was unwittingly participating in some kind of teasing dance, as he answered our queries with as many naughty puns for me to translate as possible. The word he uses to describe his bread was a new one to me, something not quite the usual word for "organic" and we wondered why. It transpires that to be certified organic, you have to pay a fee and have somebody come inspect your practices. Georges does not relish the thought of lining the pockets of bureaucrats to take a look at his... ahem...private habits. Oh, sure, he buys his flour from the mill down the road a few miles, and he knows which of his farmer pals send their grain there. He knows they raise their crops without pesticides (which you would have to pay money for in a store!) and that they are all-natural beautiful grains, heaven forbid! never grown from genetically modified seed churned out by unconscionable dolts in a distant laboratory. Hah! Only an American lady who hasn't experienced the uh, real thing... would ask that kind of question. Maybe other bakers are willing to shell out for the official "organic" certification, but not Georges. So he calls his bread *hihobiologique*, or "hihorganic" which has the added advantage of sounding like an ass braying and hyper-organic at the same time.

Georges answers to a higher authority, one of his own creation, being from what in France is known as the generation of '68, the year students and others took to the streets of Paris to revolt against authority, injustice, and lock-step mentality in all its many guises. Georges and I are the same age, as it turns out, though as a young woman I was more into peace, love, and a flower behind my ear than throwing cobblestones at *les flics*. Thirty-plus years later, he's on a mission to preserve his pre-French Revolution stone oven, and to provide his customers with a wholesome loaf every day. Even if he rarely sleeps more than two hours at a stretch. Even if he has to home deliver the occasional loaf to a shut-in or aged granny with hopeless legs. And if he can enjoy some *amour* from *les mademoiselles* along the way, well then, *la vie est belle*.

There is nobody to follow him in the business. Young people, he says, don't want to work this hard for so little money. After Georges bakes, he leaves by the door a small stash of loaves for his regulars to come pick up, plus a bit more, and takes the rest of his product to one of several colorful open-air Provençal markets where it is snatched up by those in the know. None of his doors have locks. There's a handwritten sign in the bakery that says, "Take what you like, leave me the money, and enjoy." The youth of France would find such practices laughable, he says, especially in light of the long hours and the scant

> I recall innumerable drives I have made, by ancient crumbling roadside walls, past hillsides of purple and green, on tiny winding cobbled roads that lead into sun-baked town squares bordered by the herb-seller and the *fromagerie*, the *boulangerie*, and the patisserie. At the last you stop to buy bread and it is always brown and crusty and when you break it in half the smell of the earth fills your nostrils.
> — Don George,
> "My Private Riviera"

remuneration a hundred loaves a day might bring. Georges is proud of his work, and understandably so, living the naturally honest life of a good man who's found his calling. The carousing part is of course just for fun. It's only natural, he says. Georges is nothing if not natural and good.

Presently, Georges spins around, sensing the exact moment that he should spring into action. He sets up a creaky old misshapen bread crib to receive the morning's bounty, on the floor right in front of the oven opening, making one end of the rolling crib higher by propping it up with the ancient boulder—aha!—giving it just the right angle so he can sweep each long loaf out of the huge oven with his formidable twelve-foot baker's peel. Seeing him slice and shove the giant spatula into the deep oven in quick jerks and pokes, we all press against the sides of the room to avoid being bashed by its handle. Each loaf is swished and slid into the crib just so, stacked up, all pointing at the same precise angle which doesn't allow for any to slide down sideways. Once the last loaf is in, fitting exactly, Georges kicks away the boulder in a time-honored tradition of efficiency, his one swift gesture setting it perfectly back in its usual spot beside the oven.

We buy more bread, croissants, and *pains au chocolat* than we should, entirely seduced by the yeasty aroma of hot bread and pastry, silly jokes, and the giddiness of being up and about before daylight. Georges and I exchange the customary three-cheek goodbye kisses and my little troop heads back into the chilly twilight. As we are getting into the van, I look back to wave a last goodbye. Is someone standing in the doorway with Georges? Is it Jennifer? Good lord, are they kissing?

Connie Barney Wilson is a Californian happily married to an Englishman despite the culinary traditions of his homeland. Together, they lead food and wine tours for their company, Provence on Your

Plate, for people who either like to eat, cook, or watch people eat and cook. An optimist to the end, Connie is looking for an affordable wisteria-covered stone cottage in the Luberon.

CLIVE IRVING

✦ ✦ ✦

Relish the Rhône

It's worth getting to know the
"alimentary canal of France."

IT BEGAN WITH A FURTIVE RATTLING OF THE WINDOW shutters and a faint howling around the medieval casements. Night sounds where there had been many night sounds through the ages. By morning the howling was incessant. I pushed open the shutters against the forcefully resistant wind. Fifty feet away, in the ruins of an ancient chapel, its nave open to the sky, the trapped wind sucked up white powdered stone and took on the form of an incubus driven mad with the constraint.

This was a pervasive, inhabiting wind. It raged across the hill above, tearing into freshly bloomed cascades of yellow broom so that the color writhed. Cypresses, the most exposed of the trees, flexed acutely in the line of the wind. They signaled its direction—and identity. The intruder came from the north, sucked down the great valley of the Rhône and into Provence like a jet stream. This was the mistral.

The evening before had been different, a foretaste of summer in a backwater of southern France called Drôme-Provençal. I had followed a minor tributary of the Rhône, the

Jabron, into a valley and to a medieval village called Le Poët-Laval. There, on a hillside, I found a commandery originally built by those ardent Christian hosts, the Knights of Malta, in the fourteenth century. The commandery is now a hotel, Les Hospitaliers. Dinner on the terrace overlooking the Jabron Valley had been serene. A light, warm breeze wafted up its scents: lavender, lime (the *tilleul*, whose fresh blossoms are locally dried for use in a soothing herb tea), broom, and even the ripe cherries that hung heavy in the orchards below.

Then came the mistral to remind us that Mother Nature can be a spoiler, too.

My memory of the mistral was of something warmer and more congenial. It had been many years earlier in the crucible of the southern Midi, at Carcassonne. Then the wind had been at my back, urging me on to Spain while it remained domiciled in France. With enduring luck, I had never felt it again.

Until now. The concierge at Les Hospitaliers admitted that it was unusually late in the spring for the mistral to strike, and offered with mathematical certainty that it would last for either three, six, or nine days.

I checked with a more scientific source. A mistral is generated when two vast rotations of pressure converge: high pressure over the mountains and plateaus west of the Rhône and, to the east, a low-pressure storm system over the Alps and northern Italy. The Rhône Valley acts as a funnel between these two systems, drawing down cold, desiccating air from the Alps. The wind can be miles high, and it gathers force as it roars toward its nemesis, the Mediterranean.

I could see one effect immediately. The sky was rinsed clean of haze. This produced a stark, intense light that seemed to curb or even eradicate shadows. Where there was shade it was suddenly chill. This polarization of light and temperature driven by violence was, I suddenly realized, very familiar—it invests the final landscapes of Vincent van Gogh.

A few days later, in the remnants of the Plaine de la Crau southeast of Arles, with the mistral tearing across the last fields before the sea and the cut grasses as yellow as corn, I was looking at van Gogh's palette, needing only art to intervene. Van Gogh's derangement, whatever its cause, must have embraced the whiplashed intensity of light as soul mate.

The blaze of colors he found when he arrived in Provence was not inert, and his olive trees have the gnarled ligaments that come from fighting the mistral year after year.

The mistral is a living force, blowing grit in your face and perspective into your vision. It shapes the lands of the Rhône as profoundly as history. Often, it drove people to extremes. On an exposed and isolated hunk of rock at Grignan, near Montélimar, is a castle made famous because it was home to Marie de Rabutin-Chantal, who, as

...The mistral hurricane
Is still blowing. The trees, greeting it
With groans, bend and shake
As if to tear themselves from their trunks. The wind
Holds back the Rhône, become smooth as a mirror.
Against water and wind the strong teams,
Nose down, march northward
With a regular step. Like a mighty bagpipe,
The resounding storm astounds the animals
And makes them prick up their ears.
The exasperated waggoners raise their hands
To their hats and plush caps,
And, with lips awry, let fly against the mistral
A torrent of full-mouthed oaths...

—Frédéric Mistral
(1830–1914)

Mme. de Sévigné, bequethed a classic of French literature, the acutely observed letters she wrote to her daughter Françoise-Marguerite recounting seventeenth-century court life. Snuckered into the bowels of the castle is a glorious church, the Eglise de St.-Sauveur—located here precisely to gain shelter from the mistral. I found Grignan a bleak and grim place, causing me to wonder whether Mme. de Sévigné wasn't really a closet masochist disguising her vice with ripe accounts of the local food. Pellets of gravel lashed at me as I composed this thought—hurled by the mistral, but also, possibly, by the lady's ghost....

Midway between the two exits for Montélimar on the A7 there is a sign, not to a place but to an idea: LE PORT DU SOLEIL. Two years ago, when I was driving to Provence on a gray fall day, the sun had actually broken through at precisely this point. A lateral valley cuts its way to the Rhône from the east, and high wooded ridges tail back toward the Alps. Today, a corona of heat fringed the ridges, the blue of a flame. The flame of Provincia Romana.

It would be wrong to accept the Romans as the sole sensual zeitgeist of Provence, despite their many physical remnants. It's more a wider Mediterranean atmosphere, with its off blend of lusts and enervation, that permeates the Rhône's southern flanks. The Greeks probably gave the river its root name, Rhodanos. Celts and tribes from northern Italy preceded them. The Roman machine, once it rolled in during the last century B.C., found much to its taste, access to plentiful wine being one. The legions were as susceptible to the natural assets as we are; Caesar sent his worn-out veterans, layered with scars from bleak and distant garrisons, to enjoy their twilight years in Provence. The Roman spine was, over the decades, helped on the way to its decay by the good life encountered in the Rhône delta.

Now the colonizing legions are Peter Mayle-inspired house hunters. The Provençal fantasy has seeped from the coast northward to the Lubéron. I gave these pastures a wide berth, heading instead for Drôme-Provençal, a regional label that was new to me. The department of the Drôme, with its capital in Valence and named after a tributary of the Rhône, has been left untouched by fantasy marketing; it's just another place on the left as you zoom south. I had briefly touched its northern border, the sheer-walled valley of the Isère River leading to Grenoble and the Alpine ski resorts. This southern flank, with its commingling of Mediterranean and Alpine light, is a borderland, regardless of departmental maps—the deeper I went into it, the more independently physical its identity became.

The road following the Jabron River was suddenly squeezed into a defile. The Montagne du Poët, nearly three thousand feet high, descended in a series of densely wooded spines from the north, and from miles away, in the dark skirts of the mountain, I saw the limestone turrets of medieval Le Poët-Laval, the only reflectors of the southern sun. The Knights of Malta must have chosen this site with care, spiritually aligned with the light they emanated from.

Les Hospitaliers is still a sanctuary. A small pool has been built into the ramparts without softening the commandery's severe outer fabric: The comforts are all within, including a series of small dining rooms with bare stone walls.

On my first evening these were empty. Dinner was served on a terrace under almond trees. In the long June twilight the valley below slowly dissolved into a shroud of river mist.

The nearest town, Dieulefit, showed no sign of creeping Mayleism. In the main square a friendly, plain bar, the Brasserie du Levant, was clearly the close kin of its namesake in the 1914 Baedeker I use to check lineage, and it faced a wonderful relic of old France, a Grands Magasins spelled out in the original Deco type—a nickel-and-dime emporium layered in junk and bare essentials. In a classic avenue of plane trees, men played boules without the histrionics you see closer to the Mediterranean.

Was I hallucinating? I seemed to be in a lost France of those Clouzot movies with the young Signoret or Montand. What would the right date be? I settled for 1957; it felt right but needed authentication.

This came soon enough. I went south and farther into the mountains, into an area known as Les Baronnies. The name lingered from three medieval baronies that ruled there and, more to the point of my mission, this was also a source of one of the Rhône's tributaries, the Ouvèze, noted for its trout. The river and the roads snake into valleys where all urgency dissipates. Slopes carpeted in broom, lavender, myrtle, and other colors I didn't recognize followed the river, but the higher reaches were wind-scoured bare with lime leeching like melting snowcaps. Mont Ventoux, a limestone massif more than six thousand feet high, blocked off the south.

The Ouvèze waters an enchanting town, Buis-les-Baronnies. A corridor of plane trees, planted in 1811 as a gift from Napoleon to celebrate the birth of his son, follows the river into the town square. It was market day. Lavender, scented soaps, honey, and lime flowers mingled with olives, pears, apricots, cherries, and sausages and charcuterie on the stalls alongside a cool fifteenth-century arcade. And it was here, in a restaurant called La Fourchette, that 1957 became edible.

Always eat where the market people eat is an infallible rule. In La Fourchette they were lapping up the three-course menu. I had a charcuterie plate, piquant hams and sausages; a grilled trout so fresh it must have leaped straight from the Ouvèze to the plate; a pear poached in red wine to the consistency of aromatic jelly; and a young, greenish chardonnay, a *vin du pays* Baronnies. A dozen or so tables were served, single-handedly and charmingly, by the patron's wife. The patron was, of course, cooking. Another of the minor miracles of France.

Later, tracking the Ouvèze upstream into the lengthening shadows of Mont Ventoux, the weather turned as Spielberg would have directed after such a time warp: weirdly oppressive. Les Baronnies are locked in their own densely bucolic theater with an occasional, really mad flourish like the church at Peirrelongue, which was built atop a sugar-loaf rock with no space to spare. The ripeness of the land fuses with stagnant, heavy air and erodes the will. Breaking free of it was a relief. But at Les Hospitaliers that evening the air had a new mischief. Diners retreated from the terrace. There was a sound in the trees like water on a reef.

The mistral, defying the triserial predictions, raged for four days. Then I began to understand better its imprint on the land, how cultivation had been defensive: cypresses used as screens for vulnerable crops, walled gardens for early-budding flowers, villages built into the wind's lee on southern slopes, with narrow streets walled off at the perimeter. Because this was a late mistral, it caught the fields of lavender and lavandin (a less fragrant hybrid) as they were coming into color and created effects of strange beauty, whole hillsides liquid in waves of color. Some lavender is grown on gravel in rows, like vines, and these fields danced like woven robes.

Leaving the valleys and heading farther south brought no relief. The Rhône Valley loses definition in the plains south of Orange, with the massifs folding back, leaving only a few sawtoothed spurs in the path of the wind. The mistral is released with renewed force. A vestigial limestone shard of the

Lubéron range called Les Alpilles, which seems to have been detached bodily and blown toward the sea, lies immediately south of St.-Rémy. It's a beguiling optical illusion, since it seems more massive than it actually is—its highest peak is only 1,312 feet.

On a spur of Les Alpilles is Les Baux, a source of legends as romantic as those of the Arthurian court. For a while from the eleventh century, the lords of Baux dominated the Rhône delta, but the surviving shell of their fortress, the Eagles' Nest, doesn't seem martial; instead, you feel the aura of the medieval voluptuaries who turned it into a love nest. During a pacific interlude in the thirteenth century, troubadours courted a ménage of beauties culled from the noble families of the south. They lived a kind of pre-Pre-Raphaelite idyll paced by lutes and poems, broken eventually by civil wars and religious repression. On the heights the mistral was an abrasive reminder of Les Baux's fall. A contest of spirits arose in the wind:

★

"Close your eyes," Laurent commanded as we drove east toward the walled city of Avignon. Then, "Open them," and I caught my first sight of the Palace of the Popes soaring upward beyond its protective walls. With the late afternoon sun playing on spires and turrets, it looked like an illustration for a child's book of fairytales.

We were crossing the Rhône River on the Pont Daladier. To our left, Laurent pointed out the Pont d'Avignon, which jutted part way into the river, then stopped abruptly. With characteristic gusto he launched into the children's melody, *"Sur le Pont d'Avignon..."* When I joined him in snatches, he shot me an approving glance, dark eyebrows raised, a smile spread across his handsome features.

—Joyce Gregory Wyels,
"Postcards from Provence"

the lashing northern air, carbolic, like Switzerland, pitted against the whole amorous embrace of the south.

But the south held out. Below Les Baux lies the exquisite and perfectly formed St.-Rémy. The Provençal gift for distilling pleasurable oils, juices, and scents, as though making manifest a spirit in the earth itself, is here in concentration. The ancient inner town, well insulated from the mistral, is a warren of delectables. Cottage-size restaurants, patisseries, charcuteries, and herbalists retain an artisanal eye over quality and presentation. The one problem is intrusive cars, driven with Gallic temper through alleys seldom wider than the vehicle—if ever a whole town would be made into a pedestrian precinct, this is it.

On the western edge of the old town, on the site of the medieval ramparts, the Place de la République is even more exposed to traffic, but it also has the best bars. I began to devise a new category: bars out of reach of the mistral. The Brasserie du Commerce, on the northeast corner, qualified. Over an *assiette de jambon cru*, washed down with a plummy rosé from Les Baux, I finally came to terms with the damn wind: The sky was picking up the tinge that foretells the Mediterranean, even when you are a good way from it. Mistral or not, I was going to go where nothing could shield me, the Camargue, to the end of the river.

Unlike almost all other great rivers, the Rhône has no final sweeping estuary to the sea. At Arles, it divides into the Petit Rhône and the Grand Rhône. I already knew the squalor of the Grand Rhône's last miles as it reached Port-St.-Louis. It falls within an industrial sprawl of ports, refineries, and an aerospace plant. I chose to follow the Petit Rhône as it slithers through the western stretches of the Camargue wetlands and meets the Mediterranean placidly.

Thirty years ago, the Camargue (it probably got its name from Caïus Marius Ager, a Roman general) was a place people talked of confidentially, a secret, wild place with white horses and black bulls with large, sharply spiked horns (the bulls bred for the bullfights at Arles and Nîmes). The mosquito-plagued lagoons to the west had not yet been cleared and turned into a resort coast, and most of the summer crowds turned east at Avignon, heading for the Riviera, missing the Camargue with its large, unmolested wetlands and exotic bird population. An attempt was made to turn the delta into a rice granary, but that didn't seem to threaten the remoteness.

I had heard stories of cars being blown off the road by the mistral on the route into the Camargue from Arles. Mine wasn't, but the wind was merciless. A few bold cyclists trying to ride north into Arles were incapable of movement, and dismounted. There were virtually no windbreaks. Lagoon grasses, sea lavender, and glasswort patchily covered salt-streaked earth (salt pans of the southern Camargue yield a major harvest of Mediterranean sea salt).

But the impression of bleakness conceals a vulnerable ecosystem. The Camargue is the only place in France where many bird species will breed, including herons, egrets, terns, and flamingos. An ornithological park at the Pont de Gau covers 60 hectares (about 150 acres) and, with a series of well-posted walks, gives access to a world that otherwise can easily be missed. But efforts like this to preserve the natural life compete with trashy distortions of the old Camargue—"ranches" promoting rides on the native horses, for example. In the mistral the horses were huddled around water troughs, rumps to the wind. They didn't resemble the white horses of legend; most were a sad, soiled gray.

The Petit Rhône meets the sea at the southern tip of the Camargue just west of Stes.-Maries-de-la-Mer. In the summer of 1888, while the yellow house at Arles was being repainted, van Gogh took a trip to Stes.-Maries-de-la-Mer, then a small fishing port. He made drawings that were to guide his painting, and one of these paintings, *Fishing Boats on the Beach*, explodes with a new energy of color. The beached boats have spiky masts piercing a yellowing sky that seems to boil with heat and wind. It's as though van Gogh trapped on canvas not just the equivocal light but the strange, gaseous forces energized by the Rhône as they hit the Mediterranean.

When I finally reached the Mediterranean, it was at Stes.-Maries-de-la-Mer, and there was the same combustible quality in the light. The mistral confused horizons, mixing driven yellow dust and water into a foaming mist. But no sailboats had left harbor, and the beach van Gogh painted was now bordered with a spreading ribbon of villas. Stes.-Maries has become a resort, like many on this coast, a place dedicated to summer without the culture to support any other life.

The last bridge on the Petit Rhône, the Pont de Sylvereal, reminded me of many in the Carolinas and Georgia, a single metal span without ceremony. In its final stretches, the Petit Rhône is an amiable, unhurried river devoid of the roiling currents I saw on the Rhône's upper reaches in Savoie. A lazy day of fishing can be had from its banks without even realizing that these are the dissipated waters of one of Europe's greatest rivers.

A little west of the Petit Rhône, farm stands sold sweet Muscat wines and sacks of rice and olives. There were vineyards on the vast alluvial plain that don't appear on any appellation map, owned by the same company that harvests the Camargue salt.

It was an unprepossessing site, with wind whipping sand through the vines, but, at 4,200 acres, it produces the largest wine crop in France. In his *World Atlas of Wine*, Hugh Johnson

praises the vintners and says that under their brand name,
Listel, the light and fruity table wines show promise. Much of
this stuff, though, will end up as cheap supermarket wine in
wine-glutted Europe.

The late gourmand A. J. Liebling, whose girth eventually
cleared sidewalks, is a dangerous muse for a writer in France.
He rightly instructed that "the eater's apprenticeship must be
as earnest as the cook's." His appetite eventually killed him. I
had been earnest all the way down the Rhône, but Liebling
would have thought my intake risible. There was one last
gesture to make to him, though. Of all the wines he imbibed,
Liebling kept returning to Tavel.

Tavel's color, mingling burnt orange and cherry, is a root
pigment of Provence, suspended in a bottle. At its best it hits
the tongue with an instant recognition of the place: earth and
sun consummated. I'm not a rosé fan, but Tavel stands alone
and, in salute to Liebling, I wanted to drink it within reach of
its source. Tavel is one of the most Romanesque vineyards in
the southern Rhône. It's encircled by the Gard forest, and the
village roofs have a roseate shimmer.

A few miles southwest of Tavel is Castillon-du-Gard,
where the core of a medieval town has been converted to a
hotel, Le Vieux Castillon. This has been done so discreetly
that the hotel is virtually invisible. The rooms are spread out
in a cluster of medieval shells linked by courtyards and alleys.
The hotel's restaurant is at the highest level, giving views over
many vineyards. It was here I had my Tavel moment: a bottle
of 1992 Domaine de la Forcadière.

By pure luck I had found what the wine guru Robert
Parker ranks as the finest Tavel, from an estate with 114 acres
and a demand that often outstrips supply. It was a double hit,
because with the wine I had a whole grilled *dorade*—the

French name for Mediterranean bream, which, so legend has it, was sacred to Aphrodite. If she'd tasted it with Tavel, she would certainly have been even more wanton.

Taking a walk at dusk, I saw what at first seemed a Tavel-induced crepuscular phantom—three tiers of perfectly sculpted arches stretched, pale pink, across a valley against the darkening outline of a high plateau. But it was real enough: the most spectacular piece of Roman engineering I have ever seen, the Pont du Gard—the Golden Gate Bridge of 19 B.C.

The Roman obsession with pure water has left its traces all over Europe. As Augustus Romanized the cities of the southern Rhône, the demand for water outstripped supply. In Nîmes the Roman hedonists found their baths running dry. Nobody knows exactly who should be

> When the vague twilight began to gather, the lonely valley seemed to fill itself with the shadow of the Roman name, as if the mighty empire were still as erect as the supports of the aqueduct; and it was open to a solitary tourist, sitting there sentimental, to believe that no people has ever been, or will ever be, as great as that, measured, as we measure greatness of an individual, by the push they gave to what they undertook. The Pont du Gard is one of the three or four deepest impressions they have left; it speaks of them in a manner with which they might have been satisfied.
>
> —Henry James, *A Little Tour in France* (1882)

credited with the solution—Augustus allegedly put Agrippa on the case. In any event, the engineers fixed on the water source the Fontaine d'Eure, thirty-five miles north of Nîmes, as their salvation. The terrain between the source and Nîmes is a folding of gorges and the high, rocky scrubland called *gar-*

rigue. To span this distance with an aqueduct required a variety of works: troughs, very long tunnels, covered ducts, and, to leap the Gard at a narrow-necked gorge, an aqueduct carrying a canal 160 feet high and 900 feet across.

The engineers' solution was as elegant as it was breathtaking: three vaulted levels, the first with its piers implanted on the embankments and spanning the river; the second, on top of the first straddling the gorge; and the third, the actual aqueduct—all of this built from quarried limestone, with some blocks weighing six tons, positioned without mortar. Over the course of the thirty-one miles, the gradient was precisely planned to achieve a flow of 44 million gallons a day.

And here it was, two thousand years later, still intact. I've seen Roman waterworks from Budapest to Bath, but always remnants whose original scale was lost. The scale of the Pont du Gard is astonishing. In the morning, when I reached the gorge, some people immune to vertigo were cavorting across the highest span; I took the middle, which was converted to a road bridge in the thirteenth century. Kayakers were coming down the gorge beneath. Others were picnicking on the banks. The scents of sage and mint drifted from the *garrigue.* The mistral had died the night before. Provincia Romana was back in balance, ripe and content.

Clive Irving is the author of four books, Axis, Comrades, Promise the Earth, Wide-Body, *and the coordinating editor for the tribute to the victims of the Oklahoma City bombing,* The Spirit of the Heartland. *He is a frequent contributor to* Condé Nast Traveler, *where this story first appeared.*

CAROL DRINKWATER

* * *

Pressing the Olive

It's a virgin birth of a different kind.

FINALLY, AT LONG LAST, THE MOMENT HAS ARRIVED. MY husband Michel and I are about to begin our very first harvest: *la cueillette des olives*. It is a critical period because the fruit has to be gathered at precisely the right moment and in the correct manner. The olives do not produce top-quality oil if picked too green. On the other hand, if the fruit is left on the trees too long and it overripens or grows wrinkled, then the drupes begin to oxidize, which gives a bitter, unpleasant taste to the oil.

This year, our first as olive farmers, we have a bumper crop. We will lose some of the fruit if it is not gathered and delivered to the *moulin* within forty-eight hours. René says we will need help, particularly in light of our lack of experience. We accept his counsel, and the following morning—the first occasion since we met him that he turns up on the day he said he would—he brings with him a motley collection of harvesters. Each of the five gatherers, one woman and four men, is presented to us, and each steps forward to give us his or her name and profession. They treat us deferentially, with what we suppose is the respect normally shown to proprietors, *oléicul-teurs*, of a *grand domaine*. This puzzling behavior makes us both a little awkward. We have not come across this class barrier here before. We would prefer a rather less formal relationship, and I offer them bottles of water, for the day is warm and I want to lighten the mood.

"*Nous avons, nous avons tous*," they assure us politely and retreat. They set about unloading their cars, parked on a flat grassy bank which skirts the base of the hill and the lowest of the terraces. It is a beautiful morning. The birds are chirping. There is heat in this late-November day. We leave them to their work and head off to begin our share of the picking at the top end of the land, promising to return later to see how their share of the *récolte* is progressing. I suspect René has divided us into two groups so that should we, with our city fingers and clumsy unskilled ways, damage the fruit—all too easily done—our basket loads need not be mixed in with those collected by the professionals and won't destroy the acid balance at the pressing.

What excites me is the thought of that first taste. There are over fifty different varieties of olives, and I have bought and tasted and cooked with an assortment of oils. Some were virgin, others were extra-virgin, while a few bottles were of lesser quality or mixed varieties of olives. We will soon be trying a single-variety oil cold-pressed exclusively from our *cailletier* olives. Perhaps at some point in my life I have used oil pressed from this southern French variety, these rocky coastal hills, without being aware of it. Even if that were the case, they were not from here, not from this very hill. A modest geographical nuance, but it makes a world of difference to us. Part of the thrill lies in the expectation. Does this farm, our humble terraces, produce fruit that can be classed as first-class oil? We can only wait and see. Until then, there is hard work to be done.

The gathering is backbreaking. And time-consuming. And there is no way around it. René does not hold with wooden rakes. No, every olive is gathered from the trees by hand, stretching from ladders or climbing up in the branches and reaching out to pick each olive individually, for they do not grow in bunches.

"But I read that the wooden rakes are good. They're used on many of the well-known estates," I protest.

He shakes his head adamantly. "No. Whatever anyone says, the rakes can cause damage. Two or three olives growing close to one another, almost a cluster, the rake is bound to bruise at least one. No, we will climb the trees. You, Carol, can take the ladder."

So here I am, battling with branches flicking me in the face, wobbling and gripping for dear life. On top of which, when I have managed to clutch hold of an olive or two, I must take care not to squeeze it too hard or hold it too long in my sticky palms and overheat it. And the nets, both white and green, that encircle the base of the trees have to be considered for fear they may split. Worse, if the foot of the ladder gets caught up in the netting, I and the ladder will topple over, spilling two hours' work on to the ground. It is about now that I am beginning to wish we had bought a vineyard. At least cultivation and harvest are at ground level.

Our first visit to the *moulin*. Heading off into the hills with René once more, we are planning to visit two mills, about twenty minutes apart. René wants us to choose where our fruit is to be pressed, particularly given my preference for all matters organic. Our first stop is at the mill he recommended. He brings the harvests from his other farms here, and like so many of these traditional land matters, it is family-run. Altogether, on his four farms, including ours, he is husbanding

720 trees, so, not surprisingly, he is a familiar and well-loved face at the mill. When we arrive, he takes us first to the shop that the family runs above the mill. Set on a cobbled hill, this is the tourist arm of their trade.

Once inside, everybody kisses and embraces and we are introduced as the *patrons* of the villa-farm in the hills over-looking the coast. During a brief tour of the merchandise—Provençal napkins, various jams and soaps, and objects such as pepper and salt shakers carved out of olive wood—we observe the steady flow of men with children, or lone adolescents, bringing their farms' early season pickings. Their olives are delivered in large woven *panniers*, about the size of a modest laundry basket, resembling those which in bygone days were strapped to the sides of donkeys or packhorses. Other loads are delivered in plastic crates, and a few arrive in bulging sacks that look like outmoded coal bags—though these are discouraged now because they do not meet the latest European Union standards of hygiene. The fruit is placed on a whacking, great metal scale, where it is weighed and then stacked on the floor in a line alongside a chute which will shunt the gathered drupes down to the level of the mill....

To reach the level where the mill is operating, René ushers us back out of the shop onto the cobbled street, through another door to the left of the one we have just exited and down a rickety flight of narrow wooden stairs. I feel as if I am going backward in time. Added to which, the temperature is falling. At the mill level, it is almost arctic. Every exhalation is visible.

We *have* gone backward in time.

As we enter the mill, our senses are socked by the thumping and turning of a whole array of machines, and the air is so thick and heavy with the dense aroma of freshly pulped olive paste you feel you want to shove it off you, just like a blanket.

At eight-thirty in the morning, it makes my head reel, as does the rough red wine handed to us to accompany thick wedges of locally baked bread topped with ham cured from the pig reared and slaughtered in the village. It is a peasant's breakfast offered to us by a wan girl of no more than fourteen, who is accompanied by her brother of about nine.

Once we have been fed, the children retreat politely to stand guard at the table groaning with the family produce. Silently, arms at their sides like small soldiers, they await the next batch of ravenous *oléiculteurs*. René is battling against the din to explain the mechanics of the machinery, but I am more fascinated by the children. They look like waifs, serious-faced with dark penetrating eyes that, though kindly, might have witnessed a thousand hard seasons. It seems incredible to me that our farm is situated somewhere equidistant between this world and the gaudy glitz and *escroquerie* of Cannes.

The noise down here is impossible. I cannot hear or understand a word that is being spoken. René talks on, lips moving.

---

*P*rovence *was not really a place!* It is not really a separate entity with boundaries and a separated, self-realized soul, as, say, Switzerland is. It is a beautiful metaphor born of Caesar's impatience with a geographical corridor stacked with the ruins of a hundred armies. The capricious rivers which scribbled over its surface often flooded and inhibited the free movement of regiments and of trade caravans alike. The Roman roads, when they came, did much to render the place coherent, and to clarify the prevailing doctrine and predisposition of the country's inner being, its true soul which could be summed up by the word "dissent."

—Lawrence Durrell, *Provence*

I have no idea what he is explaining. I turn to the miller, who says nothing. He has returned to his work. Both he and his assistant are wrapped in scarves knotted at the neck and substantial jackets, although they are moving continuously, shunting trays of mashed olive paste and enormous bottles filled with freshly pressed green oil. All around me, machines are milling, thrumming, spewing out liquid or excreting dried paste. A fire is roaring behind a small glass window, no bigger than a portable television screen. It is fueled by dried olive waste. Each ancient machine feeds the next, it seems. They are interconnected as though it were some enormous Rube Goldberg invention which today, according to the miller— who beckons us over into a corner away from the racket—is taking four and a half kilos of olives to press one liter of virgin oil. Most of these early-season fruits are not quite ripe enough, he explains. The fruit arriving after Christmas, when it has had longer on the trees to plumpen and grow black, should be better and produce the optimum.

We are led through to a cave where labeled bottles glow with oil growing gold instead of green as the sediment settles. They await the return of their owners, who will cart them away and store them safely in cool, darkened depositories. This mill, I see, is rigorous about making certain that no grower's olives are mixed with another's if they are a single-estate press such as ours will be.

I am fascinated by how the remains are put to good purpose. Olive oil soap is made from the residue of the third or even fourth pressings, and the desiccated paste is burned in the fire which heats the water and operates as the central heating system, such as it is here. Ecologically speaking the olive is an all-rounder. Nothing goes to waste. Every last drop of oil is wrung out of the fruit, and only in the making of *tapénade* is the pit extracted and thrown away.

Before we set off for the second mill, the longer-established of the two, everybody shakes hands enthusiastically. "Next time, Christophe will be here," we are assured. He is the *patron* and has "*parti pour faire la chasse.*" Gone hunting. There is much kissing and backslapping and promises to meet again soon. They enjoy the idea that foreigners take an interest in this most venerable of trades.

"*Beaucoup d'Americains visitent içi,*" we are told. Thumbs and fingers are rubbed together, heads nod gravely, all to express the sums of money handed over by the Americans in return for trinkets, souvenirs, and glossy books detailing the history of the olive and Provençal life.

"And the English?" I ask hopefully.

As one, the family shakes their heads. I appear to have touched upon a sensitive and sorry subject. "*Mais, non,*" returns Madame in a conspiratorial tone. "*Les Anglais* have no interest in anything!"

The second *moulin* is an altogether different affair. Situated in a field at the end of a deserted lane in the middle of nowhere, it was founded in 1706. It looks as though it originally must have been a peasant farm with an outbarn, which at some early stage was transformed into a mill and never decorated since. The crumbling outer walls of the edifice are of a washed pink which is popular in certain parts here but which I feel belongs more comfortably in Suffolk. First impression: there is little about this place, aside from the surrounding countryside and mountainous backdrop, that is welcoming.

One step in the door and we are directly in the mill, a cavernous space, with a room temperature barely above 40 degrees Fahrenheit. It is sunless and gloomy. There is no shop here, no tourist attractions of any sort, which rather pleases me. As before, we are instantly knocked backward by that dense, palpable odor of crushed olives. Here, though, there is no offer of comforting slabs of bread and ham and red wine to douse our senses. There are no trimmings whatsoever. The place has one function: the coldpressing of extra-virgin oil.

The pressing wheel and floor have been honed out of massive slabs of craggy stone rendered smooth by centuries of use. Somehow, the heavy stone adds to the keen wintry atmosphere. I exhale and watch my breath rise like smoke. Ahead of us are two farmers engaged in business with the lady miller, or the miller's wife, who appears to be discussing their accounts. René, because he has visited here only once before, is not quite sure who she is. We are all strangers, which suits me because it allows a sense of discovery.

René guides our attention toward the stone wheel that crushes the fruit. It is so imposing, almost monolithic, that I shiver at the thought of getting any body parts trapped beneath it. It is stained with what look like clumps of dark peat, but on closer inspection we see that, of course, it is coated with trapped olive paste. Passing along to another completely indescribable contraption, we find oil at its base, trickling at a snail's pace into a dustpan-like box made of olive wood. The arrival of the oil appears to be a discreet, low-key affair; none of the slosh and flow of the last establishment or the horrendous ear-splitting noise, but then to be fair, the machines here have completed their last pressing for the day, even though it is only a little after half past ten.

Looking closely, with René drawing our attention here and there, we learn that this system requires more fruit for less yield. It takes approximately six kilos of fruit to produce a liter of oil here, even with the ripest and richest of drupes. René closes his eyes and goes through a swift mental calculation. If we use the other *moulin*, Appassionata [the author's farm] can expect, on average—depending on the weather and the harvest—to press approximately two hundred and fifty liters of oil a year. Here we could net fewer than two hundred.

"Yes, but here it is cold-pressed, extra-virgin."

"The other too," he assures us.

"In any case, two hundred liters is more than sufficient for our needs," I counter.

Michel quietly reminds me that our share would be, in the first instance, eighty-three or -four liters, while here, somewhere around sixty-five. The remainder is René's. I glance at René, who merely shrugs.

The miller woman, who wears her gray hair slicked back in a tight, uncompromising bun, boots, a full woolen skirt, and velveteen shirt, is paying us no attention, engaged as she is with her clients. They are weighing *panniers* of violet olives and calculating figures: the cost of the pressing, no doubt. Perhaps for the first time, I am made acutely aware of this as a business, not a dream. Olive farming and oil pressing is a livelihood, and these people are close to the land, bearing its vagaries and hardships. They cannot afford the romance that swims about in my head. I wander off to investigate further and to be alone.

Beyond the mill, though still under the same roof, I discover a cave with storage spaces dug out of rock and cut with stone-shelved corners. It is windowless and dark. Two or three dozen glass jars cased in wicker are stored there. Each must be capable of holding fifteen or twenty liters of liquid.

"They are called *bonbonnes à goulot large*." It is René. He and Michel are once again at my side. "In the olden days, the Romans stored their oil in tall clay jars which were originally turned or baked in Spain and then shipped to Italy. They were not dissimilar to the oval terra-cotta pots you keep in your garden and fill with flowers. These are a more modern version, if you can describe anything in here as modern."

Some of these thick-necked demijohns, the *bonbonnes*, are still empty, while others have already been filled with a deep green, freshly pressed oil, which from this distance and in this crepuscular light, resembles seawater or steeped seaweed juice. Judging by its color and the juice slipping heavily into the dustpan apparatus, the quality of the oil here is richer, more luscious and aromatic.

"I like this place better," I whisper to Michel, who laughs and replies *"Mais, oui, chérie.* The question is which mill would better suit our needs. Not which would serve us as a film set!"

"I still prefer this one," I confirm calmly.

Outside, the morning is warming to a bright clear day, so clear that we can see the shrubby details on the surrounding hills and valleys and the snow caps on the high, distant Alps. I close my eyes and inhale the fresh air, rich with the smell of pine resin. The heat of the sun against my eyelids is a comforting relief.

Strolling back to our car, we learn from René that there is an olive tree growing in Roquebrune which we might like to take a look at. There are several villages down here with the name, but the one he refers to is the rather glamorous Roquebrune-Cap-Martin situated on the mountainous road between Monte Carlo and Italy. Michel knows the place. In fact, he has visited it on several occasions. Its marvelous restaurant, le Roquebrune, which has been owned and managed by the family of Mama Marinovich since its inception, has been a favorite of his for years. The village is also known for its medieval houses cut into the rocks. There, a few kilometers from Menton, the gateway to Italy, grows an olive tree believed to be a thousand years old. Who planted it? Does anyone know? Who would have looked upon it?

It is fifteen hundred years too young to be a souvenir left

by the Greeks and almost a millennium too young to have been planted by the Romans during their marches north from the heart of their empire while constructing the via Aurelia, the great highway stretching from Ventimiglia to Aix. The Romans, with Agrippa as their consul, were building roads and tracing out this land of Provincia, creating cadastral surveys and scientific mappings before the tree was ever in existence. Even Charlemagne, crowned emperor of the West in 800 A.D., preceded it, as did the Saracens, who were looting and sacking the littoral even while Charlemagne and his children were dividing up the country for their heirs.

Might it have been a peace offering to the counts of Provence from Rome?

A thousand years after the birth of Christ, somewhere around the date the tree was planted, Provence was being returned to Rome and inaugurated as part of the Holy Roman Empire. The Saracens, having created havoc and terror for a hundred years, had been conquered and driven out, and Provence, though back under the ruling thumb of Rome, was enjoying a certain independence, a bit of peace and quiet after so many centuries of strife. Alas, it was not to last. Within a century or two, the counts of Provence ceded the province to the counts of Toulouse and they to the counts of Barcelona and so the chain goes on, right up to the liberation of Provence by the Allies from the Germans in August

> Provence is simply a corridor down which, or up which, people have rushed bound for other landfalls. Yes, but underneath it all the place has a spirit of its own which starts to modify the invader if only he will stay long enough, starts to model his sensibility, invest him with its own secret lore.
>
> —Lawrence Durrell, *Provence*

1944, which our friend, René, standing beside us now, bore witness to.

Still, this noble tree is believed to be the oldest in the world.

By what stroke of fortune has that one single specimen survived. Michel suggests we make a detour, a slightly elongated one, approximately one hundred and ten kilometers round-trip, and pay homage to this most holy of trees. This I agree to wholeheartedly. René, who does not want to come with us, bids us *bon appétit* and leaves us to it.

Less than an hour later, our car is swooping and turning like a bird in flight along the mountain road. It is a giddy, spectacular altitude. The endless hairpin bends on this infamous descent, then ascent, from La Turbie with its magnificent Roman ruins, make you catch your breath when you look down to sea level and pray to God your brakes won't fail. There is precious little chance to enjoy the view if you are driving. Michel is at the wheel. He drives fast, but with great skill, and I am leaning out the window, unafraid, hair flying in the wind and whipping my face, eyes watering, thrilled by the panorama all around me, following the sweep of hundreds of meters of rocky face which lead dramatically to the Med.

Somewhere near here, Princess Grace of Monaco lost her life when her sports car went over the cliffside. She was killed instantly. From where I am now, you see why. The memory of that accident sobers me for an instant, and I crawl back into my seat and gaze at the rock faces towering to the left of us.

It's then that I spot the village high above us, rising out of the stone toward a linen-blue sky. It resembles a picture from a book of fairy tales illustrated by Arthur Rackham; even more so when I realize that, perched atop its pinnacle, is a castle with a tower.

We park the car at the foot of the village in what was the

ancient castle's barbican and hike the winding lane to the *vieux village*. Much to our dismay, because we are starving, every single restaurant is closed. This is not about being closed for lunch. It is that time of year, *la fermer annuelle*, November 15 to December 15, when so many businesses shut up shop in preparation for the upcoming festivities; Christmas and the New Year are a busy season on the Côte d'Azur. But we are not too disappointed, even if our stomachs are rumbling. Our noontime is flooded with warm winter sunshine.

We stride and puff and arrive at a perfectly empty place, and what strikes me instantly is that there is not a soul about, though there is no sense of this as a ghost town. In the center of this pleasingly airy square is an olive tree, fenced and surrounded by benches. It is unquestionably an aged specimen and well preserved, but I had expected something more spectacular. The girth of its trunk is probably three meters which is barely more than our own trees. I stroll to the cliff's edge and look out across the rippling water, lambent in the sunlight, toward Cap Martin and, in the other direction, to the kingdom of Monaco with its curiously out-of-place skyscrapers. Michel comes up behind me and wraps his arms around me.

"I've had a good look. I don't think that's the tree we're after," he says. "Let's investigate."

We make our way through the *vieux village* up a hill, down a winding stairwell—everywhere tiled and cobbled and polished with the gleaming shine of a proud housewife's stoop—passing through Place Ernest Vincent with its obsolete prison, until we spot a sign for the *olivier millénair*.

"Look," I cry.

Triumphantly, with the air of adventurers whose navigations are confirmed on track, we begin to descend. A profusion of hillside trees fluffy with green leaves similar to the willow—a variety of tamarisk, if I am not mistaken—overhang the pathway. We are plunging down a steep path. In former days a donkey trail, no doubt, used to transport victuals from the fields at sea level up to the homes carved out of the rocks. We are walking in the footsteps traced by a billion and more travelers, by soldiers, other lovers, by farmers and farmhands, to pay homage to a tree. And lo and behold, two hundred or so meters farther along, there it is, growing out of a wall on the terraced cliffside. This elephantine miracle is not fenced in. It is not on display. It is simply there. Being. Its roots, like a banyan tree's, sprawl everywhere. Branches, roots, reach ing out like an octopus, stretching, bursting its banks with the sheer determination to live, to survive. Its force is taking earth and stone with it.

Michel and I stand side by side, silenced, gazing in awe at this monumental symbol of creation. Then we spin around, seaward, to take in the view unfolding before us; flocks of starlings swoop and tack against a vigorous blue sky. Even at this precipitous height, we can hear the gentle lap of the water washing the coastal rocks and beaches so far beneath us. We incline our heads and gaze down upon the coastline, eyes eastward to the cap of St.-Martin, where Yeats once spent a holiday, Queen Victoria was a regular visitor, and the architect Le Corbusier drowned.

Everywhere is warm and still and calm; *calme* in the French sense, meaning untroubled and at peace. Without a word, we reach for each other, and I feel the warmth of the sun on Michel's skin.

"*Je t'aime.*"

Rarely have I felt so in harmony with life, so humbled by its magnificence. I pace out the distance between the farthest visible reaches of the trunk extensions and measure fifteen meters. Here we are, some nine hundred feet above sea level, in the presence of a growing organism that has stood sentry over this landscape for ten centuries. I can comprehend the millennia of reverence given to the olive tree, to its wisdom and unmatched nobility.

For a heartbeat, all seems clear. The world is pure, and the miracle of life washes through me.

Carol Drinkwater is a British actress, screenwriter, and author of The Olive Farm: A Memoir of Life, Love, and Olive Oil in the South of France, *from which this story was excerpted. She and her husband, Michel, live in a village just outside of Cannes.*

YVONE LENARD

Days of Pastis and Lavender

*You can try to bring home the Provençal way
of life, but it may be impossible.*

BY JULY, LAVENDER (OR RATHER *LAVANDIN*, BUT THE TWO ARE
hard to tell apart) planted in great clumps on the terrace has
already put out long spikes. A few days later, these are tipped
with ears of violet blue, intensely aromatic, rugged little
flowers, whose perfume begins to rise under the morning sun
and wafts through our open window.

We know bread was baked earlier, in the lower village
bakery. We could smell it just about the time the six peals of
the belfry bell rang out. We also know one should not tarry
too long before the croissant run, for by eight, they'll be all
gone. The baker still hasn't adjusted to the influx of newcomers like us who are beginning to descend upon the village,
so his output remains stubbornly too low.

Walking barefoot on the terra-cotta floors, my husband,
Wayne, brews espresso. Sitting on our terrace we sip, and scat-
ter croissant crumbs for insistent sparrows, who scoop them
right off the table. On a nearby tower, one of the few still
standing out of the fortification's original twenty-two, a pair

of magpies raucously yells at us greetings, or, more likely, warnings. A calico cat sits on the very edge of the overhanging roof and stares down at us with total concentration.

Yet, breakfast can be only so languid, for there are inflexible rules to be learned. Everything will close down at noon sharp, except food stores, which may remain open a little longer: shops, post office, gas stations, garages, city hall, banks will shut tight, since their employees shall be going home for *déjeuner*. And *déjeuner*, as practiced in France, holds nothing in common with what we Americans know as lunch. Some places will re-open around two, or two-thirty, or three, some not until four, and others not at all. So, all errands should be completed before closing time, and if you have plans for the afternoon, or guests over for dinner, get going before it is too late. Besides, nobody wants to miss out on the best part of the morning in town: the hours devoted to food shopping.

In Pertuis, our nearby shopping *bourg*, the streets are hosed down in the early A.M., so they stay wet and cool all morning. Doors are wide open for business, and great displays of fruit and vegetables crowd the sidewalks: lush tomatoes picked with their vine; tightly bunched pink radishes; varnished courgettes; new onions like white jade veined in celadon; strawberries glowing scarlet; and the small, musky cantaloupes with an aroma you can smell from the end of the street.

Bakeries are crowded, because the second batch of the day has just come out of the oven, and everyone is stocking up for the day, carrying away baguettes and *ficelles*, the thinner, crustier version of the baguette, in a thousand imaginative ways: tucked across a baby carriage; strapped over a backpack; firmly grasped with a briefcase handle; or brandished like a conductor's baton, the better to point to a direction, or stress a point in conversation.

In the *charcuterie*, which, according to an age-old royal edict still in force, is privileged to sell only pork meat and pork-meat products, *jambon de Paris*, cooked ham, and air-dried *jambon de Bayonne* are thinly sliced, giant salami are unhooked from the ceiling with a hooked pole, chunks of pâté are wrapped in wax paper.

We hurry from shop to shop, composing menus as we go. We'll have tomato salad for *déjeuner*, followed by *ravioles de Romans*—tiny goat-cheese raviolis you just dip in boiling water and serve with a touch of butter and cracked pepper—fruit for dessert. Since we expect guests for dinner, we'll need some of the paper-thin *jambon de Bayonne* to drape over slices of cantaloupe, courgettes for a gratin, a lamb roast, and mesclun salad to drizzle with dark-green olive oil from the village mill. Mesclun is composed of baby leaves of all kinds: lettuce, escarole, arugula, romaine, endive; some sweet and some bitter. We are all set now, except for dessert, and for that, we know exactly where to go.

We return to our car, parked in the parking *payant*, where one always finds plenty of space, since the French prefer to park more creatively—on sidewalks, in front of doors, or even double-park on the street—to save some money, yes, but much more likely to exercise that Gallic sense of indiscipline that brings zest to their life.

A vegetarian in Provence is a novel concept, or so it appeared to me. The French/English dictionary I carried contained a word for vegetarian in French, but "*Je suis végétarienne*" only elicited blank stares from waiters and waitresses. My French phrase book also offered a translation for "I do not eat meat," but "*Je ne mange pas la viande*" only resulted in a series of fish and poultry suggestions.

—Cassandra Dunn, "A Vegetarian in Provence"

We are already opening our doors, when, from the terrace of the Café Thomas, someone waves energetically and calls out to us. We recognize Monsieur Estain, one of our neighbors, sitting there with a friend he wants us to meet. Everybody shakes hands. Custom demands each man buy a round of drinks, and what would anyone drink near noontime in the summer but pastis?

Bébé, the owner's great white poodle, ambles over to identify these newcomers, gets a sniff and a scratch on the head, then languorously paces over to the next table. The waiter brings a tray with glasses, ice cubes, a carafe of water, and a bottle of pastis. It seems that, sitting in a café, ladies may accept *one* drink with the men. Refusing refills shows good breeding. We beg for a pastis *léger*, just a little of the golden liquor poured in before the glass is filled with water. It is lovely to watch the yellow liquor turn into swirls of milky opal as it mixes with the water, and a strong *anis* aroma fills the nostrils. No *léger*, though, for the natives. The recommended formula is one part pastis to five parts of water, but they prefer their own *tassé*, practically half and half.

At other tables, they're having *perroquet,* parrot, the same as ours, but with the addition of a dose of cream of mint. Others tint their pastis red with grenadine: that's a *tomate*. Adding almond syrup, called orgeat, makes a *mauresque*. Even so, pastis is never sweet; it remains briskly tart and truly refreshing.

In the middle of a pastis-induced euphoria, I idly observe a young parking officer examining cars, but I fail to connect his interest with any potential problem. As he leans over Chipper, our car, Monsieur Estain calls out: "Eh, Lucien! How about a drink?"

The officer walks over, removes his cap, wipes his brow, shakes hands all around, and sits down. "I wouldn't mind," he allows. "The sun's beating down." He turns to us: "Isn't that your car, over there, by the fountain?"

Monsieur Estain interrupts: "Lucien is from the village. I've known him since he was that high. His dad and I go hunting together." He turns to Lucien, roughly jocular: "So, you rascal, you found a job, at last? About time, too, I'd say. But don't you go bugging honest people, now. Try and catch some criminals, instead. Plenty of those, I hear. Right here, though, I don't see any crimes being committed."

"Ah, but," stammers Lucien, "it's not crooks that I chase. I am a parking officer. And their car, over there, it's over-parked by fifteen minutes." You feed coins into a meter that delivers a ticket stamped with date and time, to be placed on the dashboard. Ours obviously shows overtime.

"What!" roars Monsieur Estain, turning red in the face. "And so what? This isn't the Lord's good earth anymore? You have to *pay* to just sit on it now?"

Lucien tries to argue. He's got the law on his side, after all, as well as a job to do. "*They* can sit all they want," he insists, fairly. "It's only their *car*. The parking time has expired…."

Monsieur Estain is now purple with righteous indignation, and makes it abundantly clear that if Lucien, that good-for-nothing strippling, thinks he can bother good, honest *Américains*, yes, the same who landed in Normandy to liberate us in '44, and personally vouched for by Monsieur Estain *lui-même*, he'd better think twice. Monsieur Estain happens to be a municipal councillor, don't you forget, and he'd have only one word to drop in the proper ear to send Lucien right back to unemployment.

We try to protest.

"No, no, Lucien is right. He's only doing his job, nothing personal. Give us the ticket, Lucien, we don't mind at all, we'll pay it. Come on, Lucien."

But Monsieur Estain's hand clamps over my wrist. He's teaching us a lesson in village life and doesn't mind at all displaying in the process, the awesomeness of his authority. Meanwhile, Lucien's drink arrives, glasses are clinked: "*Santé!*" and Monsieur mock-angrily crams the ticket pad into Lucien's uniform pocket, as Lucien protests he would never give a *contravention* to friends of Monsieur Estain. Now that he knows our car, he'll tell his colleagues to watch for it.... By the way, he's heard we're from California. Is it true he looks like Tom Hanks? His girlfriend swears he's a dead ringer.

The resemblance is far from striking at first glance, but now, in profile, I can see something indeed of the character Tom Hanks created in *Forrest Gump*. So, I assure him truthfully that, yes, his girl is right, he does have that certain look about him, especially the right profile.

"Maybe you should go to 'Ollyvood and become a movie star, eh?" suggests Monsieur Estain scornfully. "But you see, these guys, they may *look* dumb, but they're *smart*. So, you're better off here."

No hard feelings. Lucien turns his profile to me even as we shake hands all around. And we rush to Chipper, now over an hour overparked, but unpunished, thanks to powerful protection.

Now, for the dessert run.

Yvone Lenard served as a model for the famous painter Jean-Gabriel Domergue in Paris, then left her native France as a young adult for California where she earned a master's degree in French and Classics at UCLA. She became head of the Language Division of the French Department at UCLA, then Chairman of the Foreign Language Department at California State University, Dominguez Hills. Her highly successful textbooks on French language and culture have been recognized by the French government with many high honors. Yvone divides her time between homes in Los Angeles and Provence. In both, she enjoys gardening, cooking and entertaining. Some of the best times in her life are at a dinner table surrounded by friends. This story was excerpted from her book, The Magic of Provence: Pleasures of Southern France.

PIERS LETCHER

* * *

Winemaking
in the Lubéron

There is art, science, and love in this venerable activity.

I GRABBED A HANDFUL OF THE WORLD'S SWEETEST CHERRIES off the nearest overloaded tree, and then helped Richard load the red wine into the trunk of his beaten-up old station wagon. We laid the dusty unlabeled bottles tightly, end to end, to avoid breakages.

"How many do you need?" I asked.

"If I can't get it done for 120, then it will have to wait—it's all I can spare," he replied cheerfully, rolling up another wheelbarrow full of bottles.

We laid an old blanket across the top row, slammed shut the trunk, and set off in search of a local garage who would agree to paint the car in exchange for 90 liters of the best Côtes de Lubéron. That's the way things still work in Provence, if you make your own wine.

Richard and his wife Jenna (my godmother) bought their house in Provence in 1980—though it wasn't so much a house back then as an uninhabitable ruin. But it had potential, and it had land. More importantly, it had vineyards.

The first season's *recolte*, however, once bottled, matured and tasted, turned out to be filthy. The whole lot—the craft, the art of Richard's first summer and autumn, the result of tired shoulders and aching backs, the pressing, the care and the attention, the hope and the labor of love—was poured down the drain.

Fortunately, Richard's not just an indomitable spirit (he was taken hostage in Lebanon in 1975, and survived *that* experience), he's also an industrial chemist. Not the kind of chemist who decides to "fix" a wine with the use of filters and additives, but the kind of chemist who quietly tweaks the *process* of winemaking.

In the meantime there was also the small matter of the house being uninhabitable. You wouldn't know it today, but for that first summer and autumn, whenever nature called, Jenna and Richard were off up the hillside with a bucket and spade. Heating and hot water were things that would arrive "some day." The "garden" was the area of land surrounding the "house."

So—already in their fifties—Richard and Jenna taught themselves to be builders. They restored the first rooms, paved a terrace, pruned back the vines and planted a small garden. Their neighbors—still getting over the shock of last year's "wine"—were impressed.

Within a couple of years, things were looking up. Not only did they now have a fully operational bathroom, but hot water ran, fires burned, and even the wine had started to improve. Guests no longer politely wrinkled their noses and pushed their wineglasses away, with a muttered "*très intéressant*" as the latest batch was uncorked.

Richard invested some useful time in eavesdropping at local café terrace tables, where the hidden secrets of new grape varieties were traded in low voices, and was soon joining in the more voluble discussions over the clandestine art of cellaring. How often to perform the *soutirage* (running the wine off the sediment)? Which mix of wood to use in the barrels? How long to mature? How on earth to keep the temperature stable? When to bottle? And most importantly of all, when to drink?

Their house gradually became a meeting place for the neighboring *vignerons*. Given authority not just by his steadily improving wine, but also by the great scientific mind behind it, Richard became something of a local wine oracle, trusted even more for being the only foreigner in the area running his own little winery.

By the mid-1980s, Yves—the local *paysan* who helped with the vineyards—was beginning to show definite signs of anxiety. What if the wine were to become too good? Why, it would need to be *regulated*. It would need to be *labeled*. It would need to be—his eyes rolled and raised to heaven at this—*taxed*.

Richard chided him for his fears. "This is *our* wine, Yves," he reassured him, eye-to-eye, hand firmly on one solid green-overalled shoulder. "This isn't *commercial* wine. It's just for you and me. It's for our families. It's for our families and friends."

And so it was—and indeed so it is. A couple of thousand bottles a year, with a growing reputation drifting across the dry hills of the northern Luberon.

During the night, with a frightful crack, one of Jenna and Richard's cherry trees split right down the middle, the trunk rent asunder by the sheer weight of fruit straining its boughs. First thing in the morning, with Yves's help, we set to binding the trunk together, first with strips of canvas, and then with a length of heavy rope.

The tree secure, we harvested the cherries. They were ripe,

sweet, heavenly-firm beauties, known locally as *cœurs de pigeons* (pigeon's hearts). By afternoon, Yves reckoned we had more than a ton, just from the one tree—and you could see him mentally totting up what they might be worth at the cooperative. (Yves gets to sell the cherries in exchange for some of the time he puts in on the vines.) We loaded the wooden crates into the back of Yves's truck, and he sailed off down the lane with a friendly wave and a toot.

We played a game of boules on the gravel drive—deadly serious stuff at aperitif time—and waited for the evening breeze to settle before dinner. Jenna made dips and served *niçois* olives to accompany our gin and tonics, our whisky and sodas, our chilled rosés, and we sat quietly around the heavy wooden table on the flagged terrace, sheltered by an ancient vine trailing across a trellis overhead.

"War can wait—the vintage cannot," goes an old French saying. Wine grapes are perfectly ripe for a few days of the year, at most. If inclement weather threatens, that window of opportunity can shrink to a few hours. Thus whole villages have been known, in centuries past, to ignore hostile armies at their gates in order to bring in their grapes. "War can wait" subtly celebrates the agrarian heroism of people keeping faith with nature in the face of bloody conflict. It also reminds us, sadly, how often such heroism has been required.

—Thom Elkjer,
Adventures in Wine

The sun set behind the hills, and it seemed to me that the heart of Provence really hadn't changed at all.

Sure, property prices have gone through the roof, since the 1989 publication of Peter Mayle's *A Year in Provence*. And sure, most of Jenna and Richard's neighbors are now holidaying

English, Belgians, Dutch, Austrians, Germans, and Americans (*Gladiator* director Ridley Scott has an enormous place a few miles away), rather than the French *paysans* of yesteryear. But the essence of the place is unchanged. The peace and quiet of an early summer evening is still remarkable—with just the upper branches of the great chestnut tree creaking in the tail end of the evening breeze, and the quiet rustle of conversation over a sheltered terrace table to disturb the silence.

Until a dreadful whining moped crests the hill and burns along the long road at the bottom of the drive, and then back again. Revved up to full speed in the lowest possible gear by a local French teenager, the noise is like a magnified hornet, and twice as irritating.

"How do you put up with that?" my wife asks, once the buzzing subsides into the distance. "It's awful."

Richard throws up his hands, in resignation. "You didn't think you could have *everything*, did you?"

The next day we load the car with cherries, rosemary cuttings, dried grasses, and jars of Jenna's famous apricot jam—and two dozen bottles of Richard's wine—and set off with a heavy heart for home. They may not have everything, but these Provençal vignerons get pretty close.

Piers Letcher has been traveling for twenty-five years and travel-writing for twenty. British-born and educated, he has spent most of his adult life in France eschewing alliteration. He has published more than a thousand newspaper and magazine articles and a dozen books. His most recent books are Croatia: The Bradt Travel Guide, *and* Eccentric France, *a guide to France's bizarre buildings, ridiculous royalty, quirky collections, impossible inventions, and peculiar people.*

ALAIN DE BOTTON

* * *

On Eye-Opening Art

Can we see what an artist saw?

THE TOURIST OFFICE IN ARLES IS HOUSED IN AN UNDISTIN-
guished concrete block in the southwestern part of the town. It
offers visitors the usual fare: free maps, advice on hotels and
information about cultural festivals, child-minders, wine tastings,
canoeing, ruins, and markets. One attraction is emphasized above
all others: "Welcome to the land of Vincent van Gogh," exclaims
a poster with the sunflowers in the entrance hall; inside, the walls
are decorated with harvest scenes, olive trees, and orchards.

The office particularly recommends what it describes as the
"van Gogh trail." On the 100th anniversary of his death of
1890, van Gogh's presence in Provence was honored by a series of plaques—fixed onto metal rods or stone slabs—positioned in some of the places he painted. The plaques feature
photographs of the relevant works and a few lines of com-
mentary. They are to be found both within the town and in
the wheat and olive fields that surround it. They extend as far
as St.-Rémy, where after the ear incident, van Gogh ended his
Provençal days at the Maison de Santé.

I persuaded my hosts to spend an afternoon following the trail, to which end we stopped in at the tourist office to collect a map. By chance we learned that a guided tour, a once-weekly event, was about to start in the courtyard outside, and that there were still places available for a modest sum. We joined a dozen other enthusiasts and were first taken to the Place Lamartine by a guide, who told us that her name was Sophie and that she was writing a thesis on van Gogh at the Sorbonne in Paris.

At the beginning of May 1888, finding his hotel too expensive, van Gogh had rented a wing of a building at 2 Place Lamartine known as the Yellow House. It was one half of a double-fronted building that had been painted bright yellow by its owner but left unfinished inside. Van Gogh developed a great interest in the interior design. He wanted it to be solid and simple, painted in the colors of the South: red, green, blue, orange, sulphur, and lilac. "I want to make it really an artist's house—nothing precious,

For two months van Gogh and Gauguin lived and worked together, sharing a little yellow house in Arles. Vincent believed his dream of an artists' community was beginning to come true. But living and working together was hard for both artists. They were an odd couple. Gauguin liked things to be neat, while van Gogh was extremely messy. Gauguin liked quiet, serene surroundings but van Gogh was full of nervous energy and talked a lot. They also painted very differently. Gauguin could paint entirely from his imagination. He liked to reflect and dream before he began to carefully plan the shapes he would paint. Van Gogh liked to have his subject right in front of him as he painted.

—Wenda O'Reilly, Ph.D.,
Van Gogh and Friends

but with everything from the chairs to the pictures having character," he told his brother. "About the beds, I have bought country beds, big double ones instead of iron ones. That gives an appearance of solidity, durability, and quiet." The refurbishment complete, he wrote elatedly to his sister, "My house here is painted the yellow color of fresh butter on the outside, with glaringly green shutters; it stands in the full sunlight in a square that has a green garden with plane trees, oleanders, and acacias. It is completely whitewashed inside, with a floor made of red bricks. And over it there is the intensely blue sky. In this house I can live and breathe, meditate and paint."

Sadly, Sophie had little to show us, for the Yellow House had been destroyed in the Second World War and subsequently replaced with a student hostel, which itself was now dwarfed by the giant Mono-prix supermarket that had gone up beside it. We drove next to St.-Rémy and there spent more than an hour in the fields around the asylum where van Gogh had lived and painted. Sophie had with her a large plastic-coated book containing the main Provence paintings, and she frequently held it up in spots where van Gogh had worked, letting the rest of us crowd around to look on. At one point, with her back to the Alpilles, she held up *Olive Trees with the Alpilles in the Background* (June 1889), and we admired both the view and van Gogh's version of it.

But there was a moment of dissent in the group. Next to me, an Australian wearing a large hat said to his companion, a small, tousle-haired woman, "Well, it doesn't look much like that."

Van Gogh himself had feared he might encounter such accusations. To his sister, he wrote that many people already said of his work, "'This really looks too strange,' not to mention those who think it a total abortion and utterly repulsive." The reasons for such opinions were not hard to find: the walls of his houses were not always straight, the sun was not always yellow or the grass green, there was an exaggerated sense of movement in some of his trees. "I have played hell somewhat with the truthfulness of the colors," he admitted, and he played similar hell with proportion, line, shadow, and tone.

Yet in playing hell, van Gogh was only making more explicit a process in which all artists are involved—namely, choosing which aspects of reality to include in a work and which to leave out. As Nietzsche knew, reality itself is infinite and can never be wholly represented in art. What made van Gogh unusual among Provençal artists was his choice of what he felt was important. Whereas painters such as Constantin had expended much effort in getting the scale right, van Gogh, though passionately interested in producing a "likeness," insisted that it was not by worrying about scale that he would end up conveying what was important in the south: his art would involve, as he mockingly told his brother, "a likeness different from the products of the God-fearing photographer." The part of reality that concerned him sometimes required distortion, omission, and the substitution of colors to be brought to the fore, but it was still the real—the "likeness"— that interested him. He was willing to sacrifice a naive realism in order to achieve realism of a deeper sort, like a poet who, though less factual than a journalist in describing an event, may nevertheless reveal truths about it that find no place in the other's literal grid.

Van Gogh elaborated on this idea in a letter he wrote to his brother in September 1888 about a portrait he was planning: "Rather than trying to reproduce exactly what I see before my eyes, I use color more arbitrarily, in order to express myself forcibly.... I'll give you an example of what I mean: I should like to paint the portrait of an artist friend, a man who dreams great dreams, who works as the nightingale sings, because it is his nature [the portrait was *Poet*, of early September

1888]. He'll be blond. *I want to put my appreciation, the love I have for him, into the picture.* So I paint him as he is, as faithfully as I can, to begin with. But the picture is not yet finished. In order to finish it, I am going to be the arbitrary colorist. I mean to exaggerate the fairness of the hair, even get to orange tones, chromes, and pale citron yellow. Behind the head, instead of painting the ordinary wall of the mean room, I will paint infinity, a plain background of the richest, most intense blue I can contrive, and by this simple combination of the bright head against the rich blue background, I will achieve a mysterious effect, like a star in the depths of an azure sky.... Oh, my dear boy...and the nice people will see the exaggeration only as a caricature." [*Emphasis added*]

> I am risking my life for my work, and half my reason has gone.
>
> —Vincent van Gogh

A few weeks later, van Gogh began another "caricature." "Tonight I am probably going to start on the interior of the café where I eat, by gaslight, in the evening," he told his brother. "It is what they call a *café de nuit* (these are fairly common here), one that stays open all night. Night prowlers can take refuge there when they have no money to pay for a lodging or are too drunk to be taken in elsewhere." In painting what would become *The Night Café in Arles*, van Gogh abandoned adherence to some elements of "reality" for the sake of others. He did not reproduce the proper perspective or color scheme of the café; his light bulbs metamorphosed into glowing mushrooms, his chairs arched their backs, his floor buckled. Yet he was still interested in expressing truthful ideas about the place, ideas that would perhaps have been less well expressed if he had had to follow the classical rules of art.

*

The complaints of the Australian man were unusual within our group; most of the rest of us came away from Sophie's lecture with a newfound reverence both for van Gogh and for the landscapes he painted. But my own enthusiasm was undermined by the memory of an exceptionally acerbic maxim that Pascal had penned several centuries before van Gogh's southern journey: "How vain painting is, exciting admiration by its resemblance to things of which we do not admire the originals" (*Pensées*, 40).

It struck me as awkwardly true that I had not much admired Provence before I began to study its depiction in van Gogh's work. But in its desire to mock art lovers, Pascal's maxim was in danger of skirting two important points. Admiring a painting that depicts a place we know but don't like seems absurd and pretentious if we imagine that painters do nothing but reproduce exactly what lies before them. If that were true, then all we could admire in a painting would be the technical skills involved in the reproduction of an object and the glamorous name of the painter, in which case we would have little difficulty agreeing with Pascal's description of painting as a vain pursuit. But as Nietzsche knew, painters do not merely reproduce; they select and highlight, and they are accorded genuine admiration insofar as their version of reality seems to bring out valuable features of it.

Furthermore, we do not have to resume our indifference to a place once the painting of it that we have admired is out of sight, as Pascal hints. Our capacity to appreciate can be transferred from art to the world. We can find things that delight us on a canvas first but then later welcome them in the place where the canvas was painted. We can continue to see cypresses beyond van Gogh's paintings.

Alain de Botton was born in Zurich and educated in Switzerland and England. He is a philosopher and author of five books, including How Proust Can Change Your Life *and* The Art of Travel, *from which this story was excerpted. He lives in London.*

PART TWO

SOME THINGS TO DO

✦ ✦ ✦

Cassis

Drink it where it was born.

As one enters Provence from the north, there is a place that never fails to have a magical effect on my spirits. After Montélimar, the road passes through a gorge that pinches right up to the shoulder of the *autoroute*, then opens out upon a vast, vine-covered plain. The effect is emotionally exhilarating, like the untying of a mental knot, a release and a shock of open space within that mirrors the widening landscape without.

Shortly afterward, a large road sign announces: VOUS ÊTES EN PROVENCE.

Provence is good for the psyche. By the time I approach Cassis and that first breathtaking view of the glistening Mediterranean, I am singing, I am happy, I am *chez moi*.

Cassis produces the one wine I buy whose vines actually look upon the Mediterranean. This fishing village just east of Marseilles, long a weekend retreat for the wealthy Marseillaises, has nothing whatsoever to do with Cassis the black-current liqueur. This Cassis is one of the least spoiled, most picturesque seaside villages in Provence.

The bay, the village, and its little harbor are visible from the *autoroute* far above. As you wind down to the sea, you see some of the geological formations that make Cassis so special; aeons of wear and tear have uncovered a series of huge, crown-shaped prominences the color of bleached bone that rise from the grayish-green, scrub-covered mountains. It is as if the timeless stony core of the mountains stands revealed. This rugged landscape has protected Cassis from undergoing what I call Rivierazation, the transformation of something deliciously inviting into something to be avoided. Developers run into problems erecting their high-rise condominiums at Cassis.

The roadway down from the *autoroute* cuts through one of the finest Cassis vineyards, those of the Domaine de Paternal, whose proprietor is Monsieur Cathinaud, a sly old gentleman who has seen ninety years come and go. In his youth he nearly learned English by studying Shakespeare in the original, and he uses my presence each year as an excuse to dust off his heavily accented Shakespearean vocabulary and grammar. He takes pleasure in concocting plays on words, so I laugh along as merrily as I can, although I rarely understand a thing he says. I am not about to let him know his English gabbling is incomprehensible, for fear of wounding his obvious pride.

Centre ville Cassis, the old section, is a lively colorful place with a beach, a mast-filled harbor, and a row of outdoor cafés where everyone is very animated, sipping pastis, soaking up the sun and sea air.

The subject of one of Frédéric Mistral's poems, Cassis also attracted painters such as Vlaminck, Dufy, and Matisse. Today it is not uncommon to see a movie crew at work, using the alluring site as a backdrop.

The main beach is too crowded and pebbly to be interest-ing. Continue east half a kilometer and you will find an inlet

with a small beach where the water is irresist[
Here is where most of the semi-naked, young
seem to congregate. If you proceed farther, follo[
to La Presqu'île, you will pay to enter a little parking
price high enough to discourage the multitudes, because once
you have parked amid the pine trees, you are relatively isolated, by Riviera standards.

There is no sandy beach, however. You sunbathe on the
rock shelf above the sea, but there are places to dip your toes
into the water, or dramatic heights from which to plunge if
you prefer a good wakening shock. The water at Cassis is said
to be the coldest on the
Mediterranean, because
springs of fresh water from
the Alps flow out from
beneath the rocks. One
advantage, however, is that
Cassis is said to have the
cleanest water on the
French coast, and this, I
assure you, counts for a
great deal once you have gazed into the murk at certain
Riviera spots where the city's waste is piped to spill out a mere
few hundred feet offshore.

> I still love the Mediter-
> ranean, it still seems young
> as Odysseus, in the spring.
> —D. H. Lawrence
> (1885–1930)

I take a mat and towel and find a flat spot on the hot rocks
and settle in. Every once in a while I try to concentrate on a
mystery novel, I get baked enough to dive into the sea, I doze,
I snack on a picnic lunch, I watch the fishing boats laying their
nets and the tourist boats that plow by with binoculars and
cameras aimed at the mostly-naked bodies scattered about
basking. And I watch a fabulous light show; across the water
the celebrated Cap Canaille, the highest cliff in France, rises
ocher-colored out of the blue sea. As the sun travels across the

ιuge sky, as clouds sail by changing the light, the massive face of the cliff changes color. Ocher to orange to rust to purple. And likewise the sea changes from blues to greens to grays, an infinite breathtaking variety. A painter would spend the whole day mixing and remixing colors. There is even a decent restaurant nearby, La Presqu'île, where one can enjoy a bouil-labaisse outdoors while the sea crashes on the rocks below and the Cap Canaille performs across the bay. The wine list offers the finest growths of Provence, including the Cassis of the Clos Ste.-Magdeleine, whose vines grow on a narrow fifteen-acre cape that juts right out into the Mediterranean. The fish can almost nibble the grapes. This must be one of the most valuable vineyards in France. However, it is not as a vineyard that it would attract a great sum, but as land to develop into a resort. This is an earthly paradise, the Clos Ste.-Magdeleine, and I wonder what Hilton or the Club Med would pay for it. I shouldn't even mention it.

Cassis produces reds and rosé wine, but it is the white that merits attention. Quoting from *Les Grands Vins de France*, 1931, by Paul Ramain: *"Ils ont une saveur particulière due à l'exposition unique des terres qui les produisent."* ("They have a special flavor due to the unique exposure of the soils that produce them.") It is a quote typical of French wine books, but what does it say to give an idea of what Cassis *blanc* tastes like? It seems to say that Cassis *blanc* tastes like Cassis *blanc*. I suppose it is true that there are plenty of wines that have no personality what-soever, that taste exactly like the wine from the next village, while the white from Cassis, thanks to the exposition of the vines and the limestone soil in which they grow, does have a character that cannot be duplicated. As to the character, most intriguing is its combination of nervosity and unctuousness. Nervosity can be found in a good Muscadet, unctuousness hopefully in a Montrachet, but the two poised together in a dry white have a special attraction. Cassis has a brilliant sun-drenched color and it marries perfectly with the local cuisine. This is garlic-and-olive-oil land, and in the local restaurants it would be crazy to drink a Muscadet or Montrachet with the catch of the day. The menus feature *oursins* (sea urchins), sea snails with aïoli, *soupe de poisson*, fresh *rougets* or *loup* grilled over coals, and, of course, the endlessly bastardized bouillabaisse.

Cassis is one of the wines that people claim will not travel well. When I read the declaration of this or that gourmet or wine guru that such and such a wine (Cassis, Beaujolais, Chablis, Dolcetto, etc.) *must* be drunk on site, I know that they were having a high time and the local wine tasted better than ever. Wine travels well if it is properly shipped, which means temperature control. Motion will not harm wine, but high temperatures will. A little heat will hurt it a little; a lot of heat—say, three or four days through the Panama Canal or the month of July in an un-air-conditioned New York ware-house—and the wine is roasted. Shipped at around fifty-five degrees, followed by air-conditioned storage, your wine will not have changed between Cassis and the United States.

But then of course Cassis tastes better at Cassis! Debussy sounds better after a walk through the foggy, puddled streets of late-night Paris. You are in the midst of the atmosphere that created it. The wine is not different, the music is not different. You are.

Kermit Lynch is a wine importer and retailer based in Berkeley, California. He is the author of Adventures on the Wine Route: A Wine Buyer's Tour of France, *from which this story was excerpted.*

OLIVIA GATTI TAYLOR

✦ ✦ ✦

Hidden Among the Hills

The author finds a French sort of Shangri-la.

NEAR TARASCON, OUR BUS EXITED THE NORTHBOUND highway as my father's voice came clearly over the microphone, a bit louder than the ongoing conversations of the forty tour participants he was addressing. "We are now approaching the abbey of St.-Michel-de-Frigolet, founded in the tenth century by the monks of nearby Montmajour...."

It was unusually cool for Provence in June, but the coolness deepened the green of the many pine, cypress, and olive trees. Lavender and rosemary bushes lined the road. The sky had been so overcast throughout our visit that I could barely imagine the blistering sun that symbolizes Provence.

My reverie was interrupted by my five-year-old sister, wobbling down the aisle. She looked excited. "Olivia, we're going to get to see where they make Frito-Lays!"

"Go back to your seat, Sophia, or you're fall down," I warned, as I tried not to laugh.

My father continued. "The monks of St.-Michel-de-Frigolet manufacture a very strong liqueur, made famous by

Alphonse Daudet in his short story, 'L'Elixir du Reverend Père Gaucher.' He depicted a monk of this abbey, the taster of the elixir, as being perpetually drunk...."

My seven-year-old sister blurted out, "Hey, a drunk monk!"

"Victoria," I sighed. My sisters did not yet hold an interest in French culture. Maybe they would when they were twelve years old....

As I listened to the rest of the monastery's history, I could see its gates through the bus's huge front window. "The abbey serves as a retreat center, so please refrain from making loud noises," my father concluded, looking intently at my two younger sisters.

The bus emptied quickly but more quietly than usual, as the group gathered into clusters of two or three. The scores of bird songs which greeted us were soon accompanied and almost overpowered by the scrunch our many feet made on the gravel walk. The powerful winds of southern France had bowed some trees in permanent welcome, and their leaves rustled against the monastery's stone wall. We regrouped by the gift shop, where the monks sold the bottles of liqueur. Someone was talking loudly in French. Curious, I moved to the front of the large group, following the voice. Our guide-to-be, Père Raymond—an elderly monk—was welcoming the group. He must have been under five feet tall. As he stood squinting at us, his small, bright eyes, sharp nose, and spiky gray hair reminded me of Beatrix Potter's kindly Mrs. Tiggywinkle. He wore a long-sleeved white robe and thick white socks under his sandals. We followed him into the church of St.-Michel.

Père Raymond explained to us that a florist's wedding had taken place the day before, as we marveled over the hundreds of white lilies and roses decorating the church. Their heavy fragrances hung in the air, an invisible but nonetheless tangi-

ble tapestry of scent. Even among the dozens of French
churches I had already visited, St.-Michel was remarkable for
its ornamentation: gold motifs flashed from columns, and
ornate flower patterns enlivened the walls. We slowly made
our way up the nave and into the side altar, the chapel of
Notre Dame du Bon Remede. Intricate designs led to the
beautiful ceiling high above, and shining arcs guided my eye
to a small stained glass circle, which shone as if...had the sun
finally come out? It would be appropriate, since the vibrant
interior of this church had been commissioned by the moth
er of the Sun King, Louis XIV, to commemorate her gratitude
for her son's safe birth.

Sitting on a long wooden bench in the chapel, I listened as
my father translated our guide's words. Père Raymond spoke
with a marked Provençal accent, gesturing with his hands and
stressing nearly every syllable. Most of the group could not
speak French, yet his enthusiasm needed no translation. He
concluded with a special blessing, leading us through a doorway in the back of the church into the cloister. Indeed, the sun
was beaming down benevolently out of the first blue sky we
had seen in days. Nothing of note was overlooked by our
guide who, after recounting the history of the roof, began to
describe the herbs growing in the small central garden to several interested women.

We proceeded into the monastery and squeezed into a room
that contained several chairs, some pots and pans, a bureau
filled with apothecary jars, and a large wooden nativity. Père
Raymond described all the items in the room for us: the huge
chairs, hundreds of years old, had been designed for the over-
sized skirts then in fashion. The glossy, abstract olive wood
nativity had been carved by a local artist for the abbey, and the
porcelain apothecary jars showed that this room had been the
pharmacy. He told us how the French Revolution had con-

verted the monastery into a boarding school where, one hundred and fifty years ago, Frédéric Mistral studied. This Nobel-prize-winning poet later wrote his beautiful, book-length work, *Mireille*, about a young woman of the Provençal region. Père Raymond told us her story with as much passion as if it had been his own. Mireille's aristrocratic father prevented her from marrying the man she loved, a penniless caner. Père Raymond sang to us the song that Mireille's lover offered to her: "*O Magali, ma tant aimable....*" His spirited voice filled the room, and though it sometimes wavered, he never missed a note.

Then he resumed his tale: Mireille set out on a pilgrimage to Stes.-Maries-de-la-Mer where, according to tradition, Mary Salome, Mary Jacobe, and their maid-servant Sarah landed after leaving the Holy Land. Mireille went there to pray to these saints for a miracle, a change of her father's heart. Yet as she traveled, her strength was taken from her by the powerful sun, and she arrived at her destination dying from heat exhaustion. Père Raymond told how the saints met the girl in a vision, and speaking with great intensity, he repeated their words to her: though Mireille would not be able to marry, she would be comforted by the greatest of all loves, the love of God.

After reciting part of Mistral's poem describing Provence, Père Raymond prayed for the group's safe return. He wished us long lives and hoped we would keep in our hearts this part of Provence which Mistral called "a bit of heaven on earth."

Our group then split up. About twenty of us went to attend Mass in the original medieval church, built in the eleventh century by the monks of Montmajour. We sat in the pews and waited for the service to begin. Finally, an elderly nun intoned a melody which we echoed. Twelve monks, including Père Raymond, sat around the altar. The quality of the music that filled the church amazed me. We became part of a divine service as our voices, raised within those ancient walls, took on a transcendent tone. In ten minutes, both my little sisters had fallen asleep.

I watched Père Raymond throughout the Mass. He held the music an inch from his face in order to read it. We later learned that he was blind in one eye and deaf in one ear. He shifted constantly, while all the other monks sat perfectly still. It was clear that he was trying his best to remain motionless but could not. He had so much energy inside— energy that had been apparent during our tour—energy that seemed to distill his enthusiastic appreciation of life itself.

After Mass was over, he called my family up to the altar. He blessed us again and prayed for our safe return. When he found out that my mother was Italian, he burst into perfect Italian, telling us that he had spent his childhood years in Italy. As we turned to leave, he summoned us back hurriedly. "You must not leave yet," he said solemnly. "You haven't seen her."

He eagerly led us to a statue, about four feet high, of the Virgin Mary with baby Jesus in her arms. He told us the history of this fifteenth-century solid-alabaster statue, a unique creation which had never been reproduced. We admired the lovely face and perfect craftsmanship, and then again we started to say goodbye.

"Wait, wait!" He exclaimed. "You have not seen her most beautiful feature!" He proudly beckoned us behind the statue: down Mary's back streamed lovely alabaster curls, flowing to her knees. Père Raymond reverently touched his hand to his lips and caressed the Virgin's hair. And so we left the man with the passionate love for life, for Provence, for God.

On the other side of the church door, the burning gaze of the sun, the poems of the birds, and the tales of the crickets greeted us. After a delicious lunch of *boeuf au basilic, frites au romarin*, and ratatouille, our group mounted the bus's steps and bid farewell to St.-Michel-de-Frigolet. But I looked back dreamily at the abbey. Hidden in these peaceful hills, it really did seem to be "a bit of heaven on earth."

As the daughter of two professors of French, Olivia Gatti Taylor's travels began in utero in 1979 and continue to shape her life. Currently, she is teaching English rhetoric at Marquette University while completing a masters' degree.

* * *

Naturally Baked

Yoga Provençal requires a good sense of humor.

WE WAKE EACH DAY TO THE SOUND OF A DIFFERENT HIPPIE instrument. Day one was a Tibetan bell; on day two, Instructor Roger plays the piccolo; today, a man we call Guido because of his oiled hair and handsome gold neck chains, walks around strumming a guitar. My brother emerges furrily from another corner of the biodynamic farm, teeth unbrushed, ready to hike to the field for our *yoga matinal*.

Fifteen aspirant yogis wait in the field for Instructor Roger. All of them are French, deeply earnest, and committed to the principles of biodynamic agriculture. At dawn exactly, Instructor Roger arrives, smiling and bright. He and Instructor Claire are leading this week-long yoga and hiking retreat in the Alps of Haute Provence. Both are disciples of the Indian guru Patanjali and dedicated biodynamic vegetarians.

The sky, like the fragrant wildflowers, is a luminous purple-blue. The air smells of lavender and wild thyme; a palomino horse whinnies in the distance. The milk cows are returning from the fields, making low cow noises, the bells around their stout necks tinkling. Instructor Roger waves *bonjour* and produces a small teapot from his baggy trouser pocket. He murmurs something in Sanskrit, then cautions us in French to watch attentively. He begins pouring water into his right nostril. It drains directly out the left nostril and on to the dry ground. My brother and I are revolted and fascinated. "I'm sure it's very healthful and all," my brother whispers, "but I wouldn't do it on a first date."

I agree that it's definitely not a first-date thing.

Roger proceeds to blow his nose boisterously, spraying the wildflowers with lavish plumes, then attends to the opposite nostril. Properly purged, he launches into a lecture about the healthful effects of proper nasal hygiene. With Roger, everything becomes a lecture. The practice is called *neti*, he tells us, making the word sound more French than Sanskrit, and if practiced faithfully, will cleanse the body of impurities, physical and spiritual.

In the distance, we can see Mont Ventoux; the dawn is so clear that it is possible to see the white flag that flies from the peak. I am not sure what the flag symbolizes. Perhaps the French are surrendering again. The earth is tinder-dry, and a breeze rustles pleasantly through the grassy slopes and stirs a chorus of beating crickets, eddies of variegated butterflies.

Every morning begins with yogic nasal hygiene. We are not yet advanced enough for the teapot; instead we practice ritual noseblowing. Surrounded by golden rolled wheels of hay, we blow our noses with huge gulping snorts to Roger's cadence. *Inspire! Expire! Inspire! Expire!*

My brother leans over and whispers again: "If you do this right, you'll get high as a kite."

I blow and I blow. Nothing much happens.

Disappointingly, none of the other yogis are below the age of forty. My brother is inconsolable. "I thought this would be, you know, a *hippie* thing," he says to me. "With great-looking blond hippie girls, you know the kind with little anklets, the ones who just really like to pass the bong and *stretch?*"

"Maybe someone stretchy will show up tomorrow," I say.

He takes no comfort, and mutters to himself. "I can't believe it. I'm here with ten women old enough to be my mother, a fat guy with gold chains around his neck who wears a tiny leopard-print swimsuit, and my *sister*. This is *not* what I had in mind."

Josette and François, members of José Bové's Confederation Paysanne, run the biodynamic farm. They are not yogis themselves, but in the summer, the farm becomes a hostel of sorts for visiting groups of New Age *stagiaires*, students of yoga, astronomers, collectors of essential oils. The farm's sun-splashed dormitories sleep groups of four or five; there is an oak-paneled communal dining room with huge windows that open onto the mountains, and an activity room with walls made of local stone, cool and pleasant in the afternoon. The hostel is spotlessly clean and redolent of lavender oil. The dining room is filled with brochures denouncing the International Monetary Fund, leaflets decrying genetically modified organisms and battery farming, Greenpeace literature. To round out the activist palette, a prominent stack of tracts calls for the interposition of an international police force in Occupied Palestine.

Josette is a tall woman of handsome peasant stock and an imposing sternness, with a thick wedge of chin-length iron hair, high color, and broad shoulders. Her arms are muscular from years of heavy labor. She instantly conveys that she is not to be defied and will brook no bourgeois nonsense, no nonsense of any kind. The word *formidable* comes to mind. My brother and I imagine her children, sitting on the psychoanalyst's couch. "My mother was a *formidable* woman," we imagine them saying. She is clearly running this show; François stays in the fields and wears a series of proletarian uniforms: gray overalls, green overalls, thigh-high rubber boots suitable for mucking stalls.

In the dining room, at lunch, we examine the leaflets about biodynamic agriculture. We learn that the principles of bio-dynamic agriculture were delineated by the Austrian mystic Rudolph Steiner, in 1916. The ideal farm should be self-con-tained, he argued, with just the right number and combination of animals to provide the manure needed to revitalize the soil. These animals in turn should be fed from the same land. Biodynamic agriculture forbids the use of chemical fertilizers and pesticides, relying instead upon crop rotation and com-posting. Steiner, influenced by the Theosophists, posited subtle cosmic formative forces on plant growth, and claimed to be able to see back in time to ancient events imprinted on the cosmic ether. In his portrait, he is wearing a high starched collar and a heavy black overcoat; his eyes are wild, staring and mad.

As Steiner would have wished, the farm we are on strives for self-sufficiency, and the vegetables we eat—carrots, beets, lettuce, and fresh herbs—come from the garden behind the stable. François raises his own wheat, from which the daily bread is made. The bread is just awful, like lead.

The life of the farm appears to be organized around the daily rhythms of the twenty milk cows. They come in for milking, they go out to pasture, they come in for milking again. Each cow's name is hand-lettered above her stall. Jacinthe, Marguerite, Koala, and their companions are milked twice daily, herded to the fields by means of affectionate slaps on their marbled rumps, and allowed to graze freely. They appear to be in glorious bovine health. A calf is born the first morning we are there, white and brown with a pirate-patch of sorrel over one of his enormous eyes. He is hopelessly touching, following his mother around on unsturdy splayed legs. Behind the stable a family of black pigs and piglets scarf down slop, as Steiner would have wished: They are eating the acidic waste produced during cheesemaking so that it does not contaminate the soil. The pigs grunt happily. "Doesn't get much better than being a biodynamic pig on a vegetarian farm," my brother says, wandering over to scratch a pig behind the ears.

Later, we are dismayed to find a leaflet promoting the farm's own pâté. The farmers are vegetarians, evidently, but some of the customers are not. "This is disturbing," my brother whispers to me, showing me the leaflet. "*Very* disturbing."

While we do yoga, the farmhands work. They pitch hay, or whatever it is one does with hay. They sweep the stables. There is incessant labor involved in collecting the milk, making the cheese, and keeping these beasts warm, dry, and happy. The farmhands are always doing something disagreeable; someone is always brandishing a pitchfork, driving a tractor, industriously hauling something heavy from a truck.

The farm does not belong to Josette and François, but to a fraternal, nonprofit organization called the Earth and Sky Society. According to its charter, the organization exists to foster cultural exchanges and "make the world a better place for human life while finding a good relationship with the earth that nourishes us, a forum of life where respect for humans and nature forges a positive attitude toward humanity and its future on this planet." Major decisions about the farm are made by committee, and loans to the farm come from a fraternal bank. The farm is staffed by volunteers, many of them conscientious objectors from Germany.

The food is just abominable, but everyone keeps raving about it, because it's biodynamic. Every day Josette puts exactly the same thing on the long wooden picnic tables beneath the linden trees: dark bread with the weight and density of plutonium, a bowl of undressed lettuce garnished with edible marigolds, lentils, grated carrots, and stone-hard peaches. There is never quite enough, and even though it is a dairy farm, milk and yogurt are rationed sharply. After each meal the yogis lunge ungraciously for the scraps, bargaining savagely with each other for the last few lettuce leaves. The meals are dreary and monotonous. But no one admits it. "*C'est délicieux!*" the yogis declare, smacking their lips. "How much better it tastes when it is prepared naturally!" By the third day, my brother and I are desperate. At lunch, my brother looks down the table and whispers, softly, to no one in particular, "*coq au vin.*"

Half the table looks scandalized, as if he had revealed a fetish. But a dreamy look passes across the face of a plump woman named Anne. "*Ah oui,*" she sighs, "*avec des frites.*" Her husband looks at her indulgently, tenderly, but the rest of the table glares. "Of course this too is very good," she says quickly, applying herself to her naked lettuce leaves.

That evening I spot Jonas. Jonas is at least six and a half feet tall, not yet twenty-one, strapping, handsome, well-muscled, blond. He speaks excellent English, although very slowly, with a thick German accent that makes him sound exactly like Arnold Schwarzenegger. He looks as if he was born to invade Poland, but in fact he volunteered to work at the farm to avoid German military service. At first he thought he was clever, Jonas did, getting out of forced marches and night patrols to spend a year in Provence, but after a year of shoveling manure and slopping hogs—ten hours a day, six days a week—those night patrols are sounding better and better. He loathes the farm, loathes everything about it, is dying of boredom and hatred. He yearns to be in Berlin, listening to the music of Kraftwerk and taking Ecstasy at the fashionable clubs. He regards the yogis with pure contempt. He has lived for a year now on Josette's flavorless biodynamic cooking, and when we ask him one morning whether he will share his pot of real coffee with us—the yogis drink only decaffeinated chicory brew—he clutches the pot to his chest and growls like a cornered beast. "Not enough!" he snarls. "Find your own!"

We leave him and his coffee alone.

This is no life for a young man of his sensibilities. There is no one his age on the farm except for Josette's and François's daughter. She is plump and pretty, but Jonas suspects that François is the kind of man who knows how to use his hunting rifle. Jonas receives room and vegetarian board. They pay him a little bit every month in pocket money, not even enough to pay for gas to drive to the nearest city.

"Well," I say, "it's got to be better than the military. At least no one's shooting at you."

"Yes," he replies. "But maybe if I see another cow I shoot myself." As if to punctuate his comment, a cow moos stupidly in the distance.

How does it work, I ask him, doing public service instead of joining the military? Can you work anywhere you like?

"They like it if you work for one of Germany's enemies. You know, Ukraine, Russia, France, Israel. I think it is stupid. I wasn't responsible for that war. I wasn't even born."

Young Germans always want to tell me that they weren't responsible for the war. They say it as early in the conversation as they can.

He asks me what I do in Paris. I tell him I write novels.

"I want to write a novel, too," he says. "Like Bret Easton Ellis. He is my favorite writer."

"What do you want to write about?" I ask.

"This place," he nods toward the cows.

"What about it?" I ask.

"The story of how I sell my soul."

"You sold your soul?"

"I sell my soul to work on a biodynamic farm. I do it for my future, but I sell my soul."

"I see," I say. I am not sure what he means.

"I would write about these people. You know, François is a communist. A real one." He flings his cigarette into the flowerbed with a flick of his wrist.

"Which one is he, exactly?" I ask, trying to place him. Josette is a commanding presence, but François is just a specter.

"He is the one with all the hairs growing from his ears." *Hay-uhs gro-ving frum his ee-yahs.*

"You don't get along with them?" I ask.

He shrugs. "They don't like me because they think I am bourgeois. They hate all people who don't want to work with their hands. All intellectuals, they hate them."

I nod.

"Once," says Jonas in his Arnold Schwarzenegger accent, "I complain about the food. I say that it is always the same." *All-vays duh same.* "But Josette, she *freak out.*" He shakes his head to indicate that something awesome and terrible occurred. "I never say that again." *I neh-vuh say dat a-gain.*

As he contemplates his lot, the Tibetan chime sounds, summoning us to afternoon yoga practice.

My brother and I remark that Instructor Roger is a dead ringer for Marshall Applewhite, the leader of the Heaven's Gate cult who prompted his disciples to ingest poison mixed with applesauce in the hope of quitting their earthly vessels to ride the comet Hale-Bopp. This resemblance is especially pronounced when Roger dons his long white yoga robes. But Roger is jolly and good-natured, with a kind of softness to all his body parts. He prefers lecturing about the theory of yoga to practicing it. He lectures for hours at a stretch, winding his way slowly through each of the eight steps on the path to enlightenment. He begins each discourse with a rhetorical question: *Qu'est-ce que c'est le Pranayama? Qu'est-ce que c'est les Asanas?* He pauses for effect, scanning the class with his eyes. *Eh bien.* Then he reaches for the original Sanskrit authorities, a voluminous set of notes, photographs of a pretzeled Indian guru, and the illustrated Larousse, and begins methodically to answer his own question, saying nothing at great length. *Alors, j'explique.*

My brother and I came to practice yoga, not to listen to lectures on yoga theory, and we are maddened with impatience. But we are amazed to see that the other students appear to love these lectures, and pronounce Roger's endless disquisitions to be *très, très bien.* They *encourage* him. They raise their hands and ask long, complicated, completely incoherent theoretical questions. We are not sure whether this is because they are French, or because they are old. We suspect, though, that it is because they are French. After a two-hour lecture on the theory of yoga postures, as we become progressively more cramped and stiff from sitting motionless on the floor, my brother turns to me and asks, "How on earth do these people make love?"

Instructor Claire is deathly thin. She is nothing but bone and veins covered in translucent skin, like a jellyfish. Her spine can be viewed from the front as well as the back. My brother and I worry about her. When we go hiking, I ask what we would do if she suddenly dropped dead.

"No problem, just sling her over your shoulder and skip down the trail," my brother says.

"Could probably fit her in your backpack," I agree.

We can't figure out why she is so thin. She seems to be filling her plate with biodynamic food at every meal. Later at lunch, my brother leans over to me and whispers: "She's a chewer."

"Huh?"

"Watch how many times she chews each bite."

I watch. She is chewing every bite for a minute or more. I ask my brother what this means. He thinks that maybe she belongs to an Indian chewing sect, one in which devotees are obliged to chew each bite thirty times. The effect is nutritionally devastating, he says: The salivary enzymes decompose the proteins so thoroughly that the body can no longer use them. There is a lecture on nutrition for yogis on the schedule, but my brother declares that we will boycott it. We are not taking any nutritional advice from Instructor Claire, he says. *No way.*

> The French rivers partake of the national character. Many of them look broad, grand, and imposing; but they have no depth. And the greatest river in the country, the Rhône, loses half its usefulness from the impetuosity of the current.
>
> —J.C. and A. Hare (1847)

In the afternoons, when yoga theory crawls to a close, the gentle stretching begins, although Instructor Roger interrupts us after every pose to correct us and then offer the lengthy theoretical justification for his correction. To my side sits a plump gray-haired woman who bears so striking a resemblance to my brother's second-grade teacher that we rename her Mrs. Loeb, and cannot thereafter think of her by any other name. She is unable to do any of the yoga postures, but greatly enjoys the nose-blowing. For the entire week, she is a one-woman nose orchestra. Especially when we try to meditate. Instructor Roger's voice urges deeper and deeper relaxation, a gentle breeze stirs the dry afternoon air and rustles the grass, we focus on our breath, inhale, exhale, and—*Snort! Blast!*—there goes Mrs. Loeb's nose.

No, they are not young and lithe, these yogis. This is not the place to come to meet hippie chicks. There is Mrs. Loeb, of course, with her orchestral nose, and Christine, a drooping creature with large hips and very pale skin and sad eyes, and Marie-Thérèse, another painfully thin woman, in her sixties with dyed red hair and a pinched prune of a mouth. She complains of constipation. But we have to admit that these yogis are the gentlest, kindest group of earnest middle-aged people we have ever met. Mrs. Loeb spends hours trying to teach us the genders of French nouns. The classification of the American states is a source of puzzlement and vexation to my brother; Mrs. Loeb goes through every state in the Union with us: It is *la Californie*, but *le Kansas*, and *oui, le français*, it is not always *logique*. They are solicitous, concerned: We have arrived unprepared, without water bottles for our hikes, without raincoats. They offer their own. "But it's not raining," my brother protests. No matter; he is the youngest. They bundle him up in an enormous raincoat; his bare legs stick out underneath and he looks like a human mushroom swaying on its stalk.

At night, the yogis sit in a circle in the stone-walled activity room and sing French songs from their childhood. Together, their voices are sweet and lovely, almost childish. They sing of picking daisies, gathering wildflowers, first love. They all know all the words to the songs. Anne-Marie becomes nostalgic when they sing a song about the train that whistles. It reminds her of her first love. "How I cried," she says. I try to imagine her as a young woman.

The farm reminds them of their childhoods; they all agree. "The cows, they look like the cows when I was growing up," says Marie-Thérèse. Everyone nods vigorously. "Cows don't look like that any more," someone says. The cows do look happy, as these things go. They are outside all day; their stalls are spacious and clean; their hay is fresh. The mother and her calf are inseparable. The food tastes awful, it is true, but in the end we are glad that meat is never served. "Imagine waking up in the morning and finding just an empty stall and a cowbell where Koala used to be," my brother says.

Once, we are attempting to meditate in the activity room, when a cow walks past the window and moos loudly, making the most absurd bovine sound, a sound of pure comic stupidity. It sounds just like Mrs. Loeb blowing her nose. My brother and I begin to giggle and can't stop. The more we try, the worse it gets. We are doubled over on our yoga mats, trying to stop laughing, dying of embarrassment. The moment one of us gets a hold of ourselves, the other one starts again, and we lose control. We ruin everyone's concentration.

On Thursday evening, we are shown a videotape about biodynamic agriculture. The video shows a woman casting astrological charts, a man spraying his crops with some kind of crystal, cows being cured of hoof-and-mouth disease with homeopathic tinctures. Then Josette gives a lecture. We sit in a circle, legs crossed lotus-style. She begins by asking us each to introduce ourselves and explain what we do in the "*marche de la vie.*" I'm puzzled by the phrase, and as we go around the room, it is obvious that everyone else is puzzled too. The other yogis stammer and babble, talking about how they do yoga to relax. Josette is looking at them as if they are fools, she didn't ask about yoga and she couldn't give a damn what they do to relax. Finally, it is my turn, and since I have an excuse, I ask, what does this French expression mean, *marche de vie*? Josette stares at me, her expression stern under her iron hair. "It means," she says in French, marching her two forefingers briskly in the air, "what do you do in the walk in life?" I am no closer to understanding, but somehow I know intuitively that she is asking what sort of meaningful physical labor I do, and that no truthful answer I give will be remotely satisfactory.

I write, I say.

Her gaze is withering. Finally, she says, "What do you write?"

Feebly, I answer: "Maybe a book denouncing factory farming?"

Her face softens, slightly. "*Ça va, alors.*"

I have joined Jonas in the club of sold souls.

Wide-bottomed Yogini Christine has been flirting with Yogi Serge all week; she slaps his bottom coyly as we hike up Mount Chamouse. She seems to be flirting with Yogi Guido, too, cuddling up to him as he plays his guitar. Watching this with puzzlement, my brother asks whether I've noticed that these middle-aged French women give off an air of hideous sexual desperation. "Insane crazed lust," he says. "Like if they got their hands on you they'd tear you to shreds."

Suddenly, we both have the same idea.

"Jonas," we say in unison, and look at each other. My brother imagines Marie-Thérèse emerging from the stable, hastily rearranging herself and shaking her short dyed hair. *Oh la la! J'ai tiré un bon coup, moi!*

We know we have a moneymaker on our hands.

Later, we pitch the idea to him. "Look, Jonas, this is a strictly commercial proposal. We arrange everything and we take 10 percent. One night of work, you could make enough to spend next weekend in Biarritz."

He looks at us, the muscles in his jaw twitching. He's not sure if we're serious.

"I already sell my soul. I don't want to sell my body." *Boh-dee.*

"Aw, c'mon Jonas," I coax. "You wanted to write a novel, right? Let me tell you, no one's interested in a novel about shoveling cow shit. But a novel called *I Was a Biodynamic Gigolo*—straight to the top of the bestseller list, man, I'm telling you."

He stares at us some more. "Really?" he says at last.

"Really," I assure him.

He is thinking about it, and his head is getting warm from the effort. In the distance, we hear the cowbells and the low cow sounds. The crickets stir and croak. The children are playing *petanque* outside the stable and their voices are a gentle gabble. Jonas thinks. Christine returns from the field with an armful of fresh lavender and Spanish broom, which she will arrange in a bouquet for the dinner table. Jonas follows her wide hips with his eyes. The Tibetan chime sounds; it is time for the afternoon yoga. We leave Jonas, pitchfork in hand, golden hair gleaming in the sun, staring into the distance, contemplating the state of his soul.

Yogi Serge insists that it is possible to feel the trees' energy. On one hike, we summit a hill and find the yogis on the other side, holding hands in a ring around an ancient oak, eyes closed, expressions rapt, attempting to pass energy from hand to hand in a circle. When they are finished, each of the yogis hugs the tree in turn. My brother and I look at each other; he raises an eyebrow. We go over to the tree to try to feel the energy too. I close my eyes and stretch out my hands just like Serge. I don't feel much of anything, but of course I say that I do; I tell Serge that the energy is *très très forte*. "Did you feel anything?" I whisper to my brother afterwards.

"I felt a sort of rumbling," he says.

"*Rumbling?*"

"It's all those lentils, I think. All this biodynamic food is making me really turbo-charged, if you know what I mean."

I know *exactly* what he means.

I have almost given up on feeling the energy, writing it off as a bad job, but on the last day, Instructor Roger leads us in special yogic breathing exercises in a shady copse in the woods. The temperature of the air is exquisite, like dry champagne. We place our mats on the ground and sit with our legs crossed and our spines erect; we inhale, holding our breath, relaxing our muscles, then exhale, then inhale again. The wind rustles in the grass and the leaves of the trees. The air is so soft, the breeze so gentle, the sky so blue, the lavender so fragrant, the light so golden, that after two hours of this gentle breathing I am transported. We breathe energy into our fingers and toes, breathe energy into our scalps and our jaws and our ankles and our fingertips. We inhale and hold, we exhale and hold, my body feels as if it is lifting off the ground. My hands and my feet feel tingly and light, as if they are humming. I think I can feel the energy, yes, *definitely* I can feel the energy. I am willing to believe that the trees are speaking to me personally, telling me their sad tree stories, I can really feel it, I can, for a brief moment I can really feel it—

Then Mrs. Loeb blows her nose—*Snort! Blast!*—

My brother begins to snicker—

And the moment passes.

Claire Berlinski is a writer and freelance journalist with a newly released novel titled Loose Lips. *Since receiving her doctorate in international relations in 1995, she has worked in print media, taught at the university level, and worked for the United Nations, living in England, Thailand, Laos, San Francisco, and Washington, D.C. She is now living in Paris.*

JO BROYLES YOHAY

✶ ✶ ✶

Loving the Middle Ages

A working holiday brings rich rewards.

I STOOD UP TO STRETCH MY BACK, WITH LEGS ACHING AND jeans covered in grime. All morning, four fellow workers and I had been on hands and knees laying ancient clay floor tiles in a medieval dovecote of a Provençal hill town. The building was a tall, cylindrical tower lined with dozens of perfectly round nest holes; no doubt some wealthy villager had once kept sporting birds inside as a sign of his prosperity. Here and there, sprigs of straw still hung from the abandoned nests. The late morning sun filtered through clerestory openings and fell in a soft half-light on our slowly progressing floor.

In the midst of one of our most gorgeous spots on earth — hadn't the Impressionists thought so? — I was paying good money to crawl around in the semidarkness of a pigeon coop. Nearby lay graceful La Roque-sur-Cèze with its cobbled streets, stone houses under red-tiled roofs, gardens pungent with blooming lavender. I could have been lingering under chestnut trees or strolling sweat-free through a museum. Had I really traveled all the way from my Manhattan apartment to

swelter in the hot June of southern France—to mix mortar
with shovels, to haul great loads of cracked tiles up a treacherous
plank ramp into the second-story opening of a pigeon coop?

Yes. And my husband, Victor, had too. We were on vacation—part of an international team of volunteers convened to
help a French organization, La Sabranenque, restore abandoned medieval sites in the villages of Provence.

We were tired of conventional trips: wrestling with road
maps in a rental car, grumbling, starved, and exhausted while
we hunted for the perfect hotel at the right price. Two weeks
in one spot sounded just right.

As a veteran of one other volunteer vacation—a botanical
expedition to the jungles of French Guiana—I had a pretty
good idea that we were in for some serious work, a certain
amount of discomfort and, most likely, a rich personal experience that would stay with us forever. And that we would come
to know a place in a way that standard touring doesn't allow.

Victor, an architect, was game, delighted by the prospect of
hands-on medieval construction. I had no particular qualifica-
tions outside of a keen interest in the history of building, a
strong back from summers of gardening, a passion for France,
and a willingness to roll up my sleeves. But I had long har-
bored a romantic vision about groups of like-minded people
working together in fellowship, as I imagined some had in the
rural Alabama of my grandmother. I liked the idea of neighbors gathering for cotton picking, quilting bees, births. Was it
a chimera? What manner of traveler, besides us, would choose
a vacation of hard labor? So we signed on.

When we got off the fast train from Paris in Avignon, Marc
Simon met us at the station for the twenty-five-minute ride
to St.-Victor-la-Coste, headquarters of La Sabranenque. We
drove along a back road, past field after field of gnarled
grapevines clutching tiny green clusters of developing fruit;

past wineries whose signs invited us to come in and taste. Great bushes of broom grew wild, bordering the vineyards with brilliant yellow flowers on branching stems, long used to sweep French streets. On the way, we talked. American-born Marc told us he had volunteered for La Sabranenque thirteen years before, and had loved it so much he stayed on, eventually becoming one of the three directors. That sounded promising. In tiny St.-Victor-la-Coste, we passed a bakery, a butcher shop, a *tabac*, and two cafés with umbrellaed tables, cool under the spreading trees of the village square. Climbing farther, past houses bright with back-yard gardens, we twisted up tight, narrow streets toward the ruined hilltop castle of the Count of Sabran— a beacon for travelers approaching from far across the plains. Below the castle, we stopped at one of the houses for volunteers.

The first sight of our room delighted me. Clearly, we had entered another time zone. Built entirely of local materi-als—stone, wood, clay

A vignon: There is poetry and romance in the name; or, at least, in the asso-ciations it calls up. Petrarch, with the power that apper-tains to genius alone, has invested this place with an interest for all who can appre-ciate the beauty of his works; and we view Avignon with different feelings to those with which we regard more attrac-tive towns. The approach to Avignon is imposing: the high towers of the ancient palace, with their rich and warm toned hue of brown, rise above the walls of the city; and many a spire and steeple give beauty to the picture, which is crowned by Villeneuve, seen in the dis-tance. The battlemented walls are flanked by square towers, erected at regular distances, and have seven gates.

—Countess of Blessington
(1789–1849)

tiles—the room opened onto the countryside, inviting in the lush light and rich colors of Provence. Elegantly spartan, it was furnished with two narrow iron-frame beds, a French country armoire for our clothes, a small hardwood table that became my desk, and a straight-backed chair. One large window looked onto a sunny, walled yard below. The ceiling, with huge exposed beams, pitched steeply, as in an attic, drawing attention to two small windows near the terra-cotta floor. The first framed the view over village rooftops to fields red with poppies, and miles of vineyards beyond. The other bordered a fig tree holding the first green fruits of early summer.

A wooden door on creaking iron hinges gave onto a little stone terrace overlooking the Rhône Valley. Well-worn limestone steps crawled up the sharp hill toward the accommodations of our co-workers. Over the years, volunteers had restored all of this—by hand—using the same techniques we would learn. The total effect was a merging of indoors and outdoors. Somewhere in the distance a donkey brayed. The sound of a late afternoon *pétanque* game rose from the square.

By dinner, everyone had arrived. Two architects, an art teacher, a lawyer, a social worker, two interior designers, a librarian, a child psychologist, a financial manager—ten men, ten women—sat down at a huge table under the trees, surrounded by reclaimed stone buildings. The meal was simple: bread, freshly baked by the local *boulangerie*; a generous selection of cheeses on a huge wooden plate; Côtes du Rhône, bought in bulk from a winery in the town; a crisp green salad. The main dish, as it would be in the days to follow, was filling: at this dinner, a grand soufflé made with eggs laid the same day by neighborhood chickens. An enormous handmade basket brimming with cherries, just picked from nearby trees, was passed around for dessert. Two large affectionate dogs lounged near the table; a cat waited for her chance to inch closer and cadge some food.

Our first conversations consisted of the usual self-conscious "Where do you live?" and "What do you do for a living?" The group profile began to unfold: half North American, half European, ages ranging from around twenty to recent retirement. Two honeymooners, a couple married twenty-three years, two married people without their spouses, a majority of singles.

Founding directors Simone and "Ginou" Gignoux welcomed us. Soft-spoken and eloquent, Simone has lived in St.-Victor all her life. She has the haunting, expressive beauty of a dark-haired Modigliani figure. Ginou, spirited and robust from years of physical work, is the more vocal. His reddish beard and bushy eyebrows frame transparent blue eyes that reveal as much as his voice does. That evening he spoke ardently, in French, about the work and the region—laughing, gesturing, garnishing his stories with personal passion.

With Marc on hand to translate when necessary, we learned that in the early '60s, Simone and Ginou had begun to restore the house they live in, once the property of Simone's grandfather. Successful, they kept on, organizing a volunteer project to preserve the forty-five-foot-high castle wall. That project took two summers to complete. The volunteers' enthusiasm led Simone and Ginou to form La Sabranenque, with the aim of rebuilding the entire medieval portion of the village, which had been deserted in the early 1900s.

As word spread, neighboring villages asked for help to reclaim other historic sites. La Sabranenque committed itself to restoration for public use: chapels, monuments, portions of castles. Several times the French government has recognized the groups for projects well done, especially noting the integrity of the work and the value of the contribution.

The next morning set our daily routine. We ate the traditional *petit déjeuner*: coffee, cocoa, and hot milk from steaming caldrons on the stove; fresh-baked bread, butter, and home-made jam. By eight thirty we were ready to pile into vans and drive to the day's work site, where we stayed until twelve thirty or one before returning for lunch. Most afternoons were left free for relaxation or exploring.

During the two-week session, we worked at two locations. The first, a complex of abandoned buildings in La Roque-sur-Cèze, will eventually house the town's community center. Work assignments were general—and congenial—consensus. While four of us tiled the pigeon coop, others cut limestone for window and door openings. Victor, familiar with the unyielding granite of Massachusetts, was thrilled to chisel and saw limestone into rectangular blocks. Some volunteers tore out unsafe beams to prepare for new beams; others dug a drainage ditch and lined it artfully with stones.

The second site, a half-hour drive from St.-Victor, was the Château de Gicon, a deserted hilltop ruin whose villagers had solicited La Sabranenque's help. There, one volunteer group repaired a steep stone pathway, another shored up a castle vault, still another shoveled earth aside to uncover a fortification wall.

La Sabranenque's able directors worked alongside us. They gave expert instruction at the beginning of each session and cheerfully supervised our progress. The more we labored together, the more I came to understand their intentions. Every detail reflected their tastes and values and respect for history.

The Sabranenque methods of working—with simple regional raw materials and rigorous, manual techniques of stone masonry, stone cutting, and vault construction—are fast-disappearing crafts. Simone and Ginou hope to do more than restore the actual sites; they also want to preserve a rural way of life. They speak of the industrial world that threatens to homogenize us, that swamps us with "produced" things yet robs us of basic process. Ginou feels that volunteers, even those who work for only a short time, take something valuable back with them into the mechanized world. A Provençal farmer once would pick up rocks from his field to build his house; he located it on a hilltop to save arable land for crops; he placed his roof tiles at a certain slant to minimize erosion. The process was direct—firmly rooted in human need, in the topography and climate. Simone told me: "The spaces we use mold us. In these rural places, where there is no separation between the inside and the outside, people walk differently." I thought of myself, apartment-bound, in the damp, gray winters of Manhattan. True, by February, I too felt damp and gray and yearned for places pastoral.

With each day, as our connection to the work developed, the group relationship deepened. We lingered over meals. We gathered in the evenings at local cafés to mingle with villagers; on free afternoons and a Sunday off, we explored the countryside in small groups. One Saturday, La Sabranenque vans took everyone on a day's outing to the lively market of Uzès and a picnic at the Roman Pont du Gard. Personalities emerged: two stand-up comedians found their audience; a couple of serious snorers caused roommate problems; a woman, on vacation from her husband, committed indiscretions. But stronger than anything else, the work bonded us and gave us a depth of purpose. And it was sharing the work that finally left us with the empty-stomach feeling of loss when, at the end of the two weeks, we hugged goodbye.

Performing physical labor side by side left plenty of time for conversation. We advanced into the stuff of friendship. We talked about architecture and books and travel and boyfriends and families and dreams and feelings. And always the work.

One morning, for example, six of us were clearing rubble before we could shore up a castle wall. The conversation moved from movie preferences, through a few bawdy jokes, to a recitation of knock-knock jokes way beyond the usual third-grade level (plays on "Euripides trousers" and "Odoriferous rising"). Hilarity was what rose. When we had recited all the limericks we could remember, a Canadian barrister, all the while shoveling dirt, quoted verbatim a segment from Monty Python. The pace quickened. Still working, Carrie unselfconsciously began to quote e. e. cummings: "O sweet spontaneous / earth how often have / the / doting / fingers of prurient philosophers pinched / and / poked / thee..." The instant she was done, Brendan recited, "Whose woods these are I think I know..." Birgitte followed with *"Frühling ist wiedergekommen, Die Erde / ist wie ein Kind, das Gedichte weiss...."* ("Spring has returned. The earth is like a child who knows poems.") As if the morning had opened up something fresh inside our hearts, we went on and on, one beginning when the other finished, quoting poetry drawn from deep within our memories. So, I thought, my notion of people working together was not just romantic after all.

Another day, at the end of an especially hot work session, we were all gathered around two huge barrels of water, cleaning mortar off tools and buckets before putting them away. One playful comment led to another, a splash of water led to a splash back, and a full-fledged water fight broke out. We all shrieked like children at the beach, exuberant. I felt pure joy: in the people, in the ability of my body to perform hard work, in the act of doing something satisfying and enduring, in the pleasure of being alive.

The work was hard. Stones inevitably are heavy and must be moved from here to there to build paths and walls. Summers in Provence are hot. The mistral sometimes whirled dust into our eyes and mouths as we worked. But it was worth every callus.

One morning Victor and I worked side by side with five other people, scraping centuries of accumulated earth and vegetation from a pile of rocks that formed a crumbling fortress wall around the eleventh-century Château de Gicon. We were the first volunteer team to work at this site. Early that morning when we started, the wall had barely been visible— a pile of rubble, silent for centuries beneath the plants and soil that had claimed it. Several hours later, tired and drenched in sweat, I put down my trowel and looked out. Beyond our hill-top, 360 degrees of Provençal valley stretched over miles of vineyards, ancient olive groves, and cherry trees—branches drooping with ripe, scarlet fruit—to the roofs of the farm town Bagnols-sur-Cèze on the horizon.

I said to Victor, "Let's stop and see how it looks." Stepping back, we were astonished to see that where there had been nothing, now there was something. While we worked, stone after stone had come to life, revealing an imposing fortification wall. Massive rectangular stones at its base indicated that the wall was older than suspected—Roman, perhaps even pre-Roman. It started at what was once a castle's edge and marched across the hillside, stopping only when the hill dropped into the valley below.

For the first time, I fully understood the addiction of an archeologist's search, the exhilaration of uncovering something that no one now alive on earth had ever seen.

None of us would ever again look at stonework casually. I knew that whenever I could, I would return to this spot. Because in some indelible way, this wall—which would now give pleasure to people for ages to come—belonged to me.

Jo Broyles Yohay—wife, mother, adventurer—lives in New York.

✦ ✦ ✦

Côte d'Azur

A visit after a long absence brings an orgy
of memory, but also new sensations.

SUNLIGHT, SUNLIGHT, SUNLIGHT. CASCADING OVER ROOF TILES and palm trees and grillwork balconies and café umbrellas like a waterfall, glinting off the shimmering Mediterranean, painting mountaintops and hillsides, cobblestone squares and pebbly beaches like an artist's brush.

The supple, languorous light seduces as it illuminates, revealing all the deepest colors and corners of country and city even as it wraps you under its spell.

This is the sunlight that seduced Matisse and van Gogh, Chagall and Renoir, Cocteau and Leger—and so many other artists and writers, from Cole Porter and F. Scott Fitzgerald to Pablo Picasso and Françoise Sagan.

It is the galvanizing element in the alchemical mix of hillside and sea, herb and bloom, art and architecture, craft and cuisine, that makes the Côte d'Azur one of the most enchanted places on the planet, a land where soul and sense are celebrated, and where the layers of artistic inspiration and sensory sanctification fertilize the ground and enrich the very air.

But it was neon and lamplight that greeted me when I arrived in Nice a little before eleven p.m. on the night of July 27. Even so, the streets were luminous, and after getting settled at the palatial Hotel Negresco, I immediately made for the broad Promenade des Anglais.

The air was moist and warm, the palm trees rustled in a light breeze, and the whole city seemed to be out in easeful embrace of the balmy night. Kids rattled by on skateboards; teenagers smoked and joked and simulated the French version of cool; American parents pushed strollers and exclaimed at the softness of the air; young couples kissed in passionate oblivion, and silver-haired couples strolled hand-in-hand, lost—or rather found—in their own reveries.

And the moonlight flickered on the scraping sea, proffering a little piece of destiny, a midnight lesson for them and for me—the moonlight flickering on the ceaseless sea.

I headed for the Cours Saleya, a centuries-old square in Old Nice. The scene was amazingly vibrant, the square crammed with tiny tables showered with lamplight from the surrounding cafés, and resonant with excited conversation and leisurely laughter—the music of people with no morning duties or deadlines, of people wrapped in the endless enjoyment of the moment.

I installed myself at a far table, ordered a demi-carafe of the house rosé, and looked around. I sighed, and something inside me opened, like a flower blooming. "I'm back!" I exclaimed into my journal. "And already the Côte d'Azur is casting its spell."

The air oozed sensuality—the wine and the lamplight, the caressing air and the laughing, lilting people in t-shirts and sandals, shorts and short dresses. I remembered what I had written about the people here on my first visit to the Côte d'Azur: "If they were blessed enough to grow up here, they

have it in their bones, but if they have come here from elsewhere, they have knowingly abandoned whatever they have
abandoned because they want what this region cultivates: a
reasoned abandonment to pleasure."

The next morning I returned to the Cours Saleya and had
a *café crème* and a croissant at a café called Le Long Cours that
looked right onto stalls selling a colorful collage of flowers,
fruits, and vegetables. As I sipped and watched, and wrote,
elegant older women with well-coifed dogs smelled melons
and eyed glistening red and yellow peppers. A trio of breezy,
baguette-bearing women in floppy t-shirts and espadrilles
bought pears and peonies; housewives in sun hats and long-
sleeved dresses stuffed garlic and grapes and guavas into
woven baskets.

"*Bonjour!*" and "*Merci!*" pealed through the morning air,
past the graceful shutters and grillwork balconies on the
salmon- and peach- and wheat-colored apartments that overlook the stony square.

I spent the morning exploring the winding alleys, imaginative shops, and intimate eateries in Old Nice. For lunch I
stopped at one of the many small sidewalk places with bright
umbrellas, and had the justly renowned local specialty, *salade
niçois*, an extravagant composition of tomatoes, anchovies,
radishes, olives, artichoke hearts, cucumbers, green beans,
hard-boiled egg, tuna, and a few lettuce leaves.

After lunch I made my first visit to the Musée Matisse. This
splendid museum is set in a handsome seventeenth-century
Italian-style villa in the hillside section known as Cimiez, not
far from the artist's last residence in Nice. Engagingly intimate,
the museum's collection—68 paintings and gouache cut-outs,
236 drawings, 218 engravings, and 57 sculptures—nevertheless offered some large-scale illuminations: I was captured by a
display that presented a small canvas entitled *Tiny Pianist, Blue*

Dress, Red Background, and beside it the red cloth backdrop and easy chair Matisse used as props in the painting; viewers could see just how the artist appropriated and rendered these to suit his creation.

A series of sketches for the mural *The Dance* illuminated Matisse's painstaking efforts in the creation of that monumental masterpiece, and in a specially designed room, models for the Chapelle du Rosaire in Vence illustrated the extraordinary attention to light and line that makes the nearby chapel a luminous triumph.

And I especially liked a pairing of sketched nudes, the top one from 1950 and the bottom one from 1924, whose differences in composition, stroke, and goal elegantly embodied Matisse's evolution from naturalism to an abstractionism designed to present essences and effects rather than appearances.

For dinner I returned to the alluring alleys of Old Nice and waited in a line at a place called Nissa Socca, a four-table hole-in-the-wall that a worldly friend told me made the city's best *nissa socca,* a grainy, olive oil-flavored flatbread made with chickpeas. Accompanied by a green salad and a great house rosé, this was a simple feast that confirmed for me the notion that quotidian life in Nice is an ongoing celebration. And this notion was enhanced by the sudden presence of sidewalk musicians who serenaded my *nissa socca* with stringy guitars and even stringier voices.

The following morning I returned to Cimiez to visit the Musée National Marc Chagall. The museum houses sculptures, mosaics, sketches, and lithographs, but the spectacular core of the collection is a series of seventeen canvases inspired by biblical tales. Graced with Chagall's characteristic mix of innocence, fantasy, surreal image, and dreamlike intensity, these paintings offer an extraordinary one-stop immersion in Chagall's charismatic art.

I next picked up a rental car and drove out of Nice and into the green, flower-bright hills to Vence and the Chapelle du Rosaire, better known as the Matisse Chapel. Matisse designed and decorated the entire chapel—from candles and vestments to murals and stained-glass windows—from 1947 to 1951, in gratitude for the loving care the Dominican sisters associated with the chapel had given him during a long illness. Matisse prized this work as much as anything he did in his life: "Despite its imperfections," he wrote, "I think it is my master-piece...the result of a lifetime devoted to the search for truth."

Sacred in its spareness and simplicity, the chapel's interior is all white save for one wall, where the *Stations of the Cross* are sparingly sketched in black and white. The only other colors in the room are in the heavenly stained-glass windows, whose deep yellows, greens and blues, dazzling in their intensity, seem intimations of otherworldly ecstasy.

Moved almost to tears by the stark power of the chapel, I sat in a pew and felt Matisse's love filling the space, and then the sheer calmness of the place washed over me. It seemed to reduce all the complexities of the universe to the bare essen-tials, and in that context the stained-glass windows seemed to symbolize the radiant riches that await us when we journey beyond complexity to the simple heart of things. Perhaps this was Matisse's "truth," I thought: life reduced to yellow, green, and blue—like the Côte d'Azur itself, a luminous liberated vision, a celebration of the simple and everyday.

In a sense, my next stop, St.-Paul-de-Vence, is a worldly version of the Matisse Chapel. It bestows something of the same tranquillity, and something of the same realization that life, simple life, everyday life—the common human gift to delight in color and shape, taste and texture and smell—is a great blessing in and of itself.

St.-Paul-de-Vence is a particularly happy marriage of the

old and the new: a meandering medieval village of cobbled lanes and broken battlements, whose stony dwellings now house galleries, restaurants, crafts shops, and cafés. The only invaders today are the tourists who squeeze through its narrow streets, but because cars are effectively prohibited, the village seems a supremely liveable place. Green vines arch over alleyways, purple tendrils clamber up sunsplashed walls, crimson flowers burst from window boxes—and the tourists and the residents come and go in easy harmony, a harmony that seems to draw its steadfast power from the stones and the hills surrounding.

I especially love the texture of St.-Paul, and the way the whole village seems to embody tranquillity and tastefulness: The galleries are in themselves artful compositions of colorful canvases and provocative sculptures; in the shops, the platters and bowls, scarves and shawls, are composed of the same rich, earthy tones as the hills and the gardens and the houses outside; and in the alleyways, the fragrances of specialty store herbs and perfumes mingle

The other day we hiked through a slot canyon with rocks rising five stories high. The next afternoon, we walked along the famous limestone crests of the Petit Luberon, visiting the remains of a fortress which Louis XIV destroyed in 1660. There were enough walls left to imagine what it might have looked like. Often we come down from the trail and walk through a village on market day. For sale are shawls, handmade jewelry, lavender oil and soap, cheeses, olives, dozens of different types of tapenade, and fresh bread. We load up on food, then hike to the top of the village, past the church, always on the highest point, then back down onto the trail.

—Margie Goldsmith,
"Hiking in Provence"

with the scents of garlic and pizza. As dusk fell over the village, I felt I had stumbled upon a French version of Brigadoon, a place that preserved old secrets and treasured them, and gave them to you if you knew where and when to look.

Stained-glass windows, stony walls, pine-green hillsides and straw-colored, terra-cotta-roofed villas, a *café crème* and a *crème brûlee*, a Provençal pizza, and a house rosé—"Look around you," everything seemed to say, "the meaning you seek is there."

I devoted most of the next morning to a place I remembered with particular wonder from eighteen years before: the Fondation Maeght, *musçe extraordinaire*, an astonishingly imaginative and inviting shrine to modern art.

Sunlight sluiced through the cool trees and spotlit the sculptures in the magnificent open-air exhibition garden at the entrance, where works by Miró, Henry Moore, Giacometti, Calder, and Arp are enhanced by the tangled boughs, freshening breeze, and play of shadow and light. When I first saw this sculpture garden many years ago, I was awed by its boldness and brilliance; over time it had grown in my mind, so that I expected a setting twice as large, but once I absorbed that initial disappointment, I was as entranced as ever. All sculptures should be able to stretch their limbs this way, I thought.

Then I wandered through the interior galleries of the museum and lingered again before its small but exceptional collection of modern masterpieces, works by Miró, Bonnard, Kandinsky, Braque, Picasso, Leger, and other giants. The thrilling theories of the surrealists came to life again for me, the impassioned and impassioning collaboration of poets and painters, the breaking of barriers and exploring of possibilities, and the fervent sense that art could make a difference in the world.

As I wandered again outside into the wonderful Giacometti courtyard and then to admire a pine-framed, enigmatic sculpture by Miró called *La Fourche*, I felt as if the years were slipping off my shoulders, as if the combination of art and light were somehow reawakening me, pouring robust new colors and energies into my own artistic palette—I felt like a pine tree, or a Chagal painting; and I savored the sense, once again, that the only real limits on our aspirations and achievements are the limits we impose on ourselves. Perhaps it was just old romantic blooms opening again in the Provençal sun, but I felt these artists and their works were offering one more crucial Côte d'Azur lesson: the nurturing necessity of living—celebrating—life to the full.

From the Fondation Maeght I traced a switchback trail toward Cap-Ferrat over rivers, past golden meadows and green hills, and into the picturesque villages, centuries-old towns perched precariously on overgrown hillsides like terracotta-roofed rock outcroppings. At one point, I turned off the road and explored the wind-swept, vine-tangled ruins of an ancient castle. From its promontory I surveyed a synthesizing 360-degree scene: on one side, cultivated patchwork fields, deep green forests and the hazy Alps in the distance; on the opposite side, the sprawling, sophisticated streets, chic beaches, and shimmering seas of the Mediterranean coast.

Another high point of the trip was a stop in tiny Peille. The annual lavender festival was due to begin the following day, and purple piles of the flower—ready for distilling in the morning—perfumed the rocky byways. Peille was like an untouched, untouristed version of St.-Paul, with bright bouquets of flowers around the town square, a mix of gregariously welcoming and shyly smiling residents, and rocky buildings and lanes that seemed to have arrived miraculously intact from a much earlier age.

The following day brought visions of yet another facet of the Côte d'Azur: the verdant and pastel seaside resorts of Cap-Ferrat and Villefranche-sur-Mer, with their magnificent Mediterranean-style mansions, sleek yachts, and placid harbors. Cap-Ferrat conferred a sense of easeful elegance, and Villefranche charmed with its photogenic waterfront, all bobbing boats and umbrella-shaded sidewalk tables, palm trees and potted plants, and pastel buildings festive with flags and flapping laundry. In Villefranche, I was also charmed by the Chapelle St.-Pierre, a tiny waterfront former fisherman's sanctuary that was painted from top to bottom, inside and out, by Jean Cocteau in 1957—a fertile, almost feverish counterpart to Matisse's stark masterpiece in Vence.

When I departed the Chapelle St.-Pierre, I had about half a day left in my Côte d'Azur stay and about half a month of exploring I still wanted to do. I wanted to visit Renoir's former home in Cagnes-sur-Mer and the Picasso museums in Vallauris and Antibes. I wanted to visit the Cocteau museum in Menton and the Musée National Fernand Leger in Biot.

I wanted to visit Cannes and St.-Tropez, Monaco and perched villages like Eze and Saorge I had only been able to glimpse from afar. I wanted to visit Haut-de-Cagnes, where I had fallen ineluctably in unrequited love many years before, and Cap d'Antibes, to pay homage to Sara and Gerald Murphy and the enchanted world they had created for a few brief years half a century ago.

Alas, the end of my own enchanted stay was approaching, and already the trip was beginning to take on something of the quality of legend and myth in my mind.

So I motored back to Nice for a final night at the Hotel Beau Rivage, a luxurious place with an artistic legacy—Matisse lived and painted there on his first visit to Nice in

1916, and Anton Chekhov was inspired to write *The Seagull* there in 1891—just off the Promenade des Anglais.

I decided I couldn't leave the Côte d'Azur without at least one quick dip in the Mediterranean, so I made my way to the pebbly beach, stepped gingerly among the bronzing beauties who had staked their bathing-towel-sized claims since early morning, and dove into the cool, salty water.

After half an hour of floating and flailing, I repaired to the Beau Rivage's beachfront restaurant. Lunch there, unfortunately, was expensive and otherwise unremarkable, but the enclosed setting right on the windy beach was consolation: the sun-washed coast stretched and arced as far as eye could see, like an arm raised in salutation or extended in embrace. Surveying the scene, I thought again about the sheer sensuality of the place, of how the beach and the air, the sea and the sun have become such a seamless part of Nice's culture that skimpy clothes and prodigious

---

"There was this girl on a bicycle with her skirts hiked up on the beach where we landed. We were surprised to see her in Downtown World War II, and she was surprised to see a hundred American Rangers."

My friend in the steam room at the San Francisco Press Club would find St.-Tropez somewhat changed. (For one thing, that girl is probably a grandmother.) But sensual surprise is still part of the deal in this French Riviera village, where *le high life*, Brigitte Bardot, and movie madness took over from the sleepytime centuries. Something in the sun, sea, cobblestones, and faces still keeps faith with a history of Roman settlement and Gallic culture.

—Herbert Gold, "St.-Tropez," *Travel & Leisure*

flesh, the carefree liaison and the public caress all seem part of a coherent and coalescing whole.

That night I returned to the Hotel Negresco for dinner in its celebrated (Michelin two-star) Chantecler restaurant where the chef created an extraordinary feast that was both an illumination and celebration of Provençal ingredients, with such imaginative concoctions as a puff pastry tuna tart with sun-dried tomatoes and basil; a terrine of local rouget fish with zucchini, tomatoes, basil, and aioli; sauteed langoustines with broad beans and fried onions; roast lamb with potato cakes; and a warm chocolate tart with almond-flavored cream. Hours later I waddled out into the soft, humid, embracing night and headed for a final espresso in Old Nice. As they had four nights before, the streets lilted with light and music and laughter, and a sense of well-being seemed to effortlessly infuse the air. I sat and sipped in one of the town's central squares, surrounded by cafés, crafts shops, and a medieval cathedral, and tried to put the four fervid days into some kind of perspective.

I took out my journal and read the first entry I had made on the flight over, a time that now seemed inconceivably long ago: "Sipping champagne somewhere over the Atlantic, I begin to dream of the life Fitzgerald and Murphy had created in the heady days of the early 1920s on the Côte d'Azur. They were the artist-pioneers, crafting what would become one of the world's chicest summer resorts out of what had been a royal retreat in winter and a scene of abandonment during the sun-flooded, skin-burning middle months of the year.

"I had crafted my own Côte d'Azur in 1975, when, fresh out of college, I had stopped there en route to a year-long fellowship in Athens, after a summer in Paris. All the world was magical in those days, and nowhere more magical than the land of lyrical landscapes and laughing eyes, exhilarating art-work and alfresco feasting—of the good life made palpable—

I had found in Cannes and Nice and St.-Paul-de-Vence.

"Now I am returning years later, a four-day birthday present to myself, and wondering how the Côte has changed, and how I have changed, and if it can possibly be as magical as it had been before, and if I can possibly be as open to that magic as I had been half of my life ago."

I looked up at the cathedral and the bright cafés and the buoyant faces around me, listened to the jazz dancing through the night's caressing air, smelled the lingering scents of gardenias and pizzas, and thought: I will never lose this moment, never leave this place. I have it inside me now.

And I took out my pen and wrote: "Now I think I understand what this pilgrimage is all about: It has something to do with passion and possibility, something to do with responsibility and love. It has something to do with chevre and *foie gras* on a sun-splashed terrace, and cypress and olive trees, the moonlight shimmering on the Mediterranean Sea—and painting and poetry.

"It is the infinite variety of the world, the celebration of the body and the senses, the liberation of the self and the immersion in human creation and human history. It is connection, with a culture and a place, and falling in love—with places old and new, people old and new, and with yourself old and new, too."

Donald W. George was the award-winning travel editor of the San Francisco Examiner *for nine years before becoming travel editor of* Salon.com. *Currently he is global travel editor for Lonely Planet Publications. His career as a peripatetic scribbler started in Paris, where he lived and worked and fell in love (several times) the summer between his junior and senior years at Princeton. He is the editor of* Wanderlust: Real Life Tales of Adventure and Romance, *and co-editor of* A House Somewhere: Tales of Life Abroad *and* Travelers' Tales Japan.

$\star \overset{\star}{} \star$

Sportif!

A cyclist discovers the heart of Provence.

"No SPORTIF!" EXCLAIMS THE GAP-TOOTHED SHOPKEEPER, flapping his hand across his chest as if to indicate a palpitating heart. There is a line behind us, but the man isn't in a hurry to conduct our transaction. He points to our tandem bicycle leaning against the outside wall.

Naturally, he says, cycling is something he would do himself, if not for the fact that he is woefully out of shape and a bit portly. The line presses forward, but our friend has further questions. After all, one does not rush things in Provence. He wants to know: How far have we come that day? Where will we stay? Are we tired?

We answer each question in turn, and I begin to wonder: Could this be France? Or have we somehow slipped across the border into another country?

After countless trips to this land, including some as a journalist covering the Tour de France, there is one rejoinder I have come to expect to almost every question—the single word that most represents the maddening intransigence of these enigmatic but lovable people: *non*.

"Can you change some money?"

"*Non*."

"Are you open for business?"

"*Non*."

"Do you know the way to Nice?"

"*Non*."

But not here. Time and again, the Provençal people display a hospitable nature I have not known elsewhere in France. Directions are given gladly. Shops remain open after closing to supply baguettes for a picnic. Tools are proffered for an impromptu bike repair.

Here, the word is *oui*.

The amiable shopkeeper follows us to the door, wearing a slight smile. He has one final question: using impeccable sign language, he asks if Meredith rides the tandem with her feet up. Laughter all around.

"*Bon courage!*" he offers as we clip in and begin pedaling the last few miles to the hotel.

Yes, I begin to think, things are going to be different this time. But why? Is it our conspicuous *velo por deux*? Is it the season? Or is it just Provence?

Provence is a region that measures roughly 150 miles across, bounded by the southern cities of Nîmes and Marseilles and the stark, towering Mont Ventoux to the north, site of a controversial Tour de France death in '67. It is known for its gentle countryside, dotted with the traditional crops of lavender and olive, but also for the rough, serrated ridges of the Lubéron and Alpilles ranges. And of course there is the vast Mediterranean coastline and its Côte d'Azur, where the surf seems made for human immersion. The water is nearly perfect, in temperature, visibility, and color—a luminescent blue that seemingly draws half the

French population, like a vast and colorful magnet, each July and August.

Cyclists are also drawn here. Tiny hilltop villages dot the landscape like stepping stones for a traveler. A thicket of narrow country lanes overlays the countryside, making it easy to find traffic-free routes. The climbs are scenic, with plentiful switchbacks—perfect for a tandem.

Almost all who visit come away with the traditional Provençal prizes of flowered linen and lavender soap, obtained from the boisterous outdoor markets that are a fixture in nearly every town almost as much so as the sport of boules, a simple throwing game that is at once entertainment, religion, and determinant of social strata.

All told, it is a region that is as much a destination for the French themselves as for outsiders. And from that fact, one can surmise that it is a very fine destination indeed.

France certainly has its mountains—huge ones, of Tour-de-France proportions—but we did not

---

Surely the attribute as unique to Moustiers Ste.-Marie as the gilt star that hangs suspended above the ravine is the pervasive sound of running water. Open spouts spill into the *lavoirs* that dot almost every block. Where once the housewives did laundry, today visiting dogs lap, babies dangle and splash, and their parents lave sweaty arms and foreheads as they pause in their trudge uphill in the summer heat. Shopkeepers still gather bucketsful to douse their entryways after the street sweeper has droned by, agitating the dust and leaves along the curbs or edges of the buildings. Even as I pushed open the shutters of my bedroom in the little studio to view the valley below, the rushing roar of the cascade flooded over me.

—Ethel F. Mussen,
"L'Amoureuse de Moustiers"

expect to find any of them in this bucolic corner of the country. Nonetheless, by trip's end, our Cat Eye cyclecomputer has tallied a couple of Everests worth of climbing: 53,000 feet, or almost 6,000 per day. Normally, such numbers would be anathema to tandem riders—gravity latches firmly onto a 340-pound bike-and-rider package. But to our surprise, Meredith and I find the climbing almost effortless. The switchback ascents are scenic, long, and rhythmic. We sit and stand alternately, telegraphing the move with a quick shift between two gears. Pretty soon we are inspecting the map for more climbs—seeking them out.

But today we are to traverse France's Grand Canyon du Verdon. For much of it, the slope is a leg-deadening 13 percent, with none of the accustomed switchbacks.

"*Bon courage,*" yell bystanders. After an hour of this we arrive, panting, at what our altimeter tells us is the highest point of the trip—4,100 feet.

But as it turns out, the climb is the least of our worries this day. Now we must deal with the descent. Like so many mountain roads here, there are awesome views but precipitous drops—and no guardrails. A moment's inattention will land you in the tiny blue ribbon of water snaking its way through the canyon below. Like a trucker, I feather the brakes and am constantly on the lookout for escape routes, but there are none. To avoid overheating the brakes, I alternate between the two cantilevers and rear disk. At one point we stop to check things and discover the disk pads are worn to uselessness. What's more, the disk itself has changed from silver to black, as if worked over by a blacksmith. A spritz of water dances across the surface and is gone, like drops on a hot griddle.

We eventually find the others in our six-tandem group. They've foregone the climb and are enjoying a glorious

Provençal picnic of three types of olives, sausage, fresh fruit, bread, and apple pie amid the views. Provençal food is legendary, and we enjoy it with the vigor that can only come from riding four to six hours per day. Each night, the entire group assembles at a vast table and dines en masse. This night we are served fresh melon, a cheese tart, roasted chicken, a salad with local olives on a vast bed of greens, and potatoes.

Meredith and I are tired from a day of climbing, and so refuse the offer of *tarte de pomme* and begin heading up to bed. The chef grudgingly allows this, but not without ample compensation. She hurries to the back, and emerges with a beautiful pink rose.

Our mount for the week is the superb Green Gear Tandem Two's Day, which disassembles to fit in two Samsonite suitcases and thus avoids the onerous airline shipping fee. At one point I slip the chain, whereupon it wedges under the derailleur cage and bends the frame tab. *Merde.* Half an hour of work with all types of improvised tools brings no result, and we put the derailleur in our rack pack and pedal to the next town in the middle chain ring.

Luckily, we find a full toolbox. Some judicious blows of the hammer to the derailleur hanger, and we are in business.

At the end of day three, just twenty kilometers from our hotel and the requisite *café au lait*, a wind rises ominously from the west, blowing directly into our faces. We figure it is nothing to be worried about.

We are wrong.

By six A.M. the shutters are slapping, and a quick look out the window reveals olive trees bent sideways in the wind. It has come. The mistral.

In his acclaimed book, *A Year in Provence*, Peter Mayle says that the famed mistral has been rumored to "blow the ears off a donkey." Or the helmet off a bike rider, we might add. So strong is the gale that heavy tandems left casually leaning against a wall are immediately deposited on the ground. Bushes are uprooted and blown across the road. Ceramic roof tiles become airborne like so much paper litter.

For much of the day our computer reads six to eight miles per hour, on the flats. For hours, we never stray from the small ring. My ears hurt from the din, and my upper body aches from the exertion of holding the handlebar. At times the wind shifts to the side and the bike, with all its weight, must be leaned to compensate, making us look oddly crablike as we inch our way down the road.

At one point, near Aurons, we crest a small hill and a forceful gust rips across our path from the side. In a second, we are in the ditch. We dust ourselves off and continue. Thankfully, no damage.

Though we are equipped with picnic supplies (our normal fare: bread, fruit, cheese), and the views are spectacular, we are in no mood to find a vista in the howling gale. Seeing no other option, we crawl inside a bus stop that is covered on three sides. Given the beauty that is all around, it's a rather ignominious picnic. But we don't mind. For the first time all day, it is quiet.

We continue at walking speed, or slower, as we climb gradually through the vast park that is the Alpilles mountains. After what seems like hours, we arrive in Arles. Though the town is famous for its Roman ruins, few of us have the energy to explore. Overall, it is the hardest day of the trip. We all go to bed hoping the mistral goes to bed, too.

In Castellane, we watch what seems to be the entire town playing the venerable game of boules in a dirt square that surrounds the town fountain. Boules has the simplistic appeal of soccer, without the athleticism. A small ball or *cochonnet* is thrown into the courtyard a distance of some thirty yards, whereupon each player in turn tries to heave their three heavy iron balls toward it, as close as possible, without hitting it.

One side of the court is reserved for the best players, characterized by their jaunty style and the fact that they have brought their own balls in plush carrying cases. These men throw with amazing accuracy. On the other side of the court, eager young novitiates practice with an element of wildness; balls occasionally career into the street. Each expert has his own style. One stands nearly stock still and uses spin to achieve exact placement. The ball hovers above the ground, and then lands as if in clay. Due to counterspin, it moves hardly an inch. A lean man with a cigarette prefers a brisk running start—his forte is to loft the ball and score a direct hit, knocking the interloper across the court. Great billows of smoke celebrate the achievement.

In an impressive show of egalitarianism, the elders yield the court entirely to the novices late in the evening, and the chatter of the boules goes well into the night. At eleven P.M. we ascend the stairs to bed, throw open the shutters, and fall asleep to the pleasing knack, knack of the steel balls striking one another in the square below. Another perfect Provençal day.

"There is something about the French," two expatriate cycling friends are fond of saying. "Whatever they do, they do well."

To us, this is nearly everything.

Each morning I am awakened by church bells in the village square. I lie on my back and count the chimes—one, two, three—to determine whether it's time to rise. It makes me wonder: Why can't all alarms work so perfectly, gently? I look outside, and witness a valley view that invites taking pictures from the bed. Small pillars of smoke rise from countless country farms, where lavender is being burned for soap and perfume. The smell permeates the air.

Though the trip is winding down, and we are reluctant for it to do so, the scenery inspires us all morning, and we jam through the valleys in the company of one other tandem, even sprinting for the requisite town-limit signs. In one village we enjoy *salade niçois* and *café au lait* while overlooking a gorge. Above the ancient stone village, the neon wings of paragliders soar, forming a curious juxtaposition of old and new.

That night we witness a parade in which the older men of the village don traditional Provençal clothes and walk the streets singing ballads, guided by young people with candles. At each bar—and there are many— the revelers are invited in for a complimentary cognac, whereupon they resume their increasingly meandering path down the street. The children, being the only sober elements of the procession, serve as fence posts for the listing and inebriated men.

The parade ends in a small cement square, where loud French rock music echoes off the building walls. It is a truly egalitarian event. The traditional dancers mix with the young in a whorl of motion. Suddenly, a friend is pulled into the dervish by a French woman, and obliges with some spinning, reckless steps. In that moment, all of us are French.

No, more than that; we are Provençal. For in the end, I realized, it was Provence. Only Provence.

Oui.

Geoff Drake is a writer, magazine editor, and website content editor. His specialty topic areas include cycling, running, fitness, nutrition, and training. He works for Bicycling Magazine *and lives in California.*

Taureau, Taureau!

An afternoon's entertainment lasts a lifetime.

"*VENEZ!*" THE MEN SHOUT. "*C'EST UN PETIT BEBÉ! IL s'appele Eduard.*"

The "little baby" weighs about five hundred pounds, and he's frisky. Eduard comes roaring past the wooden gate, horns gleaming in the sunlight. He takes an energetic lap around the pit, and looks for some nice, soft human flesh to gore.

I am in the south of France on a student exchange program. My group has twenty-three other students from countries around Europe. I am the only one from India in the group, and until now, have not discovered anyone else who can speak English. So French it is, from morning till night. To keep us occupied, our hosts at the Lions Club provide us with three-hour lunches, bottles of dusky rosé, cheeses that melt on the tongue, and all that Provence has to offer.

Today it is a mock bullfight.

We are at a private ranch near Avignon. For the last hour, the ranch hands have entertained us by fighting bulls in a huge pit dug into the hard, dry ground. We lean over a thin wood railing watching them, and around us, lavender blooms wild and purple, the flowers scenting the hot Provence air. The pit is walled in concrete and has another ring of wooden barriers along the outer edge with slender man-size openings, which the bullfighters use to skip behind the barriers when they cannot outrun the bulls. One after another the bulls are let inside. The men are clad in startling white pants and shirts (cricket whites to me, but this is no leisurely summer afternoon cricket game). They prance nimbly around the bulls, metal claws in one hand, with which they swipe at the little piece of cloth tied around the bull's horns. When one gets the prize, he runs up to us and with a flourish, presents it to a woman in the group—like a chivalrous knight of yore.

When the last bull is herded from the pit, the men huddle together, then look up, teeth flashing in the afternoon sunshine.

"A treat for you," one of the men says with a bow. "You can fight the bulls now."

They let Eduard in. He's a bull-in-training, or as they put it, a *petit bebé*.

"Come," the men yell again.

Those of us foolhardy enough to face the bull (count me in that number), tumble down into the pit. One of the bullfighters, young, blond, very handsome, smiles winningly at me and holds out his hand. Under other circumstances...but the *taureau* is simmering in one corner, eyeing us for sudden movements. The bullfighter runs up to me, feet pounding on the dry dirt, and grabs hold of my hand. Then he pulls me toward the bull. I am protesting, but in whispers.

"Let me go," I hiss.

The bullfighter pays no attention.

We walk toward the bull, or rather he walks, and I drag along behind, trying to pry his fingers loose with my other hand.

The bull watches us. It paws at the ground. It snorts. It lowers its head to show off deadly horns, eyes menacing on the top of its head. Shouldn't we be running already?

The bullfighter does not think so. We keep walking toward the bull. When we are ten feet away, Eduard decides enough is enough. He draws himself up and plunges at us.

"Run!" the bullfighter shouts, and whips away to his left.

I stand mesmerized, watching Eduard barreling his way toward me.

"Run!" my friends shout. "Run, Indu!"

I wheel sharply to my right and start to flee toward the wooden barriers. Eduard, despite his height and weight, and his now-speedy run, expertly shifts bearing (on a dime, as carmakers like to say) and careens in my direction.

I have never run so fast before. If there was a world record to beat—for fastest short-sprint-with-raging-bull-at-heels—I must have decimated it. I can hear Eduard pounding in my wake. As I near the barrier, I realize that it looms six feet high at least, well over my height. The opening is a few yards to my left. Eduard and I will surely collide before I can get to the opening—I have not his dexterity at turning and maintaining speed.

Fear lends flight to my feet. I am soaring off the ground even before I reach the barrier. I scramble desperately, finding finger- and footholds on smooth wooden planks, heave myself over the top and fall onto the ground beyond.

The little *bebé* crashes into the wood a few seconds after I have disappeared. From my vantage point on the ground, the planks groan, bend, and then right themselves.

People clap and cheer. I hear a bullfighter say, "Now, isn't Eduard playful?"

My back aches, my lungs are empty of air, the sun spins in circles in the sky. A hawk twirls lazily past. Strangely exhilarated, I find the niches in the concrete wall and climb up to willing hands. Everyone is smiling at me.

"Well done," they say, patting me on the back.

I accept the congratulations, but I do not know why I am being lauded. For outrunning Eduard? Safe now, I am quite ashamed that I could not neatly sidestep Eduard's charge and flick the bit of linen from between his horns. He was a little baby, for pity's sake.

Many years later, Gerda, an Austrian who was part of my group, sends me a postcard. On the top is a drawing of a soccer field. The players, in their striped shirts and shorts, are huddled behind the goalie's net. A magnificent bull stands snorting in the middle of the field, defying trespass on his new territory. Gerda writes, "*Tu étais plus courageuse, Indu!*" You were much braver.

I wasn't. But she is awfully kind to remember it so.

With bulls chasing her only in dreams now, Indu Sundaresan settled down enough to write a historical novel. The Twentieth Wife *is the story of an almost abandoned child who grows up to become the most powerful empress in the Mughal dynasty that built the Taj Mahal in India. The sequel, titled* The Feast of Roses, *was recently released.*

JULIE JINDAL

* * *

More Cheese, Please

She learns the secret of French dining.

ONCE AGAIN, ON THIS FINAL EVENING IN PROVENCE, IT WAS time for the cheese course and the overloaded cart rumbled our way.

Anticipation mixed with dread in what little space remained in my stomach. Resisting the cheese was a struggle I'd fought and lost the last three nights. I wanted to sample a few of the dozen cheeses artfully displayed under a glass dome. I also wanted to exit the dining room gracefully after the meal. Indulging in cheese guaranteed that when dinner officially ended, instead of rising from my chair with quiet refinement, I would act like my grandfather after Thanksgiving dinner: waddling, groaning audibly, and rubbing a distended belly.

My husband Ajay and I were staying at a lovely inn outside of Joucas (not far from Gordes) overlooking the Luberon valley. Long, skinny patches of yellow and pale green carpeted the valley. April was still the off-season for Provence—the lavender fields were merely large expanses of tiny brown sticks—making this sanctuary, which normally caters to the well-heeled, fall within our price range.

We arrived that first night after eight, weary from the day-long drive from Paris. Fat raindrops spattered the windshield as we turned into the parking lot and found a small spot for our economical Renault sedan. As we cracked open the car doors, the legendary mistral grabbed the doors and tried to fling them outwards to bash into the neighboring BMW and Mercedes. We frantically grabbed the doors, pulling them towards us while sliding carefully out of the car. The icy wind sliced through our spring jackets, shoving us like a schoolyard bully across the parking lot to the low, white stucco building.

After checking in, we peeked in the dining room enroute to our room. Several subdued couples filled half of the ten round tables. Formal white linens, padded chairs upholstered in apricot damask, and the muted clink of fine silver confirmed that our travel-stained khakis needed an upgrade. Rich aromas followed us to our room just around the corner.

Whitewashed walls and arched doorways enhanced our large, pleasant room, and the hotel's terrycloth slippers offered welcome relief from frigid tile floors. What we truly craved was a hot bath and bed, but the smells of dinner were simply irresistible. I changed into a skirt and pumps as Ajay donned a dress shirt and tie.

Shivering when the wind rattled the windows, we entered the dining room. An aperitif sounded like an excellent way to chase away the cold. An inky black sky filled the glass doors near our table, and luxurious curtains turned the doors into enormous picture windows. A few yellow dots marked far-away farmhouses. I sipped the sweet orange liqueur and my shoulders began to unknot.

Slowly, sensuously, I experienced my first multi-course French meal. Tiny samples of flawless food, cooked in imaginative ways, arrived at our table as though a conjurer were at work just out of our sight. Delicate crisps of fried duck skin in a crystal dish. A sampling of marinated figs and seasoned olives. A small, exquisite Parmesan cheese and bacon tart garnished with roasted hazelnuts. Bread studded with succulent olive bits. Three bites of tuna shaped into a perfect circle accented with a savory sauce. A short tower of artichoke hearts layered with beef, topped with breaded, deep-fried lamb. And these were merely the appetizers.

The main dish was grilled *foie gras* with a light carrot sauce. Then came the cheese course—silky Camemberts, piquant chevres, complex Roqueforts—accompanied by more fresh bread. Next came a palate cleanser of mint sorbet and herbed cream custard before the main dessert: a baked apple with caramel, resting on pie pastry and topped with ice cream. Placed between Ajay and me, a small rustic basket made of twigs displayed six different types of miniature cookies. And to leave a delightful taste in one's mouth, a decorative ceramic spoonful of chocolate mousse beckoned, paired with fresh fruit chunks skewered on a brightly painted wooden toothpick and drizzled with milk chocolate.

Dinner was thrilling, but utterly exhausting.

The next morning we strolled along the single-lane country road nearby, trying to work off the previous night's excess and develop an appetite for breakfast. Mud puddles shrank in the bright sunshine. We also noticed various exhortations and sample menus for other inns' restaurants displayed on their respective wrought-iron gates. Chefs' pedigrees and triumphs vied for supremacy. Apparently all the lovely little hotels in the area battled ferociously for patrons. It didn't matter whether there was a vacancy or how much the rooms cost— the most important questions were: What's for dinner, and who's the chef?

While we fantasized about the meals other hotels could provide, we had no intention of giving up the dinners that were included with our stay. Besides, weeks ago we notified the chef that Ajay was vegetarian, and we weren't sure other hotels could accommodate him on short notice. Most significantly, we saw no need to change an excellent situation.

And so it went for the next few days. Ajay and I wandered the Roman arena in Arles, admired the stark beauty of the ancient Pont du Gard, imagined an austere life in the barren fortress of les Baux, then ate ourselves into stupefaction at our hotel. In Roussillon, lush potted flowers spilled from windowsills and porches to punctuate the town's red clay walls. Yet this gorgeous sight was exceeded that evening by tender lobster medallions and asparagus spears on one plate, and thinly sliced lamb laced with squash, marscapone cheese, and warm apple slices on the next.

Once seated for dinner, the fixed menu arrived first, printed on heavy paper for the diner's perusal, approval, and optional custody. I knew enough French to identify the various animals on the evening's menu, but often not enough French to discern the body part, which was just as well. One night I anticipated succulent lamb sautèed in Jamaican spices. When it arrived, the prized entrèe was unmistakably a brain. I told myself it would be the tastiest lamb brain possible and risked a few bites. And yes, it was superb.

After each dinner, I brought the menu back to our room and perused our French-English pocket dictionary to discover what I'd just eaten. Ajay also consulted the dictionary to learn the names of ingredients. For him, eggplants, radicchio, potatoes, and other vegetables were transformed into unexpected delights. Garbanzo beans lazily bobbed in a spicy tomato broth. Thinly sliced carrots surrounded a minute, creamy island of polenta. A half-circle of flaky crust revealed expertly grilled wild mushrooms and a hint of smoky provolone. The chef prepared four nights of meatless seven-course meals without repeating a thing.

But the glorious dinners came with a hidden price. We suffered through bloated, disturbing dreams and restless nights. Our clothes were becoming tighter and tighter. I kept the top button on my khakis unbuttoned, hoping my belt hid the truth. Before dinner I relied on control-top nylons to squeeze me like a sausage into my skirts or sheath dress. Every night Ajay and I went to bed too full to think, promising ourselves we wouldn't eat as much the next evening.

The cheese course was key—the only opportunity to control how much food we received. We tried to not finish our other courses, but the various delicacies proved irresistible. Deep down we knew we might never taste any of the chef's marvelous creations again. The cheese was merely cheese, surely we could skip it.

But night after night we couldn't. Or at least I couldn't. Our affable waiter in a starched white jacket (who spoke just enough English to understand my husband's French) would describe the different cheeses on the cart. "Madame, zis one, I tink you like very much, regardez zee poivre on zee top?" With a small flourish, his silver cheese knife moved from one cheese garnished with whole peppercorns to another powdery round, this one encircled with a dark brown edge. "And zis, three months zee bark of zee tree. Magnifique. Last one, you must try." His knife and fork deftly served anything that elicited a smile.

I asked for tiny wedges, but the waiter always provided more. "Oh no, Madame, so little, you cannot even taste, zis is better." I protested weakly but accepted the larger pieces, knowing by the way Ajay eyed my selections that I would be sharing them. After the first night he officially declined the cheese course, yet his fork was in hand before the cart left our table.

Ajay and I wondered how the French guests around us were faring. Maybe French people left more food on their plates. The first night we glanced at others' tables but our attention was diverted below the tables, not above. Several people brought small, precious dogs on designer leashes, and the dogs sat patiently near their owners' feet. The dinner guests were unapologetic about bringing dogs into a formal dining room and the staff was most accommodating. Apparently French dogs are more cultured than their American cousins, for I never saw one lunge for crumbs from another table. They sat with utter refinement and bored non-chalance rivaling the most elegantly blasè Parisian waiting at a Metro station. These dogs understood their roles as fashion accessories and fulfilled their duties with quiet dignity.

On subsequent nights, as the fateful cheese cart made its rounds, we watched our fellow diners slowly devouring the enormous chunks of cheeses littering their plates. Nothing was slipped to the dogs. Apparently these people had stomachs the size of stock pots.

So here was the last evening, the last cheese course, the last chance to exercise restraint. The waiter approached with the cart and I pulled my attention from the windows. He lifted the glass dome as the setting sun turned the valley pink, gold, and violet. Heady aromas wafted towards me, and my resolve vanished like water on a hot skillet. I accepted the waiter's offer of a little garlic goat cheese, a slice of Muenster, and a wedge of brie.

The next morning as I waited for Ajay to finish checking out, I reflected, nostalgic already, on the stunning meals. As if on cue, I sat on the lobby's black leather couch and my beloved khakis split up the derriere. I ruefully interpreted this as a sign that I must leave immediately.

Provence taught me what it means to have too much of a good thing. Next time I'll be ready for the dazzling culinary temptations, and I will acknowledge cheese as my biggest weakness. But the most significant thing I will do is this: I will bring larger pants.

Julie Jindal is a freelance writer who lives in Bellevue, Washington. Though she once prided herself on traveling light, she recently found herself hauling seven pairs of shoes to Paris.

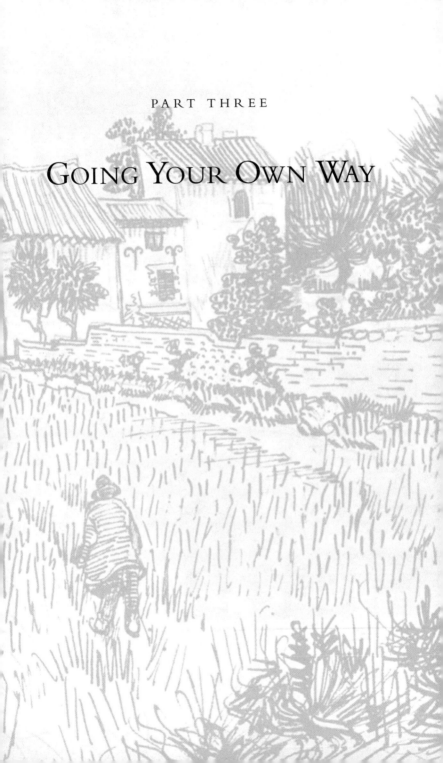

PART THREE

GOING YOUR OWN WAY

PATRICIA CLEVELAND-PECK

* * *

Routes de Lavande

Clear your nose and prepare for new olfactory adventures.

THE ABANDONED WINDMILL AT FONTEVEILLE, IMMORTALIZED in Alphonse Daudet's book *Lettres de Mon Moulin*, was encircled by twenty rabbits when the poet first set eyes on it. Now here we were, the same number of tourists, gazing up at the tiny structure. Not just any old tourists, though, but members of the Herb Society, most of us having already hopped off to explore the *garrigue*. The air resounded with excited cries of "just look at this thyme" and "come and see, wild rosemary."

The scent of the south—that delicious blend of pine, thyme, wild lavender, and rosemary—has not changed much since Daudet's day. It evokes the best of Provence: heat, blue skies, and sun-drenched vegetation. That it hasn't been bottled and marketed is not for want of trying, as we were soon to find out on this tour.

Lavender is grown commercially throughout Haute Provence and in early summer vast, blue-ribboned fields stretch toward the horizon, drenching the air with the unmistakable sweet but piquant scent. The sight is so amazing that the local tourist offices now produce a guide to encourage visitors to explore these "*Routes de Lavande*" by staying at guesthouses (including farms on which the lavender is harvested), taking walks, or visiting lavender-related festivals and markets.

At the lavender museum at Coustellet we traced the history of the industry from the days when the seasonal workers would set off with donkeys laden with their portable copper alembics to spend a month cutting and distilling the herb. These days, huge machines harvest lavender specially hybridized to yield high quantities of the essential oils— much of which ends up, rather ignominiously, in detergents. Our visit ended, as they always do, with a shopping opportunity. Here, lavender has not only been bottled but also incorporated into items such as honey and tea bags.

The next stop was Bonnieux, and as the bus whisked us along narrow roads and up steep hillsides, we chatted happily among ourselves. I began to appreciate traveling with the Herb Society members—we exchanged tips and remedies for every occasion. For example, I had never known what to do with lovage other than use it in cheese soufflés. "Try wrapping it around a piece of cheddar cheese," suggested one herbalist. "It imparts a distinct flavor." "Try frying it with potatoes and garlic," suggested another. "It's quite delicious." Not surprisingly, by the time we reached the Hotel le Prieure, hunger pangs were making themselves felt.

Not to worry. The typically unhurried French lunch, an herb menu specially designed for us, consisted of *gateau de legumes frais aux fine herbs sur une crème de tomates,* followed by *une trilogie de poissons du marche au beurre de safran,* and *figues poches au vin d'epices.* It even began with an amazing Kir-like aperitif made from wine to which lavender-flavored raspberry jam had been added. Then it ended some two hours later with a *digestif* of lavender-flavored Armagnac. Strange to report, I'm not yet sick of lavender.

That herbs are used in the production of liqueurs is well known, but I am surprised to learn that the local oregano-flavored liqueur, Origan de Comptat, which has been made by Distilleries Blanchere of Chateauneuf-du-Pape since 1835, uses some sixty different plants. The manager is happy to show me an old notebook with a handwritten list of these herbs but he is careful to cover up the quantities involved. Clearly this is one of those old secret recipes.

But our herbal journey through Provence was by no means confined to eating and drinking. We enjoyed the lively Wednesday market near St.-Remy where local baskets, pottery, and the typical Provençal fabric in vivid shades of yellow, olive green, and blue tempted some of us, while others bought local olives and packets of authentic *herbes de Provence* to take home.

And, of course, there were gardens to visit. In La Danserelle, near Lourmarin (another delightful little town with some seriously sophisticated boutiques), we enjoyed the garden of the Belgian artist Monique Lefevre, the most surprising feature of which was nine olive trees clipped to form a table. Such topiary seemed to be a common design element in the area. As well as the usual box and yew trees, I saw rosemary, santolina, lonicera, privet, and, of course, the ubiquitous lavender, sheared into round and lollipop shapes.

Although no less time-consuming than flowers to maintain, such gardens do not demand as much horticultural skill, and as many of the owners are wealthy weekenders from Paris, they leave the task in the hands of contractors. It can be expensive: one of the most fashionable must-haves for this set is a 1,000-year-old olive tree growing in grass. The tree can cost many thousands of dollars, and the special planting technique needed to keep the olive tree dry when the lawn is watered can cost as much again.

One of the most intriguing gardens that we saw is the

Jardin de l'Alchimiste at Mas de la Brune at Eygalieres. Nostradamus lived nearby, and the theme of the garden is alchemy and magic. It has fences of living willow based on medieval designs, herbs planted in beds according to the plans of Provençal magicians, and three original gardens symbolizing the alchemist's search for the meaning of life: one black with shiny slate paths, one white—planted with pale grasses and masses of the white rose Feede Neige—and one red garden, blazing with hundreds of bushes of the red rose Prestige de Bellegarde. This garden marks the end of the quest; the philosopher's stone has transformed lead into gold. It was extremely satisfying.

The Mas itself is a gem of Renaissance architecture dating from 1572. In the restaurant we enjoyed a delicious Provençal buffet prepared by the star chef Robert Brunel. Among the dozens of dishes were little artichokes stuffed with wheat and garlic and sun-dried tomatoes marinated in olive oil and basil.

Here at the Provençal monastery, midday in the garden of good and evil, Dore educates me in some of the ominous herbs such as mandrake, long known for its poisonous properties. In ancient times it was used as a narcotic and an aphrodisiac, and it was also believed to have certain magical powers. The thick, forked root (like ginseng) resembled the human form to the ancients, so was thought to hold dark earth spirits. Nearby, a waist high plant with leaves like silvery-green, rounded fingers is absinthe, the base for "Green Goddess." That deadly liqueur was the curse of poets, writers, and artists up until the early 20th-century, associated with "madness and moral depravity."

                                        Garry Marchant,
                                        "Herbs de Provence"

The visit I enjoyed the most, though, was to the fourteen-acre Ferme de Gerbaud, also near Lourmarin, where Paula and Guy Chauvin grow organic herbs for essential oils and cosmetics. We quickly realized that despite the idyllic-sounding task, this is not an easy life. Oaks are planted to protect the crops but it takes six years for the herbs to mature. But as we wandered through the rows of thyme, rosemary, sage, oregano, savory, and lavender—plucking and sniffing samples as we went, and listening to Guy's tales of folk remedies—I felt that we were as close to the essential Provence as it is possible to be.

Patricia Cleveland-Peck is a regular contributor to the London Independent *and* The Observer, *and is the author of* City Cat, Country Cat *and* Freckle and Clyde.

Beyond the Côte d'Azur

A chance encounter with an artist defines the day.

WE STRUCK OUT FROM NICE, HOPING TO SEE ANOTHER SIDE of Provence, and traveled northeast into the French Alps. Passing through the town of Grasse, we continued on for sixty kilometers, awed at the gigantic rock faces that jutted up toward the sky as if a massive geological catastrophe had coughed up the hidden depths of the earth revealing them to the light of day and to our eyes. The road wound through the old town of Castellane—ancient and picturesque, crowned by the Chapel of Notre Dame du Roc, but not for us today. We followed the signs toward the Gorges du Verdon, the Grand Canyon of the French Alps, hoping for something different— the unexpected gift of an acquaintance or an encounter that sometimes graces the traveler's day, and the hope of which sticks to our soul like a burr, spurring us on to the next adventure.

We noticed an unobtrusive sign off to the right, illegible. Doubling back, we read: *The Village de Chasteuil: buvette, creperie, poterie, sculptures turnees....* The unsurfaced road looked tortu-ous and crawled precariously up the mountain, but we took courage and began the steep climb, navigating the hairpin turns and marveling at the breathtaking views of the valley and mountains below. Suddenly a cluster of seven or eight stone houses appeared, clinging to the mountainside, reminiscent of a simpler life and another time.

Unsure of what awaited us, we picked our way along the rocky road between flowerpots, wheelbarrows, garden tools, and stone stairways. As we wondered about the inhabitants, a man emerged from a doorway, greeted us with a smile and a friendly "*Bonjour!*" He seemed a young Santa without the suit—sandy colored curly hair and beard, wire-framed glasses, an old cotton work shirt, pullover style with zipper at the neck, and dark-blue cotton work pants, a twinkle in the eye, and easy good humor. I liked him instinctively. His name was Eddy Parkiet

"Are you here to see my gallery?" he asked. Not knowing what "gallery" he meant, I nevertheless nodded eagerly, pleased that my rudimentary French had allowed me at least minimal understanding, and we followed him up a rocky twisting road that wound its way through the village. We entered what appeared to be the cellar of a nineteenth-century renovated stone house. The heavy wooden door swung aside, and we walked into a rough and rustic space. Packed on the shelves to one side, I noticed colorful lamps with plaster-sculpted bases and shades that appeared to be hand-painted. But my attention focused on the unusual wooden sculptures hanging on each wall. Track lighting illuminated the handsome designs that were carved in relief on polished wooden squares.

Eddy moved from piece to piece, describing the unusual hand-turned sculptures. He seemed friendly, sincere, and soft-spoken, and I sensed a passion about him and his work, and a bit of the artist's eccentricity. My poor French made communication ponderous, but Eddy was patient, spoke clearly and slowly, and did not hesitate to explain repeatedly until I understood. Thankfully he demonstrated as he spoke, and I suddenly saw the surprising aspect of his art—each sculpture was really composed of several pieces of wood, and each piece could be substituted for any other, creating an entirely new effect. He had created evolving works of art! Eddy showed me how I could invent and create patterns according to my mood or whim. He exclaimed that anyone could change the image and become a co-creator with the artist. His enthusiasm was contagious.

"A tableau or a sculpture is fixed and still. I wanted to create something new and unique. My sculpture has infinite possibilities." He showed me a simple sculpture composed of eight pieces of wood. Grabbing his calculator, he explained that if you calculate the number of combinations possible by moving the pieces horizontally, vertically, or obliquely, it comes to 40,320! If you also rotate the direction of the pieces, the possibilities become

---

In St.-Paul-de-Vence: Little slices of lemon float in the pitcher of water on my table, and as I take another sip of wine and contemplate the still life—"Daurade with green beans and rice"—before me, I feel a little like floating, too. To my left is a vibrant Leger mural, wrought into a section of the terrace's streetside wall. And straight ahead are the rustic interior rooms of this celebrated hotel-restaurant, where I wandered a half hour ago in search of a restroom and instead found an astonishment of modern masterpieces—canvases by Modigliani, Bonnard, Dufy, Utrillo, Chagall, Picasso, Braque, Matisse, and Miro, among others, all given by the artists when they were still struggling unknowns to the generous and perspicacious owner in lieu of payment.

—Don George,
"La Colombe d'Or"

incalculable. And this is a small, simple piece—some are more complex. But Eddy quickly clarified, "What's important is not the number of possibilities, but rather what the human mind can create with these images." I asked whether he used mathematics to design his work. He replied with a wry smile that all of life is mathematics—the cripple who uses a cane uses math. Everything is math!

When Eddy invited us to his workshop, we gladly accepted. We walked out onto the rocky road, and a young girl on a bicycle rode past and up the hill with a cheerful wave. We made our way down the path past other rustic dwellings with rows of firewood neatly stacked at each door. The smell of wood smoke drifted towards us in the crisp mountain air. The world far below seemed distant, and I wondered what hardships winter would bring to the settlement, and who besides Eddy lived here.

As we walked, he explained that, born a Parisian, he used to restore cathedrals and historical buildings. From his restoration work, he found ideas for the patterns that are now the foundation of his carving. One summer Eddy and a friend came to Chasteuil, a town abandoned and in ruins, to escape the frenetic city life. They spent the summer fixing up one of the houses, just as a hobby. Later he returned to live and work, and gradually more people joined the group. There are twenty-five people living in Chasteuil now, including children. To my question of how many of them were artists, Eddy replied with a wink, "We're all artists! You are, I am. Some make honey or crepes, others pottery…." He indicated a building to our left, and a young woman with short blond hair and a pleasant smile stood on the porch. "*Ma Femme,*" Eddy explained with a smile. He swung the cellar door aside and welcomed us into his workspace.

The room was dark with light flowing into one window.

He turned on a light, and the machinery emerged from the shadow—a large table saw, a lathe, other tools unfamiliar to me. He flicked on a CD player, and soft instrumental music set the tone. Under the light of the window, laid out on a large clean workspace, was the work in progress, his masterpiece.

Our new friend became noticeably animated as he showed us his project. Carefully laid out on the worktable, the exquisitely carved sculpture measured about two feet by two feet. The square was actually composed of six bars of wood, each measuring two feet long and two inches square. Each bar was then cut into six additional two-inch sections. The bars were held together with a long rod extending through the middle of each piece and bolted at the end. When the bars were laid out side by side in a two-foot square, an intricate design appeared. If the bars were rotated either individually or in unison, a completely new and unified design became apparent, because the bars were carved on every side. If the bolts were loosened and individual pieces were interchanged, an equally beautiful and varied design appeared.

As Eddy showed us the infinite possibilities, his excitement grew, and as he loosened the bolts, he kept repeating, "Now you'll see what I mean, now you'll see!" He explained, "Nature has patterns, but they are fixed patterns. Think of a flower, or a crystal—a diamond. They have beautiful patterns. My sculptures also have a pattern, but the human mind adds another dimension, creativity, and the patterns become infinite. Mathematically, there are many combinations—hundreds of thousands—when you add the capacity of the human mind to imagine and create, the possibilities become infinite. Every person, who ever lived or will live, creates images in his or her own way, perceives the sculpture according to his or her imagination. It's infinite!"

The thrill of creation—of engagement with something

that is like a fire within—that's what Eddy Parkiet shared with us that day. It shone in his face and leaped out through his words. It said, "Take hold of this thing called life! Embrace it, dance with it, cherish it, honor it!"

The clean smell of sawdust, the haunting notes of an unknown flautist, the last rays of sunlight that gently illuminated the room...a magical aura surrounded us. As we emerged from the workshop, evening descended on the village of Chasteuil. Reluctantly we said goodbye to our new friend and fellow traveler. Likely we will not meet again, but it doesn't matter—we touched a place that most of us call "soul," and when that happens we are never quite the same.

Deborah Abello is an elementary school principal and a pilgrim. Needing a break from the stresses of public education, she went to Europe for a year. Her two daughters are grown and on their own, and her husband and she are finding a renewed vision as they explore this new stage of their lives. Previously from Tracy, California, she currently lives in San Juan de la Arena, a fishing village on Spain's northern coast.

✦ ✦ ✦

Spies, Salads, Old Cars, and French In-Laws

They're all part of the Provençal stew.

THE CAR IN FRONT OF US STALLED AGAIN ONLY HALF A MILE after the Roman bridge. The first stall of the day had worried me, with the risk that it would bring our cocky parade through Provence to a halt, but now I kept my calm. The younger generation, I thought disparagingly of the 1938 Renault Celta 4, and patted our 1928 Citroën B14 Torpedo smugly. I had always thought things had gone downhill from the '20s. Besides, our Torpedo was a convertible and had two wind-shields, one for the front seat, and one for the back. Beat that.

My fiancé Sébastien and I pulled over to the side of the road behind the problem car—we *all* pulled over to the side of the road, the whole parade—and men thronged around the thin little hood as it was folded up. The insides of the engine looked so simple even I might have been able to put them together in a third-grade science class, and they held the power of a supermagnet. With a dozen men already gathered around the engine—all classic car experts, as proven by the parade parked along the side of the road—not one but two modern car drivers nevertheless stopped to ask if we needed any help. "Ah…saw you broken down, just wanted to check and make sure if you had everything you needed." A hand snuck out and caressed the shiny curves of the car surreptitiously. "I'm pretty good with cars. Do you, ah, want me to take a look at it?" A chin tucked in discreet but transparent craving towards the exposed engine.

"*Merci*," said the driver, which, by an odd but culturally significant vagary of French, is a polite way of saying "no." His white head bent and he blew briskly through a detached fuel line. "Got a speck of dirt in it, is all." And off we went again.

The third stall, I wandered across the road to gaze at the nearly ripe apricots that weighted the trees. Some of the other classic car drivers and long-term passengers were starting to look disgruntled.

"Him again." Sébastien's grandmother, Violette, shook her head in disgust, propping her elbow against the door of her 1952 Peugeöt. "There's a man who can't keep his cars in order." Round and stout-chested, with a hefty way of moving, she had recently come out of the hospital and was much less aggressive these days than she used to be, everybody swore.

The owner of a red 1968 Fiat convertible popped up the rear of his car and pulled out a tool chest that had been somehow tucked against his motor. A one-armed young stripling of forty-nine or so cocked the hood of the recalcitrant Celta open with his shoulder and plied a wrench. A collection of heads—38 percent of them gray and 60 percent silvery-white—gathered once more around the obstreperous vehicle and phrases like "carburetor," "air filter?" "no, maybe the spark plug" flew.

Sébastien's mother, Claudine, thin and taut and very young, only fifteen years older than I, with a modish and dynamic crop of red hair, took a picture of me and wandered over to my side of the road. "It's always like this," she said. "Fortunately these old cars usually don't take long to fix. Although I've known of at least one time when they finally had to tow a car back. Are you having fun?"

"It's wonderful!"

She smiled at that, but I kept my guard up. My stateside friends in their cozy uni-cultural couples might think *they* had problems, but this woman was a *French mother.*

And it would be a long time before I forgot last night's salad episode.

The trip south into Provence had been advertised as a birthday present for me. Isabelle Huppert's performance in *Médée* in Avignon had become a legend about five seconds after opening night ended, and I wanted to see it. Also, after a year in Paris, I hadn't yet managed to see even an acre of Provence. And the lavender fields would still be in bloom if we hurried.

Imagine someone so romantic as to arrange for such a trip for his fiancée and *get tickets* for such an event. Wow. I was lavishly admiring of this gesture all the way down to the Palais des Papes, where I learned that Sébastien hadn't, in fact, gotten tickets. *Mais non*, he had just assumed we could buy them at the door.

I took a deep breath and gazed at a woman in a nude leotard performing elastic contortions to elevator music on the steps of the Palais des Papes. We were surrounded by pale stone buildings that seemed sun-faded, irradiated with the clear dust-white heat and shirring of cicadas that is Provence in July.

"But that's okay!" Sébastien said, so sunnily it was clear that he had not only found a silver lining, but he had done so without even noticing the cloud. "My family's all down here visiting my grandparents at Chamaret. We can go spend the weekend with them instead!"

I was engaged to a man who thought spending a weekend meeting future in-laws for the first time was a wonderful birthday present, a perfectly acceptable substitute for the theatrical performance of the decade.

"For my birthday?" I reminded him, just in case he had forgotten what event we were honoring. We dodged a group of people in folk costume who were doing some hopping thing that involved smacking sticks together. Their near-white pancake make-up and heavy velvet looked insufferably hot for skipping in this weather.

Sébastien beamed. "I've been wanting you to meet my family. My mom, my stepfather, my little sister, my step-grand-parents—this is a great opportunity, you can meet them all at once!"

"That sounds just lovely," I sighed and put away the theater pamphlets that actors had been stuffing in my hand since we got off the train. "How lucky for me you didn't think to get tickets."

Three hours later, in a stifling car driven by a mad Frenchman (my future stepfather-in-law), we jerked and sped and braked and swerved through that dry heat from Avignon, past still purple but graying lavender fields (many had already been cut by then), clear green vineyards, olive orchards, and truffle-producing oak fields. Halfway there, at the shocking realization that there might not be any good wine for dinner, we swerved into a vineyard to pick up a couple of bottles, naturally with a little dégustation first. Car-sickness, like tee-totaling or an allergy to tobacco or *foie gras*, is an unfortunate malady to have around Frenchmen. I had all four of these suspicious ailments, plus I was American, which meant as an in-law I was probably doomed.

The grandparents' house was tucked below the village of Chamaret, sun-gold stone up the hill. Rosemary grew in profusion at the gates, and lavender fields stretched out before it. Not far away, in the tiny sun-bleached town of Grignan, Madame de Sévigné's daughter had found some space from her mother, who pursued her with voluminous correspondence and occasional very long visits.

As I still flinch from the memory, I will draw the veil of silence over my traditional Southern attempts to help in the kitchen and the anguished discomfort this produced. There was a truly baffling culture shock over the way I cut strawberries, for example, that continues to escape my comprehension. Still, I should have suspected something when, after all that, my potential French mother-in-law actually asked me to engage in a culinary task.

We had just sat down to the table and its big bowl of salad, rich tomatoes just picked in the garden mounding up over its brim. The scent of them—that tangy, sun-filled scent of real tomatoes, picked ripe—was making me salivate, but I knew it would be ten minutes or so before I would actually taste them. The French meal is an art in savoring.

"Why don't you toss the salad, Laura?" Claudine smiled.

To excuse myself from accusations of gullibility, I can only say that as an American I didn't at the time automatically check every dish for the ways it could be used against me as a weapon.

Past tense.

I tried my best, but a couple of those luscious tomatoes did indeed spill over the sides of the bowl and onto the bright yellow Provençal tablecloth.

I fished them quickly onto my plate, but nobody looked

unhappy about it. In fact, Claudine was grinning at her son, and said, "*Pas bon à marier!*"

Not good marriage material. I glanced sideways at Sébastien, who was trying not to laugh—the whole getting married thing was *his* idea, damn it—and back at his mother, my eyes starting to narrow a bit.

Claudine gave me a broad smile, as if I'd just handed her the world and it was an oyster. "You've never heard that? In France, we say that someone who can toss a salad without spilling anything over the sides is *bon à marier.*"

"And vice versa," Sébastien said helpfully. He grinned at me. "Want to see me mix it?"

I passed him the fork and spoon. Catching my eye as he took them from me, he abruptly smoothed his mouth out into a flat, deadpan serious line and concentrated on the salad as if his life depended on it.

"You've always been good at that," Claudine sighed with maternal pride and what I considered a certain tendency to belabor a point, as Sébastien finished mixing the salad expertly, the tablecloth untouched. Everybody around the table was grinning now, except for me. I was remembering what twisted humor all those French movies seemed to have.

For anyone trying to understand the French it must be remembered that what came with the French Revolution was repudiation of religious values but not of intellectual values. What this means in practical terms is that while the French came to reject religious absolutes, they still prize the secular opinions of he national, well-educated individual. Hence, the French have retained the air of the Enlightenment while around them stumble the descendants of the Celts, Romans, and Teutons.

—Sean O'Reilly,
Travelers' Tales France

It was in this context that Claudine suddenly leaned forward, eyes sparkling. "It's such a good thing you made it down this evening after all. This means you'll be able to go with us on the old car rally tomorrow!"

The early morning sun was burning off the fog from the nearby riverbed when we headed out, Sébastien's mother and stepfather in front, he and I and his little sister Justine tucked in back, behind the second windshield of a 1928 Citroën B14 Torpedo. The grandparents drove in front of us in a 1952 Peugeot 203 convertible, temporarily on their own because the high-riding 1928 Torpedo made all of us feel as if we were golden Twenties children, giddily beyond war or anything but living.

Sébastien's stepfather and step-grandfather collect classic cars (they have six in working order), and we met their car club buddies on the terrace of the only café in a village that would almost fit into the palm of your hand, St.-Pantaléon. The dozen cars in the gravel lot spanned forty years exactly, from our 1928 Torpedo through the 1930s, 1940s, and 1950s, to finish with three high-class convertibles—two British Triumphs and the 1968 red Fiat. A superbly fit woman with auburn hair rode in the passenger seat of this last car, wearing a tight white blouse and super-tight beige jeans, a classy scarf fluttering in the wind. From a distance she looked like Nancy Drew on a jaunt through France with Ned. Only when she reached the breakfast tables could I begin to guess that she must be in her fifties, with the car she must have wanted—or maybe had—when she was twenty.

On the shady terrace, waiters bustled, bringing coffee, hot chocolate, juice, pastries. We quickly fell behind schedule as two dozen French enjoyed their meal, caught up with everyone's news, tried to persuade me to bring a classic Cadillac back from my next trip to the U.S., and lamented the poor turnout. While we waited, Sébastien and Justine amused themselves by dancing hand-shadows across the floor of the old *lavoir* just below the café, a centuries-old stone half-building by the river, where laundry used to be washed. The café's German shepherd scrambled frantically after the shadows, trying to dig through stone to get at them.

We bounced and jounced away from the café at last, the wind in our hair, people smiling and waving as they saw the line of us pass. At a couple of intersections, we passed so close to the car waiting to turn onto the road that I could see its male driver biting his lip with envy. Or was it alarm at getting behind twelve cars that wouldn't go over thirty-five miles per hour?

A perfect speed for touring Provence! In an open convertible, the scents of lavender washed over us from those endless fields of purple. My only regret was when we passed by one of the legendary Provençal markets and I could only crane my neck at it longingly, unable to stop.

Our route wound us up into a small range of mountains, steep rock cutting up through the vines and trees. To my slight offense, the next stall was our Torpedo. The radiator acting up. A herd of goats cropped grass on a long green slope which curved downward toward a creek and then arched up again in a field of lavender, a little stone house tucked in between two bushes.

Yet another stall soon necessitated our transfer to the stouter '52 convertible. Between the weight of five people and the increasingly steep climb, our seventy-year-old-Torpedo-that-could was faltering.

She went on well enough with the lighter weight, but the Renaut Celta 4 wasn't doing so well, making some people mutter about the way a certain man kept his engines. We stalled by lavender fields, in river gorges, and in a village of golden stone about the size of a chessboard with tiny bridges arching over the well-disciplined, finger-width river, flowers growing along its banks.

A few showers of rain taught me how to roll up and down the convertibles' canvas tops, a procedure that felt vaguely familiar, as I had handled a lot of canvas and light poles camping across America as a child. But the showers lasted only enough to waken one of my favorite smells—rain on earth too long dry. A wave of wet lavender scent joined it, washing over us on a current of air as we rounded a bend.

About that time, the Renault's driver gave up and turned back down hill, with an exasperated tip of his hat and a promise to rejoin us later in a less temperamental car from his collection.

After lunch, everyone was relaxed (except for me, surrounded by salad-wielding in-laws). I eyed the olive tapenade for potential bombs, but nothing happened. Well, my future stepfather-in-law turned his full attention on me for a time, but the interrogation was exclusively focused on any old Cadillacs I might have seen or be capable of finding, whether they were pink or not, and how I might go about getting them shipped to him from America. Bees buzzed thickly among the lavender in the restaurant's garden and occasionally through the open doors over the tables and out the other side.

As we headed downhill again in the Torpedo, Claudine said, "I hope we make good time. We promised we'd be in St.-Pantaléon at four for the festival, and if we're late we'll miss the *caisses à savon!*"

Soap boxes seemed a puzzling thing to be anxious about missing. "Why did we promise we'd be there at four?"

Jean-Charles—my future stepfather-in-law, who was actually a quite sane and even amazingly impressive driver when he was behind the wheel of a car forty years older than he— grinned at me over his shoulder. "We're the starring attractions."

We were, too. The line of us swept into town at 4:30 and did a figure-eight up and down cobblestoned streets, the drivers blaring their horns in a hilarious and enthusiastic cacophony of all the toots and honks invented over four decades. To my delight, the Torpedo had by far the best—something like a cross between a scream and a car up-chucking.

We were almost too late, though. "Come on!" Sébastien's mother gestured urgently. "Hurry! We're going to miss the *caisses à savon!*"

We ran past bales of hay and a bank of men clearly set up to judge a finish line, then around the curves of a twisty, near-vertical cobblestone street.

"Here's a good spot." Claudine stopped abruptly and pulled back from the curb as a clatter of wheels from above grew louder. "It's a tradition. They have—"

Two half-size refrigerators flashed past us. They were the kind you find in student dorm rooms, only this time they were missing doors, welded together side-by-side, and packed brimful with a team of two adult males and two adult females completely equipped in helmets and paddings.

"—this contest every year, who can make the best car without an engine. They give prizes for speed and the funniest and things like that—"

A six-year-old in a tiny little concoction I don't even know how to describe came bowling down, his chin set determinedly. The purpose of those bales of hay became clear— they padded stone houses in case someone coming down too fast flew out of his curve. And a nice bulk of them protected the judges at the finish line.

"One year they had a bathtub, and the judges threw barrels of sudsy water on the driver at the finish line. Now, isn't that sweet—"

Super Papa came down at a slow and careful speed, in something like a little wagon train—a little cart hooked on behind his, three little kids buckled snugly into it. We knew he was Super Papa, both from his hand-scrawled t-shirt and because it said so on a cardboard sign, followed by the carefully printed names of the children.

"How disappointing," Claudine said at the end of all this. "It was much more creative last year."

"*Really?*"

"Oh, yes, one guy came down with a whole little café— the parasol came off his table, though." And while I tried, baffled, to imagine a café car, we went back down the hill to find all the contestants being hooked on to a long rope behind a 4WD to be towed back up the hill for another go.

We wandered over towards the café. Games for a *pétanque* tournament covered every inch of dirt that could even possibly be imagined flat, and I learned quickly to keep a sharp watch out for flying metal balls whenever turning any corner.

Conscious of the presence of French future in-laws, I resisted riding the pink cow on the imported country-fair carousel, but purely through great strength of will and true love— Sébastien would have died of embarrassment.

On the café terrace, a serious discussion was underway. Subtly jerked chins indicated a World War II veteran in pink shirt and tie, sporting a gray beret and a cane, hanging around by some trees, watching the goings-on. The Renault's driver had made his way back with a very nervous German shepherd he kept shouting orders at for no reason. "He's a spy," he said tensely. "I know he's a spy. He's at every single last festival! Standing around watching everybody!"

Claudine, who seemed to be getting over my inability to mix a salad, caught my eyes, her own brimming with humor. It occurred to me at that moment, that she might have been actually genuinely joking about the salad.

"What's the population of this village?" I whispered.

"Oh, I don't know, about a hundred and fifty people."

I looked around at the *pétanque* matches, the soap boxes being hauled uphill, and the little houses of golden stone. "They have a big spy problem, do they?"

Well, if they didn't, they had too much local pride to admit it. Besides, Provence was famous for its Résistance efforts during World War II, and apparently old habits die hard. The older drivers were now entering into a discussion of the pink-shirted gentleman's spy status with heated seriousness.

Feeling unqualified for such a high-level discussion, I went to walk across the little stone bridge above the old laundry spot, and the spy called out to me a flowery compliment on what a pleasure it was to see such a beautiful, charming young lady at one of their festivals.

May I mention that I, personally, have always liked spies? They have all the moves.

French in-laws aren't so bad either, at that.

It might be ungracious in this context to mention exactly what I had to go through to get tickets for *Médée* when it came to Paris that winter. Because the trip to Avignon had turned out to be a remarkably perfect birthday present after all.

Laura Higgins Florand has lived in French Polynesia, France, and Spain and despite intense research into fine wine and cheese still finds herself an embarrassment to her French in-laws. She is currently working on a book on the cross-cultural adventures of a Franco-American couple in France and the U.S., and is only disappointed that the title Close Encounters of the Third Kind *has already been taken.*

* * *

A Double Surprise

This was not the kind of welcome she expected.

"I HAVE A SURPRISE," CHRISTIAN SAID AS SOON AS I STEPPED off the train in Lyon. He drove me up to the hills behind the city, pointing out the yellow buildings and telling me the history of Charlemagne. His wife was at the door of their home. She ushered me into a meal that only the French can whip up with little or no effort. There was a salad with a walnut dressing with self-picked walnuts, a chicken with olives, rice with seasonings, and green beans with tomatoes and onions and an herb I have yet to identify.

"*Voilà,*" Christian said as he brought out a bottle of Nouveau Beaujolais with a flourish that would make a wine steward weep with envy.

"How wonderful. A great surprise," I said feeling like a real insider to be offered the Nouveau Beaujolais three days before the official unveiling of the wine.

"That's not the surprise," he said. "It comes after lunch."

After the last morsel of homemade *tarte des pommes*, the three of us piled into his car. Exhausted from my trip and too much good food, I fell asleep and woke to discover myself in a tiny medieval village in Provence. Christian parked the car and we wandered through the streets that a normal-sized American car could not get through without scraping both doors. At a church, he stopped and threw open the door.

The church, which had been built sometime in the 1200s, had been converted into the Salles des Fêtes. Most French towns and villages have such a meeting place for any local event. The inside of this Salles des Fêtes was as modern as the outside was old. Frank Lloyd Wright would have been proud of the design.

But it was not the architectural ingenuity that left me gaping. The entire village was inside, all dressed as cowboys and all line-dancing.

"Surprised?" Christian asked.

"Flabbergasted," I said, and then tried to find the French that expressed my shock. I couldn't.

The word quickly spread that a "real" American was there. One man came up and handed me a Budweiser. Another came to ask if I could teach them some steps. I blushed as I admitted I'd never line-danced, and making explanations about being from New England didn't seem worthwhile. However, the man quickly offered to correct this. Within a few minutes I could sally and keep my hands in my back pocket as well as the next person.

While I was eating a *saucisson*, which was billed as an American hot dog but much tastier, several people came up to tell me about their visits to the States. Those who had not been there asked about this and that place, mostly the West where I'd been on business trips but did not know nearly as well as I knew Europe or the East Coast. I found myself talking about Greyhound buses, car rentals, and the Grand Canyon, which I had seen.

The live Country-and-Western band was from Perpignan, a city near the Spanish border. They were good. They were also very loud. The leader began a series of announcements to thank the organizing committee and talk about where else they would be appearing. Then came the fatal words, "We have an American here with us tonight, and she's going to sing for us."

I knew I was the only American in the room. I also knew that when I sang to my small daughter, she asked me to stop because it hurt her ears. And she was my kindest critic. The door was too far away for an escape. Even running would have been impossible because the crowd carried me to the stage.

I looked down at a sea of eager faces. All my life I have fantasized about being a singer as only a tone-deaf person can. I imagined cheering crowds.

"What would you like to sing?" the leader asked.

"Me and Bobby McGee?" Maybe he didn't know it.

He did.

"What key?"

Key. I knew keys existed in music, keys that apparently had nothing to do with doors. I racked my brains for one that sounded real. "C?"

"C it is," he said, handed me the mike and picked up his guitar.

I looked at the mike. I imagined tomatoes being thrown, big flavorful, juicy ones that deserved local pressed olive oil and fresh picked oregano not the rejection of bad singing. I imagined the end of any decent Franco-American relations based on the auditory torture of the entire population of a French village. Then I saw the little button on the mike that switched it off. I did just that.

I indicated that the band should start and I started belting out "I was busted flat in Baton Rouge, waiting for a train." I waved for the audience to sing with me. I strutted up and down that stage like I had in a million earlier fantasies, smiling as I went. The band was great.

The crowd went wild with applause. I bowed.

The bandleader came up to me. "I'm sorry, did you know the mike was off?"

"*Ce n'est pas vrai?*" I lied, hoping my shock was as great as my fake singing.

"Do you want to sing again?" he asked.

"I'd rather dance," I said.

Christian lifted me off the stage. "You were great. I was surprised. I didn't know you could sing."

D-L Nelson worked in public relations with major U.S. corporations before moving permanently to Switzerland. She holds a master's degree in creative writing from the University of Glamorgan in Wales. Her novels and short stories have won awards and her short stories and poems have been published in seven countries and read on BBC World Radio. Her most recently released title is Chickpea Lover: Not a Cookbook. *She is the overseas correspondent for* Credit Union Times, *teaches business and creative writing courses, and coaches individual writers of fiction and non-fiction.*

YVONNE MICHIE HORN

Christmas in Provence

An off-season visit holds many rewards.

THE MISTRAL IN SUMMER IS AN IRRITANT, TURNING NORMALLY congenial souls cranky until its three—or multiples of three—days of bluster blow over. The mistral in winter cuts to the bone, making its way through double layers of mittens, wooly caps, and scarves pulled up over the nose. So it was in Aix-en-Provence the first week of December. Knifing gusts careened through the city's labyrinth of streets. Along Cours Mirabeau, Aix's legendary avenue of tree-shaded, warm-weather sidewalk cafés, icy whirlwinds piled dried leaves against the aristocratic steps of seventeenth- and eighteenth-century *hotels particuliers*.

Provence—sun and pines, scented with herbs and flowers, carpets of lavender to the left, sunflowers to the right, but not in winter. Winter, however, especially during the weeks leading up to Christmas, brings an entirely different reason for visiting. It is then that Provence lives its traditions most intensely. One comes to peer into the lives of those who live there as they prepare for the season, to watch, listen, and enjoy.

While doing so, I planned to make serious dents in my holiday shopping list. In Aix, my refuge from the mistral was the Hotel des Augustines, a renovated twelfth-century convent just off Cours Mirabeau. From my window I looked directly across pedestrian-only Rue de la Masse into the belfry of the Church of the Holy Spirit. Martins swooped in the dwindling afternoon light as the bells of the Holy Spirit struck the hour.

Aix's little shops seem designed for Christmas. Crystal bibelots, jewelry, antiques polished to a fare-thee-well beckon through lighted, paned-glass windows. I ventured forth into the winding streets enchanted by the displays until the mistral scurried me back to hug the radiator in the vaulted lobby of des Augustines. Warmed, I was off again, one excursion bringing me to the morning market in Place Richelme. Given the season, there was an amazing bounty of fresh fruits and vegetables along with tables of breads, counters of cheeses, mounds of olives, cages of live chickens and rabbits.

I ran my hand over what appeared to be miniature lawns growing in little dishes—"*Qu'est-ce que c'est?*" Wheat for Sainte Barbe, came the answer. Would I like to buy a *sachet de la blé,* so that I might sow my own? This very day, December 4, was the day of Sainte Barbe, marking the official beginning of the celebration of the Nativity. All over Provence, families were sowing wheat on wet cotton placed on three (representing the trinity) porcelain or clay plates. When grown lush and green the little lawns would decorate the Christmas table. "*Quand lou blad vèn, tout vèn ben!*" "When the wheat grows well, all goes well!"

Next day, the bells of the Holy Spirit woke me to a mistral blessedly gone, leaving in its wake the bluest of skies yet sunshine deceptively cold. I followed D17, the Route Cézanne, out of Aix through the gently rolling countryside with its ochre soil and green cypresses immortalized in the famed artist's paintings. At the foot of Ste.-Victoire, a mountain that appears in at least sixty of his canvases, I stopped to pick a bundle of wild rosemary and thyme, tossing it into the back seat of my car so that I might travel with the quintessential summer scents of Provence.

Every Christmas journey to Provence must include the village of Aubagne, capital of the Provençal *santons*. Here the clay soil is considered perfect for crafting the little terra-cotta figures that had their beginning during the Revolution when churches were forced to close. Worship took place in the homes, with custom dictating that each family should have its own Christmas crèche. In the nineteenth century, other characters began to enhance the traditional crib scene, entire villages of people with locals considering it quite an honor to find themselves the subject of a craftsman's latest cast of characters. The figures never progressed past the nineteenth century; *santons* created today remain stuck in time.

> Mont Ste.-Victoire is a massive mountain with a pyramid-like form that towers above the surrounding countryside of Provence. Cezanne was enthralled by the peak, which he painted many times. As he got older, his paintings of it grew more exuberant and spontaneous and became more abstract.
>
> —Wenda O'Reilly, Ph.D.
> *Van Gogh and Friends*

I stopped by the studio of Daniel Scaturro, third generation *santon* maker. Some sixty characters, each made in five sizes, are in his current collection. I watched as he demonstrated the process, from raw clay, to mold, to firing, and then the delicate painting of features, clothing, and accessories. Upstairs, Scaturro's mother was busily sewing clothes for the largest *santons*, creating in miniature authentic costumes from Provençal fabrics.

Leaving Scaturro's studio, I visited the *santon* fair in the town square. Kiosks filled with thousands of *santons* surrounded a central display of an entire village utilizing hundreds of characters. From the fair, I walked to what was once the town's bandstand to view the Small World of Marcel Pagnol. Pagnol, born in Aubagne in 1895, found inspiration for his novels and films in the town's surrounding countryside. Here his characters, faithfully reproduced as *santons*, were placed in settings true to his stories.

In the nearby village of Allauch, I stopped to discuss nougat with Pierre Testa at his jewel box of a candy store and tea room, Le Moulin Bleu. The Testa family has manufactured fine nougat since 1835. Today they produce annually fifty tons of the Christmas confection, all of which are sold between the end of October and December 24. Beginning October 1, Testa employs twenty-seven workers to produce naught but nougat; seven candy makers supply the shop with sweets the rest of the year.

Testa is passionate about nougat and considers it the most important of The Thirteen Desserts, essential to the celebration of Christmas Eve. The Thirteen Desserts follow the *Gros Souper*, a meal laden with tradition. The table is set with three white tablecloths, settled one over the other, upon which three candlesticks are arranged along with the three plates of Sainte Barbe wheat. An extra place is always set for an impoverished person who might stop by. The *Gros Souper*, despite its name, is traditionally simple, usually consisting of some sort of a fish stew accompanied by vegetables of the season.

But first, the *cacho-fue*. The oldest of the family brings in the Christmas log and pours liqueur over it three times. Then, with the youngest's assistance, the log is carried three times through the house before being placed in the fireplace. A match is struck and now the *Gros Souper* can begin.

Though formidable sounding, the Thirteen Desserts, too, are simple fare, consisting of a variety of dried and fresh fruits—perhaps grapes, oranges, and winter melon—oil cake flavored with orange blossom, and both black and white nougat. The black, Testa told me, contains almonds with the skins on; skins are removed for the white and only lavender honey is used in the blend of ingredients. Both black and white, symbolizing good and evil, must grace the Thirteen Desserts.

Nougat aside, Le Moulin Bleu is a delight to visit. Brioche, the fat cat, wanders through. Testa's ninety-two-year-old grandmother claims her place by the front door, with Chico, the parrot, squawking noisily on her shoulder. At the back of the shop, games of Scrabble go on non-stop, the passion of Testa's mother. Villagers drop in for tea and gossip and cheerfully put up with an occasional Chico swooping. Almost an afterthought, it seems, candy is weighed and sold.

I learned more about the importance of Christmas Eve in Le Val. I was walking with Monsieur le maire, who had a bright yellow scarf wound tight around his neck, tweed jacket straining at the buttons over his ample belly. It was crisp-cold twilight, bright stars just appearing in the blue-black sky. The mayor, Alfred Gaultier, was telling me about *pastrage*, interrupting himself to greet passersby in his distinctive gravelly voice, a voice that turned sweet and smooth when the spirit of the *pastrage* inspired him to break into song.

Pastrage, he told me, begins near midnight when the villager playing the role of shepherd wakes the miller, a role always played by the mayor. The miller goes forth to alert the village. Now the entire village is up and about, singing and dancing and costumed in Provençal clothes. Tambourine players enter in, lanterns are everywhere. Angels begin glory songs, bells ring. Entering the church, the holy child is placed in the crèche. Mass begins, and when it's over everyone gathers in the church square to discuss the wonder of it all.

Monsieur le maire took me through cobbled streets to the town's *santon* museum. Before the Revolution and the advent of inexpensive clay figures, a home crèche was only for the wealthy. In the building that once held the town's bread-baking oven, now are displayed dozens of examples of ancient crib characters and scenes, created from carved rosewood, olive wood, marble, blown glass, and collected from the far reaches of the world. Continuing our walk, we arrived at the Maison de les Oliviers where the finishing touches were being placed on Le Val's newest *santon* exhibit, this one celebrating the olives of Provence. Surrounded by miniature olive groves, a little nineteenth-century village is involved with the flurry of the harvest. The centerpiece of the scene is not a crèche but an olive press.

Outside the village of Opio, I stopped by a contemporary oil press, Moulin a Huile Roger Michel, to find it a bustling, real-life version of the scene in Le Val. It was the height of the harvest. Just-picked olives were being unloaded from car trunks and the backs of trucks to be carried in for pressing, along with glass jugs to receive the fresh and fruity finished product. Virgin oil resulting from one's own trees is considered precious as liquid gold.

The mill's gift shop followed the theme. I browsed through an array of olive-inspired items ranging from pottery to t-shirts, to stacks of olive oil soap—soap made the traditional way, simmered for three days in an open cauldron. The result is a hard, long-lasting soap, the color of light straw, never perfumed.

It was fragrance I was after, however, as I headed for Grasse, home to great perfumeries since the eighteenth century. In the center of old town, the house of Fragonard offers more than an opportunity to sample its products. Down the street is

a boutique of lovingly chosen items that only begin with perfume and its accoutrements. Special indeed are copies of the
eighteenth- and nineteenth-century jewelry that I'd earlier
admired in the house of Fragonard's Museum of Provençal
Costume, a beautifully displayed collection that includes two
centuries of women's dress representing every walk of life.

Every weekend in December, Christmas markets spring up
throughout Provence, some fifteen in the little towns surrounding Grasse alone. I was on my way to the market in the
perched village of Bar-sur-Loup when I was stopped dead in
my tracks by the Confiserie des Gorges du Loup.

Located deep in the gorge with its feet in the river, for it
was a mill for fifty years, the *confiserie* turns local fruits and
edible flowers into sparkling versions of themselves. Glistening
like perfect jewels, whole melons, apricots, cherries, pears,
violets and verbena are crystallized, perpetuating one of
Provence's oldest and best-known confections from the days
when candying was the sole way of preserving the color and
form of the fruits of summer. The result is a sugar plum-lover's
version of Noel. No wonder that 70 percent of the *confiserie's*
fruit confits are sold in the weeks preceding Christmas.

On to the Christmas market at Bar-sur-Loup, a medieval
village of steep cobbled streets with ancient houses grouped in
a semicircle around its feudal castle and church. In this square,
artists, craftspeople, and the good cooks of the village set out
their wares. The work of glassblowers, potterymakers, and
woodcarvers were on display along with bouquets of dried
flowers and jars of confiture bonneted in Provençal fabrics.
Socca, the Provençal crepe made with a batter of chickpea flour
came sizzling off pans the size of tractor wheels—Christmas
market fast food. Musicians kept toes tapping.

At Bar-sur-Loup I completed my holiday shopping with a
purchase of hand-dipped candles. In my Provençal treasure

trove I'd already accumulated reproduction eighteenth-century earrings and exquisite letter paper from the Fragonard boutique; bars of olive oil soap; blocks of nougat, both black and white; a tablecloth and napkins of bright Provençal Souleiado fabric purchased in Aix; fancifully boxed and wrapped assortments of crystallized fruits; sachets of Sainte Barbe wheat to sow on wet cotton the moment I returned home. And, of course, *santons*—the basic characters for several classic crib scenes. One set of figures I set aside for myself, thinking with pleasure of bringing them out holiday season after holiday season as a delightful reminder of my days spent peering into the lives of those who live the Christmas traditions of Provence.

Travel writer Yvonne Michie Horn is headquartered in Northern California's Sonoma County. Although her work takes her to far-flung parts of the world, she has an affinity for France, which she returns to time and time again.

ROSEMARY LLOYD

✦ ✦ ✦

Problem-Solving in Aix

It helps to be a saint—an extremely patient one.

I WAS SITTING IN MY OFFICE IN AIX-EN-PROVENCE WHEN I heard an alarmed cry for help from my graduate assistant, whose girlfriend, freshly arrived from the United States, was in his office with him. I rushed in, expecting the usual computer trouble, but he pointed with trembling finger to the balcony of his window onto which had just fallen a pair of black female underpants. What is the politically correct male graduate assistant to do in such a case? What the presence of the underwear revealed was that one of the young women who had rented the rooms above ours had hung her washing out of the window to dry—strictly forbidden, of course, in this quarter of Aix-en-Provence with its elegant buildings dating from the eighteenth century. As I carried the panties upstairs to explain the rules to her apartment mates (the student in question of course having gone out so we had to enter her room to retrieve the rest of the washing, no doubt committing an intrusion of domicile), I found myself wondering if my previous training had really prepared me for directing a year-abroad program. It was a question I was to ask myself several times a day, as we moved between the unforeseeable and the chaotic.

Certainly not even my training as a professor of literature, used to flights of imagination and depths of analysis, could prepare me for the intensity of a student gaze that spun my private life into imaginary constructions I never dreamed of in the anonymity of a U.S. campus. I became aware of this when, on a brilliantly clear blue day the program's outing took us to the ochre quarries at Roussillon. Here, against the intensity of reds, oranges, and yellows, I noticed that three students were wearing jackets whose vivid modern colors clashed most horribly with the natural décor, enough to

> Roussillon is the real name of "Peyrane," the subject of Laurence Wylie's *Village in the Vaucluse*, an excellent account of his life there in the early 1950s.
> —JO'R and TAW

warrant a photo. Our guide suggested I also add the bright green backpack of my husband. The word "husband" caused two students to look up in deep surprise and profound disappointment. It was then that I discovered that those two students, and maybe others, too, had assumed that I was taking advantage of my time in Aix to have a little love affair on the side, in plain view of the entire program contingent. Being suspected of an adulterous affair with a husband of twenty-nine years was both amusing and rejuvenating, although I could see my standing plummet in the eyes of the students concerned.

Even apparently simple matters, such as dealing with the telephone company, seemed to take on mythic proportions. Our year-abroad program was receiving many calls from people who found us in the yellow pages, under the rubric

"academic," and who therefore contacted us for anything remotely concerned with all kinds of academies. As a result,
when someone called from France Télécom to check that the
entries were correct for the next publication, I asked that our
entry be removed from the yellow pages, which indeed it was.
But as a result, and for reasons I still to this day do not understand, the removal of our entry promptly led to one of our
two phone lines being removed as well. Frantic calls led to a
visit by a charming Télécom mechanic who explained, after a
lengthy hunt for the gray box, that the problem was outside,
at second-floor level, and that he himself was forbidden by his
union to climb more than six rungs of the ladder, which he
nevertheless asked us to produce so that he could look into
the matter. When asked whether or not he intended to climb
to the necessary height (considerably more than six rungs) he
answered: but of course, I would never get my work done if
I did what the union told me. The second line was subsequently restored.

Dealing with the post office also had a charm and mystery
all its own. Sometimes service was stunning, as when my
mother-in-law sent a card to us addressed merely to our first
names, omitting the family name, and the postman delivered
it with the aplomb born of being, as he put it, thirty years in
the business. Other instances were less satisfactory. Returning
from a two-week vacation, we found a notification from the
post office that a packet could not be delivered to us (the reason given was "*trop gros*" which I assumed referred to the
packet and not to us, whatever culinary indiscretions we may
have committed on vacation) and awaited us at the main post
office. With the insouciance born of ignorance we therefore
went to the post office, only to be told that our packet could
not for the moment be found but that a search would be
mounted and we would be called the next day. Silence. Forty-

eight hours later therefore we returned to the post office. There a charming young man, no doubt specially chosen by the *chef d'équipe* to carry out disagreeable tasks, returned after a long unfruitful absence to tell us that there was no trace of our packet, that it was indeed as if the packet had never been there. Also that the packet delivery was entrusted to some other firm, based at the relative safety of Celony, between Aix and Marseilles, and that the post office merely acts as a go-between. Celony had been faxed but had no trace of our packet either. We were informed therefore, that we must contact the person who sent the packet and ask them to launch an enquiry from the post office from which the packet was sent. I protested, mildly, that in the absence of the packet I could not know who the sender was. The charming young man acknowledged the problem but insisted that this was how it was done in France.

And yet, the year my husband and I spent in Aix-en-Provence seems in retrospect to have been dominated by The Door.

My apartment was the size of a postage stamp and was situated just above a *marchand de fruits et légumes*. I had enthusiastically signed the lease as my landlord looked at me with a combination of relief and bewilderment. Now, I understand why. The owners rolled up their awnings promptly at 6:30 every morning, and at night the rue d'Italie was a thoroughfare for drunken exchange students making their way home from the pubs in the *centre ville*. I could count on roughly two hours of sleep a night. Again, it mattered little, for I was in Aix! I was henceforth known to my landlord as "*l'Americaine*," or the one crazy enough to live without a proper night's sleep for a year.

—Margaret E. McColley, "Sleepless in Aix"

We had just arrived after a flight across the Atlantic, the curious struggle across the airport at Roissy, waiting for the shut-
tle in what seemed an abandoned building site to get to the
other terminal where, inevitably, the train station is situated,
and then the ride down to Marseilles in the high-speed train.
This last was rendered more memorable by the presence near
us of two dogs whose owners had omitted to buy tickets for
them. The owner of the larger dog, when questioned on
whether her dog was actually small enough to travel at all,
asked, not unreasonably, what the limit was, and responded,
"But he weighs exactly six kilos, my dog, and if I had had him
shaved he would weigh even less." Then there was the picturesque journey in the bone rattling little train to Aix and the
clamber up the four flights of stairs with our year's luggage
and the laptop. And then, the realization that the entry door
had been forced open, breaking all three locks, and shattering
parts of the door all over the floor in a spectacular but amateur fashion. It was after hours, but a call to an SOS locksmith
brought a repairman at around eight that evening. He made
what he explained were temporary repairs to the bolts and to
the door. We were to learn the meaning of temporary over the
next few months.

Nothing had been stolen, but for insurance purposes, on
the following morning we went to the police station to make
a formal report. Although the police station was thronged
with people in uniform and in casual clothes who seemed to
be employed there, most of these seemed to be primarily engaged in kissing, shaking hands and talking, or in playing with
the children of anyone waiting to report a crime. After an
hour, we were seen by a plain-clothes officer, whose typing
and orthographical skills were limited but who was kindness
itself, and who made up for the mundane nature of his job by
covering the walls of his office with giant posters of movies

showing police in exciting and demanding roles. Nothing, of course, came from this exercise, except the report required by the insurance company.

Our insurance brokers assured us that since this was a "*ré-paration de fortune*" as French legalese charmingly puts it, there would be no difficulty if we proceeded immediately to arrange for the replacement of locks and door. The company which had supplied the emergency service agreed to inspect the door on Tuesday, August 10, and to provide an estimate. Unfortunately, the person concerned was involved in an accident in traveling to our apartment and had to delay his visit. He arrived the next morning, his right hand encased in a huge plaster the size of a baseball. Close on his heels came our neighbor, M. Declercq, who had been in Ireland when the break-in took place and whom we had not previously informed, since he was happily engaged in a curious process involving leaving all manner of equipment in the stairwell, presumably, from the sounds coming from his apartment, in order to redecorate.

After a conversation about break-ins and what most thieves look for (jewelry), the locksmith proceeded to measure the door with much snorting and sighing. "*C'est pas standard*" he announced, leading up inevitably to the statement: "*Ça va coûter extrêmement cher.*" (It will cost you a packet.) Then off he went, shaking hands with us by using his left hand held backwards to simulate a right hand and promising to mail the estimate to us in due course. We did not see him again until we went to his office and found that he was unable to solve the problem of the nonstandard door. Then our landlord's favorite workman, M. Canaux, came to inspect the door. He too commented on the fact that it was "*pas standard*" and went off to think, although apparently to no effect. Three weeks later we contacted another company in the hope that something might be done before the end of the academic year, but they too could do nothing except suggest we try a carpenter. This suggestion led at last to M. Lauret, a tubby white-haired man in his sixties who exuded competence, who told us he had already made such repairs in the residence and promised an estimate "*incessament sous peu*," a phrase I have come to realize means, in Provence, a longer and vaguer expanse of time than elsewhere in the world. By early November, I started phoning, while the estimate mailed to some mythical address traveled goodness knows where and back again.

Eventually I realized that personal contact rather than phone calls were my sole resource and tracked him to his office. In a minuscule space, M. Lauret and a smartly dressed woman who appeared to be the accountant, but may have been a frustrated customer, were dealing with a snowstorm of bits of paper. By dint of standing over his desk, while he took phone calls and sneaked outside to talk to a friend, I managed to extract the estimate from him, signed it, and returned it in person that afternoon. This dramatic gesture made him laugh so much that when I asked how soon he could come, he produced a sentence I had not imagined: "You'll want it before the end of the year, no doubt?" Why? I have no idea, but to such a sentence one simply agrees, emphatically. So on, December 22, the start of winter, our new door was installed. It fit beautifully—no more frenetic shaking whenever the main door was opened downstairs—and it would certainly deter amateur thieves. But of course nothing is that simple, and over the Spring, the lock became stiffer and stiffer until it reached the point where we feared we might snap off the key in trying to let ourselves in or out. M. Lauret promised to send someone, who did indeed eventually come, and reported that, "the building has moved, but the door has not moved." Actually I suspect that this was probably quite accurate. In any case, the door was then made more accommodating to the movements of the building. And this description sums up in a strange way our time in Aix, where what moved and what was fixed was not always what you expected. But that was what gave the town and our time there such charm.

Born and raised in Australia, Rosemary Lloyd lived for so long, first in Cambridge, England, then in Bloomington, Indiana, that she's never quite sure what brand of English she's talking. Fortunately her teaching is done in French.

⋆ ⋆ ⋆

How to Tame a Tarask

Or, how to make béarnaise sauce.

I ARRIVED AT TARASCON AFTER A SERIES OF LONG TRAIN journeys across Europe. During one overnight journey I had tried to get some sleep by lying down in the only space available, the floor of the corridor next to the stinking lavatory. I had been trodden on repeatedly.

At Tarascon there was open space and a smell of sweet herbs. I hired clean sheets at the Youth Hostel, showered, and went to sleep in a large room with whitewashed walls. I woke up bathed in honey-white light, like a blessing.

In the hostel there was a picture of a strange scaly beast. The receptionist told me it was the tarask (in French, *tarasque*), a kind of dragon, which according to legend terrorized this town before being tamed by Saint Martha.

Here is one version of the legend. The tarask lived under a big rock in the river Rhône. It breathed fire, sank ships, and devoured parties of knights sent to kill it. Martha was a young woman who had arrived in the town from the Holy Land. She went to meet the tarask unarmed, carrying only some holy water. She talked with it calmly, as though it were a suffering creature rather than a ferocious monster. Eventually she walked back to the town leading the tarask, which was now completely docile.

The standard interpretation of dragon stories is that they represent the moral struggle within an individual. Another interpretation of this legend is that it dramatizes the conquering by Christians of a people following the old Gaulish religion. Philippe Reyt's fascinating paper "*Les dragons de la crue*" suggests, on the other hand, that the tarask may have been a symbol of dangerous running water prone to floods. If so, the holy water carried by Martha might indicate the triumph of placid water over the perilous kind.

Each year, on the last weekend in July, the citizens of Tarascon celebrate and parade an effigy of the tarask around the town. I came across a parade-style effigy near Tarascon Castle. It had an enormous curved body like the hull of an upturned boat, covered with scales and with rows of defensive spikes. Its tail was a long spike. It had the head of a lion, and the face of a sad old man.

Upon the first goblet he read this inscription, *monkey wine*; upon the second, *lion wine*; upon the third, *sheep wine*; upon the fourth, *swine wine*. These four inscriptions expressed the four descending degrees of drunkenness: the first, that which enlivens; the second, that which irritates; the third, that which stupefies; finally the last, that which brutalizes.

—Victor Hugo

Many herbs grow wild in Provence. One of the ingredients of the mixture called *herbes de Provence* is tarragon. You can see it growing near Tarascon, with its dark-green pointed leaves in the shape of a three-toed claw. Tarragon grows well in hot, rocky places, but watered ground saps its strength.

Lexicographers think that the word *tarragon*, and its French translation *estragon*, may derive from the same Greek word as *dragon*. (*Le Grand Robert Dictionary* says that *tarasque* derives from *Tarascon*, but does not trace this name back any further; I wonder whether it is another growth from the same Greek root.) Medieval herbalists believed that the look of a plant indicated its use, and prescribed tarragon as an antidote for dragon bites—and by extension snakebites, which presumably were more common. Modern herbalists do not recommend tarragon for bites but say it stimulates the appetite.

Tarragon leaves are very strongly flavored; you need to mix them with milder ingredients to tame them. A classic way of doing this is to make your tarragon into béarnaise sauce. The great chef Escoffier came from Provence and would have grown up seeing wild tarragon. For his béarnaise recipe you make a reduction of white wine and vinegar with chopped shallots, chopped tarragon and chervil leaves, crushed peppercorns, and salt. Then, over a low heat, you whisk in six egg yolks and half a kilo of melted butter. Once all the butter has been incorporated you can stop whisking, strain the sauce, add extra tarragon, adjust the seasoning, and serve.

The greatest danger in making béarnaise sauce is that the mixture can overheat and curdle during the whisking stage. If this happens, whisk in a little cold water. It may save it.

Use freshly grown French tarragon, not Russian tarragon, which is very bitter. Crush the chopped tarragon leaves in the palm of your hand before adding them to the mixture. This sauce is delicious with game, poached eggs, or asparagus.

On a later train journey a passenger was shouting curses. His breath smelled of firewater. Everyone else had crowded into the other end of the carriage. I went to speak with him. Perhaps it was foolish of me. After a while he was quiet and meek, and a tear was slowly running down the side of his nose.

"How did you do that?" asked another passenger, who hadn't been to Tarascon.

So the next time you see me roaring with anger and sinking ships, don't yell back. Talk with me calmly, firmly, and patiently. Or, make me some béarnaise sauce.

Miranda Mowbray is a soprano mathematician. Her hair is red. She likes mango ice cream, and lives in Bristol, England. Her writing also appears in Travelers' Tales Italy *and* Travelers' Tales Tuscany.

The Saints and Spectres of the Alpilles

*A prodigal daughter takes her mother back
to the Provence of her youth.*

SOMETHING'S WRONG. THIS *IS* THE OLD FARMHOUSE I SAW IN
the pictures, with its mottled salmon walls and faded blue
shutters. A jigsawed figure of an angel marks the driveway. The
gardens, hedged by rosemary, are carefully tended and free of
weeds. But Le Mas de l'Ange is completely deserted. Has no one
heard the crunching of gravel under our Peugeot tires? Has
the *whoomp whoomp* of suitcase wheels on brick gone unno-
ticed? Where is the *patron*? Where are his guests? Where is the
Provençal welcome we have anticipated all the way from Paris?

Settling Mom at a café table under an arbor, I set out to
find our elusive hosts. At the main door, I announce myself
with an "*allo!*" noticing a window broken along a jagged diag-
onal. I wander along a path bound by cypresses, finding a
series of interconnected *bassins*, leading to some signs of life in
a poolside cabaña: emptied bottles strewn on tabletops, spent
wineglasses lining the bar. The only glimpse of people,
though, is a photo gallery featuring a handsome horseman in
a gleaming white shirt and black-brimmed hat.

I hear noises coming from an outbuilding whose chalky blue doors and eaves are cut into shapes more Morocco than Marseilles. "*Allo?*" I implore, peering through a spade cut-out, only to find myself face-to-face with a massive gray stallion.

Returning to the main house, I slip my arm through the gash in the window, unlock the door, and creep inside: There is the large kitchen, long loaves of bread crisscrossing a pine sideboard. There is the dining room, presided over by a giant oil painting of a nude Venus holding an urn. There is the salon, its flea-market candelabra and gold-silk-draped sofa seeming right out of the pages of *Côté Sud*. Upstairs, gossamer curtains billow in and out through French balconies, and gigantic armoires stenciled with flowers await visitors. But not a single room has the disheveled look of a traveler's refuge— no random sleeves dangling from suitcases, no shoes peaking out from under beds, no necklaces cast hastily upon dressers.

I rejoin my mother under the arbor, shrugging. There we sit, a petite matron with an elegant sweep of white hair and her somewhat disheveled daughter, adjusting our gazes as though we've just exited a matinée into unfamiliar light. We pour ourselves mineral water from an iron cart and let the surroundings do their work. The shade of a giant sycamore slowly envelops us. A chocolate lab saunters over the grass and spreads out at our feet. The blue sky deepens, and wispy clouds soften with the late-afternoon light.

Twelve weeks earlier in California, I had chosen Mas de l'Ange as the perfect base for my mother and me to explore Provence together. It would be an important voyage—her first return to France after having lived there forty-five years ago and our first trip together since I'd left for college. I rejected hotels out of hand—too expensive, too far from fields of lavender, too stuffed with tourists. Instead, I reasoned, we should find a B&B that offered the quiet of the countryside, a *petit déjeuner*, and the promise of conversation, preferably in French. Perhaps, then, we'd evade the throngs of Americans.

It's not that I hate my compatriots. It's just that as a child in Hawaii I developed contempt for tourists—their beet-red knees, their matching Hawaiian shirts, their struggles with the syllables of Polynesia. Since then, whenever I've traveled, I've recoiled from the souvenir-collecting herds, sworn off English, and gone to great lengths to seek The Authentic Experience. But by the time Mom and I were to make our pilgrimage, millions of English-speakers had bought *A Year in Provence*. They had taken to cruising the Lubéron in giant buses, retracing the steps of Peter and Mrs. Mayle, buying up antiques and old farmhouses. How could we find our own vistas, our own cast of characters, our own narrative?

"*Vous savez où elle va, la Princesse, pour récuperer?*" asked Meriem, a Belgian Algerian who had settled in Berkeley, where she worked at a chic salon and kept up with the movements of Caroline of Monaco. Meriem advised me on things French while waxing my legs. "*St.-Rémy-de-Provence. C'est une très belle village, très tranquille.*"

I then Googled my way through a series of web searches, eventually replacing "B&B" with "*mas*," the name for the Provençal farmhouse that often doubles as a country inn. Mas de l'Ange's web site showed interlocking gardens and whitewashed rooms. Reviews from prestigious publications said "country gone funky" and "what it lacked in grandeur it made up in quirky personality." The owners, Bruno and Hélène Lafforgue, were not only French, but Provençal. The clincher: for a reservation Mas de l'Ange required payment in cash. No Visas, no checks drawn on American banks, no English. And this is how, twelve weeks later, we have ended up sitting alone under the arbor at Mas de l'Ange.

✳

With sudden speed, a compact Eurowagon careens off the main road, cuts into the driveway, and crunches over the gravel. The dog rouses himself, car doors slam, voices pierce the stillness. Down the brick path come two leggy teenagers, their shiny brunette hair brushing their shoulders, their polite "*bon soirs*" brightening the shadows. Following them is the handsome horseman, in fitted jeans, knee-high leather boots, and a fluid gray shirt. "Madame Hale?" he asks, with a formality that makes me nostalgic for the "mademoiselle" of my more nubile days.

Bruno leads us up painted-white steps edged with river rocks and carries our bags into the Chambre Jaune, with two beds tucked under the eaves, a tangerine-colored armoire, and a brooding portrait of a *bourgeoise* whose steely hair is pulled into a chignon. Bruno explains the breakfast routine, advises on a place for dinner in St.-Rémy, and disappears.

The scenes of our story of Provence were laid in 1953, when my mother spent her junior year abroad. That adventure started with six weeks in Aix-en-Provence to bone up on her French before being thrown to the wolves in Paris, where she would stay through the summer.

Her junior year abroad had been one of *the* formative experiences of her life, yet she later gave up her cosmopolitan existence, divorced my dad, and settled in a ramshackle town in Hawaii. Her classiness distinguished her in a sometimes comic way: she insisted on proper grammar from Pidgin-English-speaking schoolchildren, served coffee in porcelain cups to beefy Hawaiians, and ended up with a second husband who crassly mocked her manners.

Mom may never have returned to France, but she spent the rest of her life passing on her taste for all things French to me, her eldest child. She pulled me off the beach to read *Madeline and the Bad Hat, Eloise in Paris,* and *Babar's French Lessons.* She bought me a small spiral notebook, inscribing its brown cover with MON PETIT CAHIER DE FRANÇAIS and listing words for me to memorize. Although our everyday diet consisted of things like tuna-noodle casserole and Hamburger Helper, she occasionally gave my brother and sister and me a taste of her Continental past by serving cheese soufflé or chocolate mousse. She also treated us to stories of the French Gypsy who'd taught her to read palms—then proceeded to predict our futures.

She couldn't predict that I would spend my adult life moving away from her. I loved our home in Hawaii, but hated the indignity of poverty, the crudeness of my stepfather, the claustrophobia of my family's tense domestic life. I felt hemmed in by my mother's choices. I fled to college, then headed to San Francisco, where I fashioned my own kind of rebellious existence. In short, I rejected her life.

But I never rejected her French lessons, choosing instead to *make French mine.* I lacked her elegance and easy grace, making up for it in scrappiness: I won accolades for my accent (*not* for my grammar), worked in French restaurants, traveled to Paris, and fell in love with a photographer from Bordeaux.

But as I entered my forties and my mother her sixties, I yearned to draw closer to her. In part my longing was a desire to give back to her what she

---

I was doing my usual shuffle, trying to convey something in French to a horrified merchant, when my daughter Anna, then eight years old, took me aside and advised, "Daddy, you need a lot of spit in your mouth to speak French." Alas, my drooling only caused more problems.

—James O'Reilly,
Travelers' Tales France

had generously given me. In part, I wanted to take Mom back to a time of fewer cares. But, in part, my motivation was selfish: I wanted to find a way back to our original bond, when I was the first-born and had her all to myself.

So, for Mom's sixty-fifth birthday I gave her a book on Paris and a promise: the following September we would head to France. In keeping with the relationship we have settled into as adults, I seized control, paying for the three-week trip and making the grand plans. But the journey itself becomes a more delicate dance. In Paris we share with each other the mysteries of our pasts. In Provence, which I've never visited, Mom will be my guide.

She first takes me to Aix-en-Provence. All I know of what everyone seems to call a "charming university town" comes from a black-and-white photo of Mom standing before a fountain on the tree-lined Cours Mirabeau. She is a dark-haired, lipsticked twenty-year-old, the belt of her dress sashed tightly over her wasp-like figure. Today, with my matronly Mom in the passenger seat, I am distressed to find not a tree-lined *ville* but a teeming metropolis surrounded by freeways and clogged by cars. All routes seem to be circular and I feel my anxiety edge up as I lose all sense of direction. Mom retains her bearings.

"Turn left here," she gestures. "Now right."

She points, I follow.

"We want rue Cardinale. Let's try this alley."

I do. Suddenly, "Let's park."

We get out of the car, and Mom heads straight for the nearest intersection, guided by what seems like ESP. She stops, fifty yards away, at a fountain in which four dolphins curve gracefully around a pine-cone-topped obelisk. From there she reverses, walking down rue Cardinale and stopping just short of the Eglise St.-Jean-de-Malte, once the chapel for a Knights of Malta priory. Mom studies the face of a chestnut-colored *hôtel particulier*, then approaches a forbidding set of carved doors with giant brass knobs.

"*C'est ça*," she chirps, "Number 17. This is where I lived with Madame Lanes—a widow who always wore black—and her young servant. There were four of us from the United States. She set up private vocal lessons for me, since she thought a lack of proper musical training was at the root of my eccentric pronunciation."

I have heard this story all my life. Usually, Mom tells it as a way of poking fun at the Cleveland schooling she was subjected to. And yet her joking glosses over some more painful stories. Her mother, Madeleine, was an alcoholic whom my grandfather divorced and banished just before their twelve-year-old daughter was honored as Ohio's most promising French student. My mother never saw Madeleine again. And from that point on, her family insisted on calling her not by her christened name, also Madeleine, but by the name of her paternal grandmother: Molly.

It was here, in the house of Madame Lanes, that my mother became Madeleine again.

As she continues to spin out the tales of that time, Mom's sentences begin to take on the breathy lilt of French. "Madame also arranged for us to meet a venerable *duc*." In the taxi on the way to his château, Madame Lanes tutored her wards in the intricacies of French society, giving them as she did a proprietary stake in the glories of privilege. "Dukes, you see, have a very pure blood—*plus haut, plus important, que les princes.*"

We leave the house of Madame Lanes lighter, gayer, breathier. We indulge in little levities—buying lavender soap in the *marché*, taking in the sidewalk art and the skateboard contest

that mark the civic *Journée de la Patrimoine*, and allowing ourselves a carafe of rosé in the cool interior of Le Bistro Latin.
As our waiter dotes on her, I see a trace of the schoolgirl who
came here in 1953 and has never outgrown the experience.

After lunch, we wander up rue de la Couronne, circling
around to the Cathédrale St.-Sauveur, with its mishmash of
art and architecture, including a fifth-century baptistry, a
fifteenth-century triptych, and a double nave—one Romanesque, one Gothic. The highlight is not just the sublime history, but the surprise of the present-day quotidian: we crash
the wedding of a young Aixois couple, resting in the ancient
pews and testing our French by following along with the Mass.

Unfortunately, Mom doesn't always share my taste for the
commonplace. She's especially anxious to visit Les-Baux-de-
Provence, a medieval village carved into one of the white
peaks of the Alpilles. "A whole bus of American college girls
came up here together," Mom exclaims as we wind our way
through the rocky hills, catching glimpses of a medieval
fortress through the pines. Since 1953, however, Les Baux has
become second only to Mont St.-Michel as a popular tourist
site. And tourists we find there—by the carload, the busload,
and the strollerload, jammed into soccer-field-size parking
lots, elbowing each other in the cobblestone walkways, and
packed into Soleiado-type boutiques with paisley placemats
and sunflower-print sachets.

I have a cliché attack. Depositing Mom at La Reine Jeanne,
whose homestyle cooking and dramatic views made it a
favorite of Jacques Brel and Winston Churchill, I scramble as
fast as I can up to the Musée d'Histoire des Baux. There I
learn why Princess Caroline favors this area: Les Baux was
once the seat of the Grimaldis. From here they and the other
medieval Lords of Baux ruled over some eighty towns and
villages in the south, indulging a rich culture of courtly love,

troubadour songs, and knightly gallantry. From the cool dark rooms of the museum, I escape to the seventeen-acre clifftop, where lie the Romanesque ruins of their castle and ramparts, destroyed in 1632 under orders of Louis XIII and Richelieu. The poignancy of the ruins competes with the panorama of Provence that stretches below. I can breathe again, looking out over Cézanne's Mont Ste.-Victoire, the patchwork of vineyards and olive fields, and the chalky cliffs, studded with black-green pines and pocked with rectangular excavations of the mineral bauxite.

Our best find in St.-Rémy is le Monastère de St.-Paul-de-Mausole, a twelfth-century cloister where Vincent van Gogh stayed in 1889, after he cracked up in Arles. In a small clinic here, van Gogh was treated by a psychiatrist during the last year of his life. We stand in his former room, staring out at the very wheat fields, the very cypress trees, the very crows, that he made eternal. The hackneyed images of post-impressionism are transformed before our eyes. There is also, of course, a darker side to Vincent's sanctuary. Mom seems especially disturbed by displays of the horrific treatments common for patients in Vincent's time, and pages of journals on the walls take us deep into the torment of the artist's soul.

Images of such torment strike close to home. Surely my grandmother's alcoholism masked mental illness, and depression has rippled through the ranks of her descendants. Mom has had a lifelong struggle with memories of childhood turbulence — highball glasses full of Coca-Cola, a chaotic household in which maids threatened children with butcher knives, a spectre of a mother who would wander in the rain wearing next to nothing. But she has also struggled with the hollow peace that followed her mother's final departure. The turbulences of my mother's adult life — estrangement from a severe father, marriage with a charming but distant first husband, marriage with an abusive second—have in turn posed difficulty for my sister and me, who have both battled depression.

Upon learning that the St.-Paul monastery serves today as a sanatorium for female psychiatric patients, my mother muses, "Don't we all, to a lesser degree, know mental anguish?" She casts her gaze out along the manicured garden pathways. "Don't we all deserve such peaceful beauty?"

In a gallery downstairs we walk among the savage but poetic paintings of the current patients, who, in van Gogh's shadow, are encouraged to express their visions in art therapy. In the gift shop, Mom buys a card depicting a painting by one patient. In it five crudely drawn heads, tied balloonlike to long strings, float in a sky exuberant with rose-and-aqua brushstrokes. Entitled "L'Évasion," its caption reads, "*Que c'est bon d'avoir la tête en l'air et ne l'avoir plus sur les épaules*": How much better it is to have your head up in the sky than weighing down your shoulders. Indeed. We walk the tree-lined gravel drive back to our car, our cares lifted, *en l'air*.

Perhaps influenced by the visions at St.-Paul, Mom and I begin to wonder whether our Mas de l'Ange isn't some Provençal branch of the Bates Motel. Despite our pleasant chats with Bruno—a Camargue horseman who I decide is a fantasy made flesh, the Marlboro man with a French accent—the *mas* retains its eerie quality. Much of this comes from the absence of other guests. While we are happy to have evaded the Mayle-ites, we can't help wondering whether this marks us as losers. Several days into our stay, Mom and I are taking afternoon tea under the arbor when a French couple arrives. A palpable relief settles over us. The couple—she chic in a long skirt, he preppyish with a sweater tied precisely over his shoulders—repeat our own curious approach, pausing at the front door, examining the gashed window, waiting for a welcome. The madame inches her way toward us. "*Où est la réception?*" she asks, plaintively. So we are not just clueless Americans. In my curt reply—"*Il n'y a pas de réception*"—I feel a certain complicity. By the next morning the French couple is gone and we feel like fixtures in the ménage.

And what a strange ménage it is. After a few days punctuated by glimpses of Bruno and the girls, a gangly woman in black jeans and a t-shirt appears. She has shoulder-length brunette curls and a leathery face, a cigarette perpetually angling away from her lips, and she makes her way into the domicile with evident familiarity. From our chairs under the arbor, Mom and I try to guess who she is. One of the maids? No, she seems part of the family. Bruno's sister? The way they address each other bespeaks the comfortable-as-an-old-shoe quality of siblings.

That night, Mom retires early, and I sit in the salon among the friezes and the filigree, leafing through two bound volumes of clippings about the *mas*. There I read that, years earlier, Bruno fell in love with a Provençal beauty who was a photo stylist for French decorating magazines. He convinced her to stay in the Alpilles with him. While he gutted an old stone farmhouse, carried thousands of smooth stones from the river Durance to whimsically imbed in floors, built the *bassins* and the cabaña and the stables, Hélène scoured flea markets and antique shops, styling the shabby chic rooms. Soon, two girls were born.

As I flip through the pages, learning their story, Bruno stumbles through the dining room, a book in one hand, a bottle of mineral water in the other, wishing me "*bonne nuit*" and shutting himself into the lone guest room on the *rez de chaussée*. So much for *that* story.

The following day, Bruno leaves the rumpled sheets for the

maids, dresses extravagantly in a white blouson and fitted black trousers, and walks off in knee-high, fringed boots. Soon he crunches out the driveway, towing his magnificent *cheval* behind him. The mystery woman is now in charge, laying out our breakfast and driving the girls to and from school. "*Les enfants!*" she cries out at dinnertime. "*À table!*"

Could *this* be Hélène?

We finally work up our nerve to approach her, using as an excuse our interest in finding a flea market. As the stylist of Mas de l'Ange, Hélène clearly is the one to recommend the best *marché*. My mother is perennially on the prowl for old silver, while I am anxious to add to the *brocantes* I started to amass in Paris. (This "flea-market junk"—porcelain door handles, brass latches, scrolled hinges—are souvenirs for my sweetie, a cabinetmaker back in California.) "*Il faut aller à l'Isle-sur-la-Sorgue*," she replies, and warns us to start off early.

A village to the northeast, L'Isle-sur-la-Sorgue is not really an island but an entire archipelago, cut by bucolic canals, linked by white wood bridges, softened by mossy waterwheels from the now-defunct silk, wool, and paper industries. By the time we arrive, it has been raining buckets all morning, but that doesn't deter the merchants, whose goods—everything from *brocantes* to broccoli—are laid out along the canals. My mother finds a set of six lovely spoons, as well as a nineteenth-century precursor to a Swiss Army knife. I walk away with a three-pound bronze gate pull, a medieval-looking contraption with a roped bar suspended between two formée-crosses.

Thankfully, the rain has chased away the hordes, but when we return to the car Mom announces a plan, straight out of Fodor's, for the rest of the day. She wants to cover half the Lubéron, and doesn't want one tourist stone left unturned. We get caught in a downpour in Fontaine de Vaucluse, and I become grumpy and impatient: the roads are narrow, winding, and slick; the puddles have made a mockery of my leather boots; my wool socks are soaked; my feet are freezing. And my mother is leading me straight into Mayle country.

What's worse, we get to the Village des Bories—a strange scattering of dry-stone beehive-like dwellings believed to have been in use since the Iron Age—and realize that the steep entrance fee will use up most of our cash. I fume, then despite myself become entranced by the photos posted near the public restrooms. Mom and I decide to venture on our own through fields of scrub oak, where other *bories* are scattered outside the official grounds. We marvel at how the insides of the rough-hewn huts and sheepfolds—made without mortar—have managed to stay dry, even today.

The rain clouds stay with us as we wend our way down to the Abbaye de Sénanque—a Cistercian monastery that has since 1150 A.D. nestled amid fields of lavender in a hollow of the hills. By the time we get there, the crowds are thinning, leaving in their wake the timeless simplicity of Romanesque cubes, columns, and corridors: the long dormitory where monks slept on straw mattresses, the windowless round hall where the abbot gathered his flock for readings, the stone church devoid of paintings or stained glass. The Cistercians renounced the pleasure of this world, and we renounce its comforts, waiting on hard pews as monks prepare for the six o'clock Mass. Suddenly, a terrifying series of thunderclaps shudders the air around us. The rain sluices in through a hole above the altar that leaves the sanctuary open to the heavens, crackling on the ancient stone floor. Then the bells begin to peal. We feel the hand of God, there, in the Abbaye de Sénanque.

Forgiveness often follows grace, and for Mom and me the rains washing the stone floor of Sénanque are enough to wash away a lifetime of tensions. As we leave the valley, night is nipping at our heels. The sky partially clears and the mountains turn purple under an indigo sky. We suddenly realize that we have ended up in the heart of Peter Mayle country. So why not have dinner in Gordes, the site of an elegant Parisian-style dinner party described in *A Year in Provence*? As we approach, we pass swank resorts and the luxury homes of media celebrities who have claimed the town for themselves. Somehow, at the end of this day in late September, after the exodus of summer interlopers, after the cleansing rains, after the thunder in Sénanque, Gordes seems preternaturally peaceful. The ancient stone village, perched high on a hilltop, glows like honey in the light of the setting sun, exuberant now that the storm clouds have passed. We are among the first guests at Le Renaissance, a hotel-restaurant situated inside the ramparts of the twelfth-century castle at the heart of the village. Under a ceiling beamed with dark timbers, we settle into sturdy wooden chairs at a table near the stone fireplace. In perfect harmony, we lift our glasses of rosé for a toast to Peter Mayle.

Just as our week in Provence is coming to a close, life at Mas de l'Ange perks up. Two vans arrive one afternoon, disgorging photographers, stylists, assistants, and models— sixteen people in all, sent down from Paris for a fashion shoot. Friends of Hélène's from her magazine days, they double up in the rooms, map out plans in the poolside cabaña, and eat in the kitchen with the family (which includes the now-returned Bruno).

Hélène warms up in the presence of familiar guests. She even lingers with us at breakfast, chatting about life in the provinces. We are inclined to stick around for the photo shoot, which has been commissioned by a racy lingerie company. But we are persuaded by Fodor's of the need to visit Arles: "If you were obliged to visit just one city in Provence, lovely little

Arles would give Avignon and Aix a run for their money," the
guidebook gushes. We leave ready for a city that radiates with
the brightness of van Gogh sunflowers and the rusticity of his
bedroom. Now that Bruno has told us of the bullfights—"*Les
taureaux ne meurent pas,*" he insists, the bulls don't die—we add
the Roman arena to our sightseeing list, climbing its massive
stone stairs, contemplating its medieval towers, and wandering
in a nearby garden of broken columns and melancholy arches. We see traces of Arles as crossroads to Africa, Arabia, and
the Far East, but are most fascinated by the language and culture of L'occitan, the native people of Provence. The Museon
Arlaten is filled with their literature, pottery, and birdcage-like
breadboxes; docents sit in Arlésienne regalia, lacy shoulder
scarves crossed at the waist.

And yet something about Arles spooks us. We arrive ready
for the light, but leave aware of the dark. We sense something
ominous in the swarthy visages there, the close crowds, the
blue-black shade that seems an insult to the vivid colors of van
Gogh. We can't help noticing the anxious throng of parents
waiting outside the gates of the *école maternelle* in the early
afternoon, unwilling to entrust their children to the streets.
And just before we are to leave, Mom's bag of souvenirs mys-
teriously parts our company.

"*Beh, oui,*" says Hélène, when we report our bad luck and
worse impressions. "*C'est affreux là.*" She then launches into a
disquisition on the "frightful" side of Arles, with Gypsies
roaming up from Les-Saints-Marie-de-la-Mer and immigrants pouring in from North Africa.

I, of course, blame neither the Gypsies nor the immigrants.
I blame my mother, who's made the mistake of loading herself up with the kind of trinkets I've come determined to
resist—van Gogh fishing boats, lavender sachets, and enam-
eled nameplates. Yet Mom is heartsick, and the lost souvenirs

somehow symbolize the loss we feel about our trip coming to a close.

The next morning, our last, while I'm sipping my *café au lait*, Mom snaps pictures before Mas de l'Ange starts to stir. She scurries over the grounds that just a week ago seemed so odd and unfamiliar, capturing the Roman fountain in a hidden courtyard, the chocolate Lab, even the gray stallion. Her child-like enthusiasm makes me smile, and it charms Hélène, who pauses just long enough from her breakfast preparations to throw her head back as Mom captures her laughing heartily. Rejoining me in our private dining room, Mom sets her disposable camera on the table and sits down. The models descend, their tresses gleaming, and the photo assistants lug ungainly equipment out the French doors. Suddenly, Didier, the chief photographer, enters the dining room and swoops in on Mom's Instamatic. Laughing, he positions us *comme ça* under the nude Venus, moves a candelabra in from the edge of the table, raises one hand, and clicks.

It is the one portrait of the two of us that we bring back from Provence.

Constance Hale's lifelong fascination with French is rivaled only by her lifelong fascination with English. She is the author of Wired Style *and* Sin and Syntax, *and as a journalist has written about Latin plurals and Internet clichés. She's also covered national politics, the digital culture, and the spread of hula on the U.S. mainland. She lives in Oakland, California, and Hale'iwa, Hawaii.*

✵

The Provençal Sky

The colors of imagination become the colors of reality.

UPON MY RETURN FROM TEN DAYS IN PROVENCE THE questions, of course, have been inevitable: *Did you have a good time?* (Yes.) *What did you do?* (Everything.) *How was the food?* (Wonderful.)

I try to speak but the answers, if they come at all, come more slowly than the questions, or else they come in a flood-tide of words, of whirling verbal images, too many words to be spoken at one time by one person. I open my mouth and colors escape: the dazzling blues and mauves and fuchsias of the Aix sky at sunset, the emerald greens and delicate blues of the Mediterranean; the astonishing liquid yellow of the sun.

I don't really want to talk at all; I want to find another way to transfer my experience, to take this tangled web inside of me, this inner stew of feelings, scents, tastes, images, sensations all bundled together, this fierce convergence of desire and release, a great tumbling ball of human yarn, and hand it to you, let you hold it up and turn it in the light so that you, too, may know the astonishing beauty, pleasure, satisfaction, relief, and longing that is my Provence. But alas, I am left with only the word, with inadequate human language and a tale the telling of which is beyond me. How to say something so simple and profound as that I arrived home at last, without sounding romantic and hyperbolic, a silly dreamer? Maybe I am specifically that; maybe that's how I arrived at my destination at long last, after twenty-one years of failed attempts. Perseverance furthers, I recall from my old days with the *I Ching*.

I am a talker, that much is certain. If you know me, you know this. I speak easily and often, and probably too much, imposing a constant narrative overlay onto everything I do, think, and feel. But this time it hasn't happened and what might someday be the story I tell myself and others about my time in Provence, the narrative of it all, as it were, for now still flutters in the soft sea breezes, out of my reach. I have only images to offer you.

I am standing in a parking lot on the outskirts of Toulon. A tall, thin man is shoving what looks like old, broken fence boards under a three-legged iron tripod, feeding a raging fire. On top of the tripod is a huge, battered pot into which the man, who has a cigarette hanging from his lips, dumps a couple of buckets of water, then a platter of different shapes, sizes, and colors of fish and shellfish, live, kicking crab, big round chunks of peeled potatoes all go plunging in. The water quickly turns orange with saffron; the air is filled with the scent of garlic; the temperature of the water slowly rises and finally, after an interminable amount of time, the crabs' kicking slows and stops. I watch this for a while, the man feeding the fire and pulling on his cigarette, and then I walk to the courtyard behind the house, where I am handed a glass of white wine.

Time passes. If I look far into the distance I can just barely see the Mediterranean. The sun is warmer than I've felt it in months but with the pleasant breeze I don't notice the burn, the dangerous rosy glow I will discover that night and is only now beginning to fade. From the house, a woman brings out bowls of a thick yellow sauce that I recognize immediately: aioli. *Aioli in Provence.* I stare, captivated, then raise my head and look around. Someone is carrying the fish, piled high on huge platters made of cork, to the table. Someone else fills my glass with wine and yet another person asks me a question. In French. I understand and respond, in spite of the fact that it has been years since I could hold my own in a conversation in the language I so love. I look across the courtyard and see my friend Louise. "Michele, are you happy?" she asks wisely.

Another image: I am walking through narrow streets towards the center of a tiny medieval town. A woman in a black sweater, long skirt, and golden beads is sweeping her doorstep. She is very old, older than I can ever imagine myself being. She must feel me watching her; she looks up, our eyes meet and linger. We smile.

Another day; near the end, at least for now. Overhead, the sky is the color of a peacock's breast, shimmery, nearly metallic blue. Towards the east, the drape of night is beginning to close over us, highlighting the day's lingering colors. The blue overhead fades westward into a dramatic periwinkle, which in turn gives way to an intense lavender dissolving into a brilliant fuchsia horizon. A few hundred yards in the distance, the great fountain, already lit by yellow lights, glows. The enormous ancient plane trees that line the Cours Mirabeau, in their stark winter nakedness just two days ago, are covered now with tiny buds, like stars in the fading light. Listening carefully, I swear I can hear the music of the fountains above the chatter of the clientele that lounge in café after café along the famous promenade of Aix-en-Provence. Briefly, I let myself lean against a nearby friend, needing the palpable sensation of another's presence as I feel as if I will float away into the very ether of this land I've longed to see for an eternity. If ever I have been at home, it is at this precise moment.

Another image lingers. A late dinner—the best kind, to my thinking—with a friend has left me drowsy with contentment. The next day the group will depart for the States and I will go by train from Marseilles to Nice for my flight to Paris. Closeness dissolves into ever widening distances, both personal and geographic, and I snuggle deep into the large hotel bed, my nightgown as silky and black as the Marseilles night. The arms of Europe that opened so wide in welcome are closing around me, gently lifting me if not exactly home, then certainly back to the world where, inevitably it seems, I must live, at least for now.

Michele Anna Jordan is the author of thirteen books about food and wine, including San Francisco Seafood, The New Cook's Tour of Sonoma, Salt & Pepper, *and* California Home Cooking. *She writes for a variety of national publications and hosts two radio shows on KRCB-FM. She has won numerous awards for both cooking and writing, including a 1997 James Beard Award, and makes her home in Sonoma County, California.*

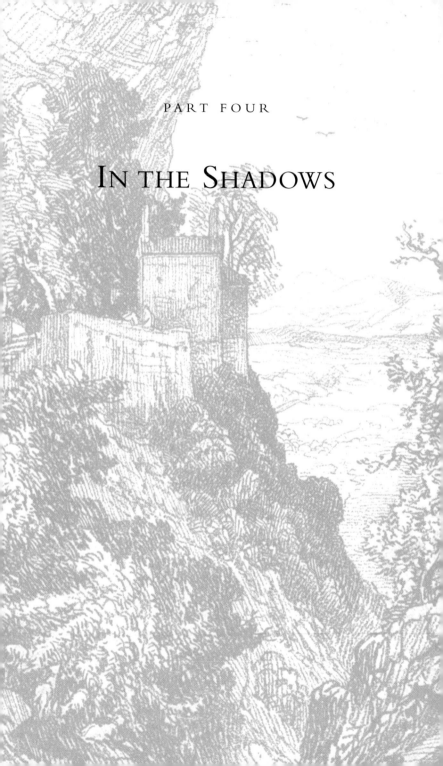

PART FOUR

IN THE SHADOWS

PAUL GAUGUIN,
TRANSLATED BY R. BURNETT

✳

Vincent at the End

In 1887, two astonishing talents cross paths in Provence.

I ARRIVED IN ARLES VERY EARLY IN THE MORNING AND I awaited daylight in an all-night café. The patron looked at me and said: "You're the chum; I recognize you." A portrait of myself that I had sent to Vincent was sufficient to explain the exclamation of this man. Showing him the portrait, Vincent had explained to him that it was a friend who was shortly coming.

Neither too late, nor too early, I went to wake Vincent. The day was given over to getting myself installed, to a great deal of gossiping, to a walk for the purpose of admiring the beauties of Arles and the Arlésiennes, for whom, as a matter of fact, I was never able to become very enthusiastic.

I remained therefore some weeks before clearly understanding the rough savor of Arles and its surroundings, which did not prevent us from working hard, particularly Vincent. Two beings, he and myself, the one a volcano and the other boiling also. But inside in some way a struggle was preparing itself.

To begin with I found in everything and with everything a disorder that shocked me. His box of colors was scarcely large enough to contain all the squeezed tubes which were never closed, and in spite of all this disorder, this mess, something rumbled in his canvases; in his words also. Daudet, de Goncourt, and the Bible burned through his Dutch brain. He had forgotten even how to write Dutch, and as one has been able to see from the publication of his letters to his brother he only wrote in French, and that admirably with an infinity of "insofar as's."

In spite of all my efforts to unravel in his disorderly mind a logical reasoning in his critical opinions, I was not able to explain to myself all the contradiction that there was between his painting and his opinions. Thus, for example, he had an unbounded admiration for Meissonnier and a profound hatred for Ingres. Degas made him despair and Cézanne was only a dauber. Thinking of Monticelli made him cry.

One of the things that annoyed him was to have to allow me great intelligence whereas I had too small a forehead, a sign of imbecility. And among all this a great tenderness or rather a saintly altruism.

From the first month, I saw our joint finances take on the same aspects of disorder. What was to be done? The situation was delicate, the cash-box being modestly provisioned by his

---

Arles, at a corner of the great main road of the Empire, never so strong as to destroy nor so insignificant as to ease from building, catching the earliest Roman march into the north, the Christian advance, the full experience of the invasions; retaining in a vague legend the memory of St. Paul; drawing in, after the long trouble, the new life that followed the Crusades, can show such visions better, I think, than Rome herself can show them.

—Hilaire Belloc,
The Hills and the Sea (1902)

brother employed by Goupil's; on my side in combination with an exchange into pictures. It was necessary to speak, and to risk blundering against his great touchiness. It was therefore only with great precaution and much coaxing, little compatible with my character, that I touched on the question. I must admit, I succeeded much more easily than I had thought. In a box [was put] so much for nocturnal and hygienic promenading, so much for tobacco, so much also for impromptu expenses, including the rent. On top, a piece of paper and a pencil for the honest noting down of what each took out of the cash-box. In another box, the rest of the sum divided into four parts for the expenses of food for each week. Our little restaurant was suppressed, and with the help of a little gas oven I did the cooking while Vincent did the shopping, without going very far from the house. Once, however, Vincent wanted to make a soup, but I don't know how he made his mixtures. Probably like the colors in his pictures. It remains that we could not eat it. At which Vincent laughed, saying, "Tarascon! The cap of père Daudet." On the wall he wrote in chalk:

Je suis Saint-Esprit.
Je suis Saint-Esprit.

How long did we remain together? I could not say, having totally forgotten. In spite of the rapidity with which the catastrophe happened; in spite of the fever for working that had got hold of me, all this time appears to me as a century. In spite of what the public may think, two men did tremendous work there, useful to both of them; possibly to others. Certain things bear fruit.

Vincent, at the time of my arrival at Arles, was up to the ears in the post-Impressionist School, and he was making a nice mess of it, which made him suffer; not that this school, like all schools, was bad, but because it did not correspond with his nature, so little patient and so independent. With all his yellows on violets, all this work with complimentary colors, a disorderly work on his part, he only arrived at soft, incomplete and monotonous harmonies; the sound of the bugle was lacking. I undertook the task of explaining things to him which was easy for me, for I found rich and fruitful ground. Like all original natures marked with a seal of personality, Vincent had no fear of his neighbor and no obstinacy. From that day my friend, van Gogh, made astonishing progress; he seemed to catch a glimpse of everything that he had in him, and hence all that series of sunflowers on sunflowers in the brilliant sunshine....

It would be idle here to enter into details of technique. This has been related in order to tell you that van Gogh, without losing an inch of his originality, found in me a fruitful preceptor. And every day he was grateful to me for it. And this is what he meant when he wrote to Monsieur Aurier that he owed much to Paul Gauguin. When I arrived in Arles Vincent was trying to find himself, whilst I, much older, was a completed man. I am indebted to Vincent for something, which is, with the knowledge of having been useful to him, the strengthening of my previous pictural ideas: then in very difficult moments remembering that there are some more unfortunate than oneself. When I read this statement—*Gauguin's drawing recalls a little that of van Gogh*—I smile.

During the latter part of my stay, Vincent became excessively brusque and noisy, then silent. On some evenings I surprised Vincent, who had got up, in the act of coming over to my bed. To what should I attribute my waking up at those moments? At all events it was sufficient to say to him very seriously: "What is wrong with you Vincent?" for him to get back to bed without saying a word, and sleep solidly. I had the idea of doing his portrait while he was painting the *nature morte* that he was so fond of with the sunflowers. And when the portrait was finished he said to me: "It is certainly I, but I gone mad."

The same evening we went to the café. He ordered a weak absinthe. Suddenly he threw the glass and its contents at my head. I avoided it, and taking him under the arm I left the café, crossed the Place Victor Hugo, and a few minutes later Vincent found himself in his bed where in a few seconds he went to sleep and did not wake again until the morning. When he woke, very calm, he said to me: "My dear Gauguin, I have a vague remembrance that I offended you last evening."

"I forgive you willingly and delightedly, but yesterday's scene might happen again, and if I were hit I might not remain master of myself, and strangle you. Allow me, therefore, to write to your brother to announce my return." What a day! Good God!

When the evening came, I swallowed my dinner and felt the need of going alone to take some air where the laurels are in flower. I had already almost entirely crossed the Place Victor Hugo when I heard behind me a well-known little step, rapid and jerky. I turned round at the very

> I feel inside me a strength which I must expand, a fire which I cannot put out, but which I must nurture. I do not know to what end it will lead, but I would not be surprised if it were a dark one.
>
> —Vincent van Gogh

moment when Vincent was on the point of throwing himself on me with an open razor in his hand. My look must have been very powerful at that moment for he stopped and lowering his head he returned running to the house.

Was I cowardly at that moment and ought I not to have disarmed him and tried to pacify him? Often I have questioned my conscience and I have made myself no reproaches. He who likes may cast his stones at me. In a very short time I was at a good hotel in Arles where, after having asked the time, I took a room and went to bed. Being very upset I could only get to sleep towards three in the morning and I woke up rather late, about seven-thirty.

Arriving at the square I saw a large crowd assembled. Near our house some *gendarmes* and a little man in a bowler hat who was the police commissioner. This is what had taken place.

Van Gogh went back to the house and immediately cut off an ear close to the head. He must have taken a certain time to stop the force of the bleeding, for the next day numerous damp towels were spread out on the flagstones of the two ground-floor rooms. The blood had dirtied the two rooms and the little staircase that led up to our bedroom.

When he was in a condition to go out, his head enveloped in a completely pulled down *béret basque* he went straight to a house where, lacking a sweetheart, one makes an acquaintance, and gave the person in charge his ear, well cleaned and enclosed in an envelope. "Here," he said, "in remembrance of me," then he ran out and went home where he went to bed and to sleep. He took the precaution, however, of closing the shutters and of putting a lighted lamp on a table near the window.

Ten minutes later the whole street reserved to the women was in movement and the happening was being discussed.

I was far from knowing anything of all that when I presented myself on the doorstep of our house, and when the man with the bowler hat said to me point-blank in a more severe tone: "What have you done, sir, to your friend?"

"I don't know...."

"Of course you know...you know very well...he is dead."

I wish no one such a moment, and several long minutes

were necessary before I was capable of thinking and restraining the beating of my heart.

Anger, indignation, pain also and shame before all the glances that were tearing my whole body were suffocating me and I could only stutter: "Very well, sir, let us go upstairs and we shall discuss that there." Vincent was lying in the bed completely covered by sheets, crouching like a retriever: he seemed dead. Softly, very softly, I touched the body whose warmth certainly assured life. It was for me the resumption of all my senses and energy.

Almost in a whisper I said to the police commissioner: "Kindly, sir, wake this man with great tact, and if he asks for me tell him that I have left for Paris: the sight of me might perhaps be fatal to him." I must admit that from that moment the police commissioner was as pleasant as possible, and he sent, intelligently, for a doctor and a carriage.

Once he was awake, Vincent asked for his friend, his pipe and his tobacco, even thought of asking for the box that was downstairs and that contained our money—a suspicion, no doubt, that glanced off me for I was already armed against all suffering.

Vincent was taken to the hospital where, as soon as he had arrived, his brain began again to become unbalanced.

All the rest is known in those circles where that is of interest and it is useless to speak of it, unless it be of the extreme suffering of a man who, looked after in an asylum, found himself at monthly intervals sufficiently in possession of his senses to understand his condition and to paint with passion the admirable pictures that one knows.

The last letter that I had was dated from Auvers, near Pontoise. He told me that he had hoped to be sufficiently cured to come to look me up in Brittany, but that now he was obliged to recognize the impossibility of a cure:

"Dear Master (the only time that he used this word), it is better, after having known you and given you trouble, to die in a good state of mind than in a state of degrading."

He shot himself in the stomach, and it was a few hours afterwards only, lying in his bed and smoking his pipe, that he died, having complete lucidity of mind, with love for his art and without hatred for anyone.

Paul Gauguin spent his early childhood with his mother's aristocratic relatives in Peru. When he was six, his family returned to a much drearier life in France. At seventeen, he went to sea for six years then settled in Paris to become a successful businessman. He married a young Danish woman and they had five children. For twelve years, Gauguin painted as a hobby but gradually art became his passion. At thirty-five, he quit his job to be an artist and abandoned his family to search for a freer, simpler way of life. He spent ten of the last twelve years of his life painting in the South Pacific, where he died at the age of fifty-four in 1903.

JEFFREY TAYLER

✦ ✦ ✦

Another French Revolution

Europe—and Provence—confront their North African future.

I'VE HIKED UP THE 500-FOOT-HIGH HILL IN THE MIDDLE OF
Marseilles on which stands the basilica of Notre-Dame-de-la-
Garde, topped by a gilded statue of the Virgin Mary. Above
the Mediterranean, clouds obscure the setting sun, but the
light is still strong, and the islands beyond the harbor show as
scattered clumps of coal in a sea of rippling molten silver.
Around me spreads a maze of serpentine lanes and zigzagging
avenues, of gabled roofs and stone apartment houses whose
ocherous reds and ashen grays harmonize with the pastel hues
of the limestone hills defining the northern limits of the city.
Such impressionistic allure is what one expects to find in the
south of France, whose landscape inspired Cézanne and van
Gogh, Daudet and Pagnol.

I'm not alone beneath the basilica. Families are ambling by,
speaking the Arabic dialects of Morocco and Algeria. The
men lead, the backs of their loafers, squashed flat, the easier to
slip them off; women follow in white head scarves and voluminous ankle-to-neck raincoats, pushing baby carriages. Their

harsh Semitic gutturals provoke irritated stares from French couples nearby, but for me they call to mind Marrakesh (where I lived as a Peace Corps volunteer a decade ago), a city that, with its sandstorms and withering sun, could hardly be more dissimilar to Marseilles. For a moment the incongruity between my sere memories of Marrakesh and the soft colors of Marseilles overcomes me, and I find myself staring at the newcomers, wondering at their strangeness here in France.

Different though they may be, Marseilles and Marrakesh, or, rather, France and North Africa, are becoming increasingly linked. Since the 1950s North Africans have been moving to Marseilles in great numbers, legally and illegally, and now make up roughly a quarter of the city's population. It is estimated that every year at least 100,000 illegal immigrants (of whom possibly half are North African) enter France, where legally registered foreigners already number 3.5 million out of a population of 60 million; the total number of foreigners in the country may be as high as 5 or 6 million. Pan-European statistics reflect a similarly large-scale migratory trend (some 500,000 illegal immigrants slip into the E.U. each year) that accelerated in the 1990s with wars breaking out or intensifying in Algeria, southeastern Turkey, and the Balkans, and with the opening of borders in countries of the former Soviet bloc. More and more, France and Europe are finding themselves confronted with an issue that parts of the United States (in particular the Southwest and the cities of the Northeast) have been wrestling with for a long time now: how to handle an upsurge in unwanted, mainly economic refugees while preserving constitutionally enshrined individual liberties and human rights....

The sun drops below the horizon and the wind gusts. From the halls of Notre-Dame-de-la-Garde echo the last hollow chants of the evening Mass, then the giant bell above the basilica strikes six, the deafening bronze blows of its gong reverberating over the darkening quarters of the city. Worshippers, mainly working-class French in scuffed shoes and coarse woolen sweaters, file out and shove their way through the Arab strollers, heading for their cars in the lot below.

From the Arc de Triomphe, which rises against the sky amid the broad and airy Place Jules Guesde, I set out for a walk across the center of Marseilles, passing the sleek glass-and-granite headquarters of the regional administration and weaving my way between joggers in spandex tights and fashionably dressed young men and women immersed in cell-phone conversations. I turn down the two-lane Rue d'Aix and enter a shadowy defile of soot-encrusted five-story buildings, and all at once I am in a different world. Arab men in *djellabahs* crowd the sidewalks. Narrow-faced youths with curly black hair, who might be from any district of Tangier or Algiers, cycle between pedestrians, zinging their bells and shouting, "*Attention!*" At the corner, a turbaned old man whining a beggar's chant in Arabic sits barefoot on a stained sheet of cardboard, his knees drawn up to his shoulders, his palm extended. Tall African women wearing floral scarves and toting bulging plastic bags talk in Wolof and make their way around Berber women with tattooed chins. Side streets weave away into a warren smelling of grilled chicken and *harissa*—the immigrant neighborhood of Belsunce, which is, from all appearances, as lively and North African as any quarter of the Casbah in Marrakesh.

Rue d'Aix widens into Cours Belsunce, where Senegalese women recline on blankets spread on the pavement, chatting, their babies lolling on their laps. Farther on, clusters of Arab men with lined cheeks gesticulate and argue. Cours Belsunce cuts through La Canabière, the city's largest commercial avenue, which, after a smattering of cheap cafés, narrows and becomes Rue de Rome, where the street fête ends and the Marks and Spencers and Galeries Lafayettes begin—where most Arabs and Africans, if there are any, are wiping windows or removing garbage.

As one might infer from this walk, the Mediterranean has shaped the history of Marseilles by favoring the migration and mixing of peoples living on or near it. Greeks who set sail from Asia Minor (now Turkey's Aegean coast) founded Marseilles in 600 B.C., and for the next five centuries it was an independent Greek city-state. Julius Caesar began his invasion of Gaul here, and the subsequent blending of Roman and Celtic peoples and cultures produced the Frankish kingdom that was to become the French Republic. Yet for hundreds of years Marseilles remained aloof and recalcitrant, proud of its independent past. It joined the rest of France only in 1481 and in 1792 sided with the revolutionaries; the volunteer force it dispatched to Paris to support the Commune sang a defiant song along the way that became the French national anthem, "La Marseillaise."

Soon after, France began its transformation from European kingdom into colonial empire. The egalitarian values of the French Revolution found paradoxical expression in the *mission civilisatrice* that served as the ideological justification for colonial expansion. The *mission* ordained that the colonized be, in effect, exploited for their own enlightenment; they were to be dragged in irons to civilization, and those who tried to sunder their fetters were savages. The *mission* had little effect on Marseilles, which prospered as the port of empire and maintained its distinct culture, accent, and population—a population that always included Mediterranean immigrants, many of whom where from the colonies. In 1891, Guy de Maupassant wrote that the city "perspires in the sun like a beautiful girl who does not take good care of herself.... It smells of the innumerable foods nibbled on by the Negroes, Turks, Greeks, Italians, Maltese, Spaniards, English, Corsicans, and Marseillais, too...[who are] recumbent, sitting, rolling, and sprawling on its docks."

Elsewhere in France at that time, however, foreigners were usually of more northern European origin. For a hundred years the country had been relying on Germans, Swiss, Italians, and Belgians to fulfill its expanding economy's need for manpower in heavy industry and mining. After the First World War the labor shortage was especially acute, and the influx of other Europeans increased to meet it: a 1931 census recorded three million foreigners in France. The newcomers provoked resentment, but they were mainly Christian and white; most assimilated, and the resentment passed.

Ye sons of France,
  Awake to glory
Hark! Hark! What myriads
  bid you rise!
Your children, wives and
  grandsires hoary,
Behold their tears and hear
  their cries,
Behold their tears and hear
  their cries!
Shall hateful tyrants, mischief
  breeding
With hireling hosts, a ruffian
  band
A-fright and desolate land,
While peace and liberty lie
  bleeding?

To arms, to arms, ye brave!
Th' avenging sword
  unsheathe,
March on! March on!
All hearts resolved on victory
  or death!
  — from "La Marseillaise" by
  Claude-Joseph Rouget de
    l'Isle (1760–1836)

It was after the Second World War that the city's present demographic outlines began to take shape. The dissolution of France's empire deprived Marseilles of status and revenue while another war-related shortage of manpower led the French to search for labor abroad, mainly to fill vacancies on construction sites and public works projects and in automobile plants. This time they looked to North Africa. France had just granted citizens of its Algerian territory full civil rights, including the right to live and work anywhere in France. Poverty and overpopulation prompted hundreds of thousands of Algerians to respond to the recruitment drive and take the boat to Marseilles. Other former French colonial subjects from Africa, the Middle East, and Asia would eventually come as well. By the mid-1970s immigrants would swell Marseilles from the 1946 population of 637,000 to 912,000.

The influx of non-Europeans did not cease after 1974, when economic recession motivated the French government to announce a policy of "zero immigration." Legal foreign residents had the right to invite their families, which they did, and then there were the illegals who kept coming anyway. By the 1980s, for the first time in France's history, primarily Arab or African immigrants were outnumbering European arrivals. It is estimated that about half of the foreigners living in France today are from Africa.

To accommodate the immigrants while quartering them separately from the French, who resented them as much as they needed their labor, Marseilles spilled beyond its traditional boundaries. From Belsunce the city grew north, adding what came to be known as the *quartiers Nord*, or northern districts—immigrant ghettos, really—that spread all the way to the limestone hills visible from Notre-Dame-de-la-Garde. Beset with crime, street gangs, drug trading, and unemployment as high as 45 percent, the *quartiers Nord* now make up about a third of Marseilles. They are not for casual touring, so I have asked twenty-six-year-old Hafid Benobeidallah, an Algerian who grew up there, to show me around. He has agreed, and offers to introduce me to friends of his in the rap group Fresh.

Hafid drives up to my hotel in a red Renault. He looks hip and relaxed in jeans and floppy salt-and-pepper sweater, a soul patch beneath his lower lip, his hair cropped short and stylishly nappy. Around his chest he carries a cell phone in a leather pouch; on his waist he wears a pager. I ask if we should speak Arabic or French. He tells me that although he understands Arabic, the language his parents still use at home, he is most comfortable in French.

As we follow the grimy Boulevard National out of the city center and into the *quartiers Nord*, heading for his old neighborhood on Rue Félix Payat, Hafid tells me his story. He was born in a village near Oran. After the Algerian War of Independence (1954–62), his father came to Marseilles to take a minimum-wage job in construction and eventually brought the rest of the family over. The minimum wage sufficed to keep Hafid and his five brothers and sisters fed: families with incomes below a certain level are eligible for welfare and other benefits. Hafid has just finished vocational college, where he earned a degree in automotive engineering, but he can't find work, and he's considering moving to Paris or Quebec if nothing turns up. His car and electronic accoutrements he bought with money he made doing part-time jobs over the summers.

The serried rows of auto-repair shops and dingy cafés on Boulevard National give way to a sparser wilderness of high-rises towering over public housing projects called HLM*s*, an acronym standing for "moderate-income housing" that has become synonymous with tenements and immigrants. In the most decrepit HLMs, the windows of abandoned apartments have been cemented over, but in places the concrete has been knocked out and smoke is pouring through the holes. "Squatters," Hafid says. The ground floors of a couple of the high-rises are paneled in glass painted unevenly in blue or green; tiny Arabic signs announce the ramshackle premises behind them as mosques.

> ─────────※─────────
>
> These Marseillaise make Marseillaise hymns, and Marseillaise vests, and Marseillaise soap for all the world; but they never sing their hymns, or wear their vests, or wash with their soap themselves.
>
> —Mark Twain (1835–1910)

We enter the neighborhood of Bassens. Here there are groups of Arab and African youths in baggy jeans and baseball caps standing in the lots between HLMs, looking tough and watching the traffic. We come upon two smashed and upturned cars, stripped of every exterior part, even the wheels. "They looted the cars," Hafid says. "For fun they turn them over after they're done. Or they light them on fire. There's nothing else to do here, there's no work." Farther on, a Peugeot chassis lies, burned out and stripped.

We race higher and higher through the *quartiers*, which never deteriorate into the full-blown slums I'm expecting to see (always they look utilitarian and basically inhabitable, if strewn with litter), and finally achieve the summit at Solidarité, a neighborhood of high-rises scattered across rocky land. There's a commotion ahead: a half-dozen helmeted policemen on motorcycles are careening off the main road into an empty lot, heading for the trash container belching smoke and flames. Arab youths are running away into the projects, and the police, circling, are left with no one to apprehend.

The sun breaks free of the clouds, and stark white light washes over the trash and smoke and concrete. We start back down toward Rue Félix Pyat. Hafid calmly explains that the kids *du quartier* ("from the neighborhood") and *d' origine* ("of immigrant background"—most of them are second-generation) quit school early, can't find work, and turn to crime as much to make a living as to kill time, knocking over stores in the city center, mugging pedestrians, or dealing *shit* (marijuana) that they buy off traffickers riding the ferries from North Africa. *Shit* serves both as a source of income and as entertainment. There's nothing to do in the *quartiers*—there are few bars, cafés, or movie theaters—and the welfare money their parents receive goes to feed the family. However, crime has dropped recently, Hafid says, as a result of the heavy policing begun by the current mayor. "The prisons are full, and the meanest characters of the *quartier* are dead."

But relations remain tense between the French and Africans, or, as Hafid puts it, whites and blacks. "I prefer not to use the word 'French,'" he says. "Most 'French' Marseillaise are just Italians or Portuguese who've assimilated, but they're the biggest racists of all. It's better so say 'whites'—the problems here are between whites and Arabs, whites and blacks. As for Arabs and blacks, we're brothers here, we're all from the *quartiers*."

Back on Rue Félix Pyat we meet Yusuf, a member of Fresh, who is of Comorian origin. Yusuf at first looks at me with startled hostility, but when Hafid tells him I'm American, his face lights up and he asks me who my favorite rap artists are—a question I can't answer, knowing nothing at all about the genre. Frowning, he steps back and says we will have to talk another day. He turns and walks off.

*

Although his father made the pilgrimage to Mecca, Hafid doesn't pray or concern himself with Islam, and neither, he says, do his friends of Muslim background; money, cars, the latest rap CDs, and cell phones mean more to them than religion. Young women from the *quartier* follow Islamic custom and tend to stay off the street, but those who venture out rarely wear head scarves, which, in Marseilles, are—like skull-caps, *djellabahs*, and three-day beards—telltale signs of recent arrival. But among immigrants Islam survives as a unifier, bonding those from the *quartiers* and distinguishing them from the white French. Muftis in Marseilles, who draw together the parents of Hafid and his friends at Friday prayers, still retain authority, and I've arranged to speak with Sheikh Abdel Hadi, the mufti of the Great Mosque of the Sunna on Boulevard National.

The Great Mosque occupies the first floor of what might once have been a hardware store or restaurant. It lacks the soaring grandeur of such buildings in Muslim countries; there is no minaret; the sign, in Arabic and French, is small and unobtrusive; and one-way mirrored windows prevent those on the street from looking inside. I arrive as noon prayers are ending. As I enter, bearded men are streaming out, adjusting their skullcaps, slipping on their loafers, straightening their jackets. Wearing gray robes and a black-and-white *kaffiyeh*, Sheikh Abdel Hadi appears. He is muscular and intense, abrupt, and possessed of arresting dark eyes; his diction, the balanced and sonorous classical Arabic of the Koran, bespeaks erudition, a lifetime of hard study in religious schools, and is devoid of traces of his native Algerian dialect or French.

The sheikh asks me to sit down on the floor in the corner, where he joins me after seeing off the remaining worshippers. We talk, or, rather, I ask questions and he orates, his voice ringing throughout the empty hall, his eyes flinty with something akin to disdain. The North Africans who've immigrated to France came in waves. The first wave were those who helped the French in the colonies; they were *jahil* (ignorant of Islam). They did not know classical Arabic, only their dialects, so how could they possibly have taught their children the Koran, which must be studied only in classical Arabic? There are no Muslims in the municipal government, and this indicates racism. The French government insists that religion and state be separate and forbids the wearing of head scarves; it does little to help the Islamic community, though Muslims have spent years working to build France. The sheikh is not complaining: his voice resounds with a sort of irritated defiance, as though the problems he describes are the inevitable lot of Muslims gone astray in a land of heathens.

In the 1970s, Islam began reviving, he tells me, and this has changed the world. When I counter that this may be the case across the Mediterranean but that here in France I've seen little sign of interest in Islam among the young and more evidence of French cultural influence, he cuts me off. "Our young have been influenced by the *zina'* [fornication] and *khamr* [alcohol] and drugs of France. This is natural. We're working to re-educate them. But they see that there's no answer to their suffering save Islam."

"Won't a resurgence in faith hinder integration?" I ask.

"*Integration?*" he responds. "We're not for integration. Islam tells us to cooperate with other *ahl al-kitab* ["People of the Book," or Jews and Christians] but not to integrate with them. We're for separation. Islam is in revival the world over, including here. It's the French who are coming to us." He tells me my time is up, rises abruptly, shakes my hand, and goes upstairs, leaving me alone in the empty mosque.

I ponder the incongruity here in France of *zina'*, *khamr*, *ahl al-kitab*, Koranic words bearing the stony resonance of the

Sunna and the commandments, of implacable struggle and sin. The sheikh's rejection of integration runs counter to the basic precept of France's nationality policy—that immigrants accept French values and assimilate. Yet his position derives from irrefutable logic: if his followers integrate, they are no longer his flock, they have been conquered and converted. France's present-day policy of assimilation is, at root, a continuation of the *mission civilisatrice* of colonial days.

If the sheik rejects integration, it hardly matters: the waning of religion (be it Islam or Christianity) in France portends a future in which race will mean more for North Africans than creed. In fact, it already does.

By reason of geography, restrictive visa regulations, and a policy of selective recruitment that favored the import of Arab labor, immigration from France's former colonies in sub-Saharan Africa has never matched that from North Africa. Black African immigrants account for only around 5 percent of France's foreign population. The Senegalese are the most numerous, followed by an expanding community of Comorians.

> No place abounds more with dissolute persons of both sexes than Marseilles, and in the abundance of prostitutes, that appear in the streets, it is almost upon a par with London.
>
> —Henry Swinburne (1776)

I'm having coffee with Nabou Diop, who was born in Senegal but just got her French passport, and her friend Agnes Yameogo, a French citizen with Burkina Fasan parents. Both are in their twenties and have worked as cooks in a Mexican restaurant near the Old Port. We're at Nabou's apartment, which is painted sunny yellow and looks out on a quiet side street splitting off from the hectic Cours Lieutaud. Haunting Senegalese music echoes from her CD player; children shout on the sidewalk below; the curtains are stirring with a breeze bringing in the warmth of the sun and the salty sea air.

Nabou is still relieved by her recent naturalization, which took six years. She has spent most of her life in France and speaks French without an accent, as does Agnes. Yet both are combative and have been stung by racism. Nabou had a hard time finding this apartment. Landlord after landlord, on hearing her French over the phone, mistook her for a white woman; when they met her, *hélas*, their apartments had "just been rented." She tells me old women sometimes grab their purses when they see her, as if she were a thief; her teachers in school tried to discourage her from pursuing a higher education, despite her good grades. She gives other examples. "When I visit Senegal," she says, clenching her small fists, "I feel European. But when I'm here, I feel black. I can't feel at home, even in Marseilles, the capital of Africa!"

Agnes pushes her glasses up the bridge of her nose and seconds Nabou, adding that Africans want to come to France because they will either "die of hunger or emigrate—it's not a question of choice. They're not going on vacation when they come here." The world belongs to the whites, she says. Whites are kings when they visit Africa, but they grudge blacks the chance to feed their families by working a few years in France. Although Agnes and Nabou have white friends, most of the people with whom they feel at ease are other Africans or Arabs from the *quartiers*, who share their sense of exclusion. On the television in the corner we see the faces of newscasters, all white; the blue screen seems to portray an artificial world from which blacks have been banished, Agnes says, and that must be by design.

The breeze stirs the curtain again, bringing in more warmth. *Le capital de l'Afrique.* The climate of Marseilles does call to mind northern Africa. Nabou and Agnes tell me that is why they chose to live here over Paris or Lyon, but wherever they go they are not at home.

The French Ministry of Justice, within whose purview fall matters of naturalization, has stated, rather loftily, that nationality means "belonging. Belonging to a single history, belonging to a single destiny...France has never refused those who want to join its community." "Never" is not exactly the word. The decree of November 2, 1945, governing the status of foreigners on French soil has been amended some thirty times, with each instance making it harder to acquire citizenship or become regularized. In 1999 alone, French maritime authorities captured and deported some 10,000 illegals landing in skiffs or stowing away in ferries. Others who manage to sneak in do so stashed in the backs of trucks, or by hiding in the restrooms on trains, or by walking over the borders from Spain or Italy. In all, some 100,000 illegals make it to France each year. Still others just overstay their visas. Foreigners caught in Marseilles *sans papiers* risk being arrested, locked up for several months in Baumettes Prison, then forcibly expelled by boat through the conveniently located detention center of the port of Arenc. Between 1991 and 1999 the percentage of those banished through Arenc's gates has almost doubled.

There is no way of knowing for sure, of course, but locals in Marseilles put the number of *sans papiers* at 20,000, though it could easily be much higher. The *sans papiers* form an easily exploitable labor pool of docile folk who staff kitchens, bus tables, drive trucks, sweep shops, scrub floors—who do, in short, all the work the French no longer want to do, often for as little as half the legal minimum monthly wage. The *sans papiers* help proprietors by saving them the social security tax that accounts for half the cost of labor; at the same time, by providing employers with an inexpensive alternative to lawful hires, they foster unemployment. However strict the laws and however rapidly deportation rates are rising, the police expel just enough illegals to appear to be enforcing the law but never so many as to interfere with the cleaning of streets or the busing of tables. This provokes suspicion of collusion— that politicians in power talk loudly but do little about *immigrés* in order to avoid alienating affluent voters (the kind who own restaurants, hotels, and trucking companies, for example), or to keep from offending the media (which has always been staunchly left wing) and the liberal sensibilities of the part of the electorate that sympathizes with the plight of the *immigrés*.

The most vulnerable *sans papiers* are the minors, mostly boys, who stow away aboard boats setting sail from Algiers, Oran, and Casablanca. Numbering around 300 at any given time in Marseilles, they gather in public parks and open squares, where their visibility protects them from police beatings and robbery. Some hitchhike out, either to farther points in France or to other E.U. countries. Many work in the jobs described above, but quite a few deal drugs, sell their bodies, or steal to survive.

At the Marseilles Palace of Justice courthouse I meet Amed Charaabi, a social worker of Tunisian origin employed by an association called Jeunes Errants. Jeunes Errants was founded in 1995 to aid runaway minors, most of whom were escaping the massacres in Algeria but who now tend to come from Sidi Bernoussi, Mouley Sheriff, and Ain Chauk—the spreading bidonvilles of Casablanca. Amed tells minors to return home (Jeunes Errants will pay for their tickets), where they at least have families; he gives them vouchers for meals and puts them up in hotels to get them off the streets.

An Algerian teenager is waiting outside Amed's office at the courthouse. His eyes are red and bleary, his hands chapped and trembling. Walking in on unsteady feet, he greets both of us with a courteous *La bes* ("Hello"), shakes our hands and taps his heart, and sits down in front of Amed's desk. The boy, whom I'll call Hussein here (Amed has agreed to allow me to sit in on the condition that I not reveal names), tells us his story in Algerian Arabic: He watched guerrillas of the Islamic Salvation Front (FIS) slit the throats of two of his neighbors. Then the FIS came after his brother, a policeman, and tried to coerce him into providing them with arms. To escape the pressure, his brother quit the police force, but then he lost his mind. Suddenly, Hussein found himself the sole family bread-winner, so he paid to stow away in a container aboard a cargo ship bound for Marseilles. Since landing he has slept behind the railway station. Now, cold and hungry and having failed to find work, he has given up and come to Jeunes Errants for help.

Amed hands him meal tickets, calls around to find him a hotel room, and then explains his only option: application for territorial asylum. The process, during which applicants must prove they've been persecuted by their government, will take months and probably result in a refusal (France rarely grants asylum to Algerians, who flee, as a rule, poverty or the FIS, not the state), but this will give Hussein a chance to collect his wits and decide to head home.

Hussein rises and shakes Amed's hand, tapping his heart, and walks, still on unsteady feet, to the hallway and heads out, this time for a hotel.

In the days of empire, France's *mission civilisatrice* purported to "civilize" the *indigènes* (natives) and gradually turn them into *petits français*—junior French who would labor with alacrity to bring in the colonial harvest. The highest-ranking juniors were the *évolués*, or the evolved ones, colonial subjects trained to work in administrative positions. *Évolués* served two purposes: they cut down on costs by replacing French manpower, and they created the illusion that colonials were profiting from their subservient status, becoming "civilized," as it were. Both *petits français* and *évolués* were to serve the grandeur of France, and one day, or so the ideology posited, in the far, far (and ever receding) future, they would become "civilized" enough to be considered fully French. When independence came, well-positioned *évolués* often ended up running their countries.

Although the colonial era had come to a close long before I arrived in Marrakesh, I found something like *évolué* culture still thriving there in places. Far from the manure-leavened dust, braying donkeys, and prayer calls of the Casbah, in the clean, once-French quarter of Gueliz, I would meet affluent young Moroccans who would gather in discotheques to speak French, show off their latest haute couture acquisitions, and argue over which Parisian arrondissements were chic, which passé. Many were going to France to study or live. As an Arabist, I found this Francophilia unsettling, even repugnant, in view of Morocco's history as a French protectorate, but the Moroccans did not see it this way: among the elite, French and Moroccan culture had merged, they said, and given them a new identity, one superior to that of the Casbah dwellers. And besides, Morocco was poor, France rich. Was their desire to head north and be French really so tough to understand?

I'm drinking a cocktail with Nadia Borde and her sister Anissa, nées Benhalilou, at their loft-style home on Rue Berceau. Both were born in Algeria and are now in their forties; their father was killed fighting for France in the Algerian War of Independence. After his death, their family moved to

Ardèche, near Marseilles, where their status as children of a veteran who had given his life for France facilitated their entry into a society still unused to North Africans. Nadia married a Frenchman and was the first Muslim to be wed in a Catholic church in Ardèche; her grandfather, although a devout Muslim, believed in assimilation and gave her away.

A librarian, Nadia has eyes that express a passion for learning, as do her flamboyant turns of phrase; her curves hint at a voluptuous attachment to good food and drink. Anissa, a speech therapist, is slender and patrician, frail from a recent struggle with cancer. Both are fair-complexioned enough to pass for French, which has helped them assimilate, but still they have felt alienated, especially when French have told them they "don't even look Arab."

Carrying our own wine, we pile into Nadia's car and drive down to Sur le Pouce, a Tunisian restaurant in Belsunce that serves no alcohol. "The owners have found a balance," Nadia says. "They observe Islam but don't bother others who have different customs. I like that." Sur le Pouce is filled with Arab and French young people downing *harissa*-flavored couscous, chicken and fries, red wine and pastis. We take a seat and order. I broach the subject of immigration. But we soon drop it: Nadia and Anissa no longer speak much Arabic and are not even accepted as Arab during visits to North Africa; Islam means nothing to them (Nadia is interested in Buddhism), and both talk about their distaste for extremists of any faith. Their hobbies are literature, travel, films (Nadia likes Oliver Stone), good wine and good food; the *quartiers Nord* are as foreign to them as they are to me.

The evening passes with couscous and wine, wine and baklava; our talk ranges over Putin and Russia, Nadia's readings, Nepal and India. They have assimilated and succeeded in their professions; they have moved beyond issues of ethnicity.

Were they not now and then reminded of their Arab blood by strangers I sense they might rarely remember it.

Nadia and Anissa chose to adopt French and drop their native language. I think back to Gueliz and my antipathy to Morocco's hybrid culture; I now see that I was wrong. One's valor and value derive from subtler things than choice of language, and that choice is, in any case, largely predetermined by circumstance: by the prosperity associated with a language, by the access that language offers to a secure life, or, as with Nadia and Anissa, by the choice of a father to fight in one army versus another. The wealth and security of France inspire assimilation. The poverty of the Casbah can incite only flight.

Hafid and I have returned to Rue Félix Pyat in the *quartiers Nord* to meet Fresh, but the group has stood us up, and we get out of his car and walk around. He shows me what used to be the police station ("the kids burned it down") on the first floor of the high-rise where he used to live; we walk past it to the back lot. There is a crash and an explosion of glass: someone has thrown a sack of garbage out of a tenth-floor window, and it has landed twenty feet from us. We wander back toward the car, passing through the high-rise's first-floor hallway— a moldering green gallery of piss-spattered walls and fecal stench, rats and rubbish, shuffled through by an old Berber man in a white skullcap. As he passes us I say, "*Salam alaykum*," but he gives me a dull stare and moves on, shuffling through more trash.

I watch him mount the stairs. Is this what this Berber, who would be so dignified in his village, has left his homeland for— to stomp through garbage in a reeking tenement? Hafid shrugs. "Well, the people here are hoping to move elsewhere. They think this is temporary. *I* moved out, after all." But the man is old, he may not have time. A decision to live in this filth screams desperation—what despair at home impelled this old man to come here?

We drive off to see Mokhtar, another of Hafid's friends, in the HLMs of Campagne-L'Evêque. At the entrance to one building we find him, a short and jumpy Comorian with manic eyes. We also meet Halim, of Moroccan origin; Berbali, another Comorian; and James, a Gypsy. Others come up to us, greeting us with *Wesh?*—slang for "What's up?" Hafid talks privately with Mokhtar, and I stand with the youths. James tells me they "steal a little, smoke a little *shit*, hang out, and have a good time...that's all." They're all second generation; they know little of their parents' homelands and care less; what counts is that they are from the *quartiers*, of immigrant origin. They owe France nothing ("We didn't ask to be born here"); they no longer go to school ("Why should we? For the French we're just Arabs, we're vandals and no one will give us work"). When a patrol of policemen roars by on motorcycles, the kids shout, "*Les condés!*" and jump inside to hide. But the police roar by, leaving a wake of exhaust drifting our way, and eventually the kids come back out.

Later we return to the center to spend the evening at Le Balthazar listening to rap. At Le Balthazar, teens—Arabs, Africans, and a few French—drink cheap beer in blue-lit murk and dance to the rumble-and-slash beat of NTM (*Nique Ta Mère*—"Fuck Your Mother") played by the DJ, Cash, a young Frenchman dressed in gangsta getup.

The kids in the *quartiers* have embraced black American culture and American rappers are idolized; their thumping verse of protest suits the anger of the second generation, but gangsta rap is winning out, eroding the old ways. One can imagine a time when the second generation will resent the illegals sneaking off boats and bringing with them the Third World, "immigrant" ways of the casbahs and villages.

Jeffrey Tayler is the author of Facing the Congo *and* Siberian Dawn: A Journey Across the New Russia, *and is a frequent contributor to* Harper's Magazine.

PART FIVE

THE LAST WORD

* * *

Tomatoes

Long live the Provençal sense of humor!

I saw Monsieur Noyer out of the corner of my eye, approaching me. It was a warm day in mid-June. The sun splashed down on the empty square. I was in the midst of loading my car with my hoe, rake, shovel and other tools, getting ready to go to the garden.

"Eh, Richard," Monsieur Noyer said when he reached me. "And the garden? How goes it?"

"It's going very well, Monsieur Noyer," I said. "Very well. I'm working hard."

"And your tomatoes?" he went on. "Do you have any tomatoes yet?"

"No, not yet." I smiled at his little dig. It was much too early to have tomatoes. "No tomatoes yet. But the plants look good. And they're growing."

He raised his hand, a thick farmer's paw, and tipped back his hat. This sixty-plus-year-old French farmer was a far better gardener than I probably would ever be, but there was a kind of rivalry going on here. Perhaps that is much too presumptuous. But there was something territorial at least. He was, remember, acknowledged to be St.-Sébastien's best gardener.

"Have you treated your tomato plants?" he asked.

At the far edge of the big square, and bathed in cool morning shadows, was Monsieur Noyer's pleasant house. Out on the terrace I could see his wife, Madame Noyer, a short, slightly bent woman, busy with something. Every so often she stopped and regarded us, leaning forward and straining, unsuccessfully, to hear what we were saying. Then she would resume her work.

"Uh, no," I answered. "Do I have to?"

He let out a low whistle. Then he cleared his throat. "You haven't treated your tomato plants with sulphur?" he asked.

"Sulphur?"

"Sulphur. Yes."

"What's that for? Insects?"

"No. No. The treatment is for disease."

"Oh."

He examined me. Then he sniffled and rubbed his mouth with the back of his enormous hand. He looked up at the sky.

"Well...to work," he said as a way of saying goodbye. He turned and walked away. After a few steps he paused and looked back.

"You will see, Richard," he said, pointing a low finger. "Gardening is an art. An art."

He walked off. His wife stopped her work and watched him approach the house. I was left standing there, in the empty square, full of doubts. Doubts about my tomato plants.

This wasn't the first time we had talked about my tomatoes. Each time we did, it made me nervous. There was usually something slightly cautionary in Monsieur Noyer's tone. He was never malicious, but he acted as if he knew something I didn't. Of course, since I knew almost nothing, it didn't take much effort to make me feel that way. I think he was just probably suspicious that I, as an American, could be serious about gardening—which to him was indeed a serious matter. I respected that. But whatever the reason, these impromptu meetings we had from time to time always left me anxious. I tried to avoid Monsieur Noyer without seeming rude.

The irony was that when it came to the produce from his own garden, he and his wife were extremely generous. They were always handing us sprawling heads of lettuce and other vegetables, or leaving these delights just outside our door. They even gave us some artichokes once, a lovely treat, since they didn't have many. Still, I have to confess that I wanted to outshine Monsieur Noyer in some small effort—peppers, maybe. I felt competitive, and that was not good, not when it was about a garden. I learned a small, unpleasant truth about myself through Monsieur Noyer.

Tomatoes. I was thinking about tomatoes.

For some reason, everyone in the village saw tomatoes as the benchmark for determining the success of my garden, or any garden. Anyone in St.-Sébastien who asked about my garden, and many of them did, inevitably asked me about my tomatoes.

Hey, Richard! How many tomato plants did you plant? Twenty? All hybrids? Ah, well. I don't know. You may get a few.

Richard. How far apart did you plant your tomatoes? Oh? Really? Hmmm.

Richard, just remember. If your tomatoes don't grow, you can have some of ours. We'll have plenty.

Why tomatoes? I suppose because tomatoes are the one thing any serious gardener is expected to grow and one which, ultimately, is not that difficult to grow. And it's emblematic of the south of France. You must have tomatoes if you have a summer garden here—fat, nearly obese, crimson things that have a wonderful weight in the hand. Dark, ripe tomatoes that, reeking with the sun, heat and land, are the essence of summer and one of its chief joys. Of course, tomatoes!

Believe me, I watched my tomato plants well. I plucked tiny, errant sprouts from the crotches of the stalks. I attached the vines to my bamboo at regular intervals, careful not to cut off the circulation with too tight a knot in the rag when I did. I dug up the earth around the plants to make it easier for them to breathe and accept water. I even treated them with sulphur as Monsieur Noyer said I should, something I wasn't enthusiastic about doing. (It was, in fact, the only chemical I ever used in my garden. But since every gardener in St.-Sébastien used it, I did, too.) There was hardly a time when I wasn't thinking about my tomato plants, or tending them.

Once in a while, I would take a villager to my garden to get his opinion on how I was doing. If he didn't say anything much, why, I assumed I wasn't doing anything radically wrong. No one ever looked at my tomato plants and screamed, Oh, my God! What have you done? (Not that that would be their style.) I wanted to show off, too. Over here, I wanted to tell them. Just take a look at these tomato plants. Twenty of them. They're healthy-looking, and they're growing nicely. Not too bad for an American in France. And I believe I will have tomatoes, in August, like you.

In late June, a week or so after my conversation with Monsieur Noyer, I drove my car one morning to the garden to do some weeding and grading. By then I had made the trip scores and scores of times, but I still always enjoyed it. The morning air was sweet and cool. I had my bucket and tools with me, the windows open. I passed by farmers on their way to and from the vineyards. Some ambled slowly by on their tractors, others went by in battered old cars they used for the fields. I waved to them, and they waved back. I honked the horn as I passed by Jules's house. His mother was hanging out the wash. She turned and looked toward the sound slightly mystified, then waved as she recognized my car. I picked up speed as I left the village.

I reached the familiar little bridge and turned off the road onto the lane next to the vineyard. I stopped at my usual place, took out my tools, and walked over the edge of the bank. I walked down the steps Jules had fashioned out of the earth and then over the heavy planks I had placed across the stream and which I had christened Pont de Jules, Jules's Bridge. As I did, the sleek frogs that had been sunbathing on the planks fled into the water. I walked over to the rise at the edge of the plateau. I was eager to see what progress my plants had made. I was expectant, as always.

I climbed the second set of steps, reached the garden and blinked my eyes. I blinked again. Then my heart skipped a beat. Each one of my twenty tomato plants had a ripe red tomato there at its base! I couldn't believe it. I had tomatoes! You could see them. It was a miracle!

I shouted "Tomatoes!" in the air. The word resounded into the heavens. Then I put my bucket down and ran over to the far side of the garden where all the tomato plants were. I had tomatoes. In June! As I came closer, though, something inside me started doubting. Isn't it a bit odd, a small voice inside me said, that every one of the twenty plants has produced a single ripe tomato? And only one? And that each tomato is at exactly the same place?

Suddenly, I realized someone had put them all there.

I laughed. I laughed so hard I nearly fell down. What a trick! I got to the plants, and, yes, it was true. Someone had obviously gone to the store, bought twenty ripe tomatoes— from Spain, no doubt—and placed them neatly one by one at the base of each of my plants. American needs help. Bad. With his tomatoes. I looked around quickly to see if the culprit was there, hiding behind a bush, stifling a laugh. I saw there was more to this. That same person had placed tin cans of string beans on each side of my bean plants. I looked at those cans with their labels displaying cut, juicy string beans, and I laughed again. This was amazingly, heroically funny. This was genius.

I had to show Iggy [the author's girlfriend] this master-piece, this astonishing visual drollness. I didn't touch a thing. I wanted her to see everything exactly as I did. The joke was on me, and I loved it.

Who had done this?

I went back to St.-Sébastien, thinking about that question the entire way. It mystified me. The joke was so witty, so dry, and that was not typical of the villagers. Or maybe it was. Maybe I had underestimated them, didn't really know them that well at all. I went and found Iggy and told her we had to go to the garden, now. I wouldn't tell her why. When we got there, I made her cover her eyes as I led her up the stairs. Then I showed her. She was just as fooled as I was for a minute. I could tell by her eyes. Then she walked closer and saw the set-up. "*Nou, zeg!*" she said in Dutch. Now, say! She automatically reverted to Dutch when something took her by surprise. Then she laughed. It was still as funny as when I saw it the first time. Tomato, tomato, tomato. Twenty ripe tomatoes, all in a row.

We speculated as to who had done it. We could only think of one name.

"Eugéne," we both said at once. Eugéne was Jules's younger brother. He was a habitual and determined trickster.

We drove back to the village and, after a short search, we found Eugéne.

"Eugéne, did you do this?" I asked.

"Do what?"

"You know," Iggy said to him.

"I don't know what."

"Come on," we said.

"You're both crazy."

Eugéne denied our accusations so convincingly, we decided it couldn't be him. We told the story to all the villagers we saw and asked them if they knew who had done it. No one knew. But they were amused. Very amused.

We ran into Monsieur Vasquez, who was patrolling the town square as usual, chewing on his small wooden stick and limping slowly along.

"Monsieur Vasquez," I asked, "have you heard anything about the ripe tomatoes in our garden?"

"Tomatoes? Ripe? No."

"Not one word?" Iggy probed.

"No."

"Well, if you do, let us know, will you?" I said.

"Yes." He looked at us oddly.

We ran into Nasim. He knew nothing, but laughed loudly, showing his blackened teeth unreservedly when we explained the situation in our garden. I even asked Albin Polge, the mayor, if he had any ideas about this, but he shook his head, seriously, no. He offered to make an inquiry over the loud-speaker—which was perched atop the town hall—at noon, the customary time for announcements, but I declined. He rubbed his chin with his hand speculatively and said, more to himself, "Ripe tomatoes." Then he produced a slight smile. The mayor had a dry sense of humor.

Did Rémy, who lived next to Marcel Lécot, know? No. Did Monsieur Valcoze? No. But he did want to talk to me about another matter.... Did Sully Valcoze know? Why, no, Richard, no. By the way, he asked in his woody voice, how was the garden?

All the people we talked to, and we talked to quite a few in the next two hours, knew nothing. What a mystery!

A little later, still in the dark as to who had done this, I saw Monsieur Noyer. I was in front of the house with Iggy, unloading the car, when I saw him approach. I paused and waited for him to arrive.

"Eh, Richard," he said, tipping his hat back. "And your garden? How goes it?"

"Beautiful, Monsieur Noyer," I said, almost routinely. Then something struck me like a thunderbolt. I waited a beat. "I've got tomatoes," I said to him. "Ripe tomatoes. Now."

He blinked. Then he had such a childlike look of open disappointment, I was almost sorry I'd said it.

"Tomatoes, you say?" he said. "Ripe?"

"Absolutely," I said. "And not just one, twenty of them."

"Oh?" he said. "Twenty? Really? Very good."

He couldn't conceal on his face what this information meant to him. Iggy saw this. She nudged me in the ribs.

"You've got to tell him the truth," she whispered forcefully in English. "Now. Just look at his face!"

Do I have to? I thought. Oh, what a low character I am!

But of course I told him. I told him it was all a joke someone had played on me. That in fact I didn't have any tomatoes, not even one. When he heard this, he shifted easily and quickly back to his familiar, commanding presence. Everything was all right again. The world was exactly as it should be.

We finally found out who had done it. Laurent Imbert! The most unlikely person in the whole village. A calm, introverted man who, though very pleasant to us, never displayed much of a sense of humor—much less such an elaborate one. But it was he. True, Iggy had worked for him harvesting asparagus, but we hadn't thought to call him till last. I hardly knew him. But we cornered him on the telephone. When he was still at the stage of good-naturedly denying he had placed the tomatoes there, I said to him:

"Well, if you didn't put them there, how did they get there?"

He waited a long beat, his timing perfect. "Perhaps," he said deadpan, "they are a new variety."

When I stopped laughing, I had the presence of mind to ask him if he needed any "ripe" tomatoes. No, he said, quite evenly, no, he didn't. I could hear his wife laughing in the background.

I never thought the same way about the villagers again. I certainly learned that some of them could be very funny. Oddly, I never thought to ask Laurent why he had done this. It didn't occur to me! I just thought it was funny. I'm sure he thought it was, too. That he didn't know me too well, and still chose my garden to act out his joke, I found endearing. My "ripe" tomatoes went on to become legendary in the village. I was always asked—by men, women and even children in St.-Sébastien—if my tomatoes were ripe yet, usually followed immediately by a hand placed to the mouth to stifle laughter. I didn't mind. Why should I? Wasn't teasing a form of affection?

But, oh, Monsieur Noyer, I ask your forgiveness now! Pardon me for taking advantage of you, for seizing what surely was a once-in-a-lifetime moment. Just for the briefest time I had you believing *l'américain* had outdone you. That somehow, I, the American, had pulled off a tomato miracle in St.-Sébastien de Caisson!

Richard Goodman is a freelance writer who lives in New York. Raised in Virginia and Michigan, he has lived in many other cities including Detroit, Chicago, Boston, and Paris. He is the author of French Dirt: The Story of a Garden in the South of France, *from which this story was excerpted.*

Index

Index of Contributors

257

Acknowledgments

It has been a pleasure to work with Tara Weaver on this project. I appreciate her dedication and energy in the research and editing of this book. I would also like to thank my family and friends for their usual forbearance while I put a book together. Thanks also to Larry Habegger, Sean O'Reilly, Tim O'Reilly, Susan Brady, Krista Holmstrom, Patty Holden, Michele Wetherbee, and Judy Johnson for their support and contributions to the book.

—James O'Reilly

A huge thank you to the wonderful people of Travelers' Tales—past and present—who are proof positive that travelers make the best friends. Thank you to James O'Reilly for letting me be his Provençal partner, to Susan Brady for making sure the trains run on time—and her wicked sense of humor. Thank you to my mother, whose love and support is unwavering and astounding; to my brother, whose humor lightens my life; and to Amanda, who has enriched and enlarged our family. Thank you to my friends near and far, who remind me what it is all about, and make the experience worthwhile. Thank you to Violeta Richards, friend extraordinaire, for her assistance with all things French and other acts of mischief. Finally, in memory of Amanda Davis, for lessons in the art of life.

—Tara Austen Weaver

Introduction by Richard Goodman published with permission from the author. Copyright © 2003 by Richard Goodman.

"Aix-en-Provence" by M.F.K. Fisher excerpted from *Two Towns in Provence* by M.F.K. Fisher. Copyright © 1964, 1977, 1978 by M.F.K. Fisher. Used by permission of Vintage Books, a division of Random House, Inc.

"The Dangers of Provence" by Peter Mayle first appeared in SALON.com at http://www.salon.com. Copyright © 1997 by Peter Mayle. Reprinted by permission of William Morris Agency, Inc, on behalf of the author.

"The Shepherd's Mantra" by Francesca Rheannon published with permission from the author. Copyright © 2003 by Francesca Rheannon.

"Provençal Dawn" by Lawrence Durrell excerpted from *Provence* by Lawrence Durrell. Copyright © 1990 by Lawrence Durrell. Reprinted by permission of Arcade Publishing.

"The Baker" by Connie Barney Wilson published with permission from the author. Copyright © 2003 by Connie Barney Wilson.

"Relish the Rhone" by Clive Irving originally appeared in *Condé Nast Traveler*. Copyright © 1995 by Condé Nast Publications, Inc. Reprinted by permission. All Rights Reserved.

"Pressing the Olive" by Carol Drinkwater excerpted from *The Olive Farm: A Memoir of Life, Love, and Olive Oil in the South of France* by Carol Drinkwater. Copyright © 2001 by Carol Drinkwater. Published in the U.S. by The Overlook Press, Woodstock, NY 12498. Reprinted by permission.

"Days of Pastis and Lavender" by Yvone Lenard reprinted from *The Magic of Provence: Pleasures of Southern France* by Yvone Lenard. Copyright © 2000 by Yvone Lenard. Published by Elysian Editions, an imprint of Princeton Book Company, Publishers. Reprinted by permission.

"Winemaking in the Lubéron" by Piers Letcher published with permission from the author. Copyright © 2003 by Piers Letcher.

"On Eye-Opening Art" by Alain de Botton excerpted from *The Art of Travel* by Alain de Botton. Copyright © 2002 by Alain de Botton. Reprinted by permission of Random House, Inc.

"Cassis" by Kermit Lynch excerpted from *Adventures on the Wine Route: A Wine Buyer's Tour of France* by Kermit Lynch. Copyright © 1988 by Kermit Lynch. Reprinted by permission of Farrar, Strauss & Giroux, Inc.

"Hidden Among the Hills" by Olivia Gatti Taylor published with permission from the author. Copyright © 2003 by Olivia Gatti Taylor.

"Naturally Baked" by Claire Berlinski published with permission from the author. Copyright © 2003 by Claire Berlinski.

"Loving the Middle Ages" by Jo Broyles Yohay published with permission from the author. Copyright © 1995 by Jo Broyles Yohay.

"Côte d'Azur" by Don George first appeared in SALON.com, at http://www.salon.com. An online version remains in the SALON archives. Reprinted with permission.

"*Sportif!*" by Geoff Drake reprinted from Volume 37 of *Bicycling* magazine. Copyright © 1996. Reprinted by permission of Rodale, Inc.

"*Taureau, Taureau!*" by Indu Sundaresan published with permission from the author. Copyright © 2003 by Indu Sundaresan.

"More Cheese, Please" by Julie Jindal published with permission from the author. Copyright © 2003 by Julie Jindal.

"*Routes de Lavande*" by Patricia Cleveland-Peck originally appeared as "Travel: France—On the Scent of the Routes de la Lavande" in the April 15, 2001 issue of *The London Independent*. Copyright © 2001.

"Beyond the Côte d'Azur" by Deborah Abello published with permission from the author. Copyright © 2003 by Deborah Abello.

"Spies, Salads, Old Cars, and French In-Laws" by Laura Higgins Florand published with permission from the author. Copyright © 2003 by Laura Higgins Florand.

"A Double Surprise" by D-L Nelson published with permission from the author. Copyright © 2003 by D-L Nelson.

"Christmas in Provence" by Yvonne Michie Horn published with permission from the author. Copyright © 2003 by Yvonne Michie Horn.

"Problem-Solving in Aix" by Rosemary Lloyd published with permission from the author. Copyright © 2003 by Rosemary Lloyd.

"How to Tame a Tarask" by Miranda Mowbray published with permission from the author. Copyright © 2003 by Miranda Mowbray.

"The Saints and Spectres of the Alpilles" by Constance Hale published with permission from the author. Copyright © 2003 by Constance Hale.

"The Provençal Sky" by Michele Anna Jordan published with permission from the author. Copyright © 2003 by Michele Anna Jordan.

"Another French Revolution" by Jeffrey Tayler excerpted from the November 2000 issue of *Harper's Magazine*. Copyright © 2000 by *Harper's Magazine*. All rights reserved.

"Tomatoes" by Richard Goodman excerpted from *French Dirt: The Story of a Garden in the South of France* by Richard Goodman. Copyright © 1991 by Richard Goodman. Reprinted by permission of Algonquin Books of Chapel Hill, a division of Workman Publishing, and Darhansoff & Verrill.

Additional Credits (arranged alphabetically by title)

Selection from *Adventures in Wine: True Stories of Vineyards and Vintages Around the World* edited by Thom Elkjer copyright © 2002 by Thom Elkjer. Reprinted by permission of Travelers' Tales, Inc.

Selection from *Guesses at Truth* by J.C. and A. Hare published in 1847.

Selection from "Herbs de Provence" by Garry Marchant published with permission from the author. Copyright © 2003 by Garry Marchant.

Selection from "Hiking in Provence" by Margie Goldsmith published with permission from the author. Copyright © 2003 by Margie Goldsmith.

Selection from *The Hills and the Sea* by Hilaire Belloc published in 1902.

Selection from "*L'Amoureuese de Moustiers*" by Ethel F. Mussen published with permission from the author. Copyright © 2003 by Ethel F. Mussen.

Selection from "La Colombe d'Or" by Don George first appeared in SALON.com, at http://www.salon.com An online version remains in the SALON archives.

Selection from *A Little Tour in France* by Henry James published in 1899.

Selection from "My Private Riviera" by Don George first appeared in SALON.com, at http://www.salon.com An online version remains in the SALON archives.

Selection from "The Perfect Meal" by Joan Haladay published with permission from the author. Copyright © 2003 by Joan Haladay.

Selection from *Pictures from Italy* by Charles Dickens published in 1846.

Selection from "Postcards from Provence" by Joyce Gregory Wyels published with permission from the author. Copyright © 2003 by Joyce Gregory Wyels.

Selections from *Provence* by Lawrence Durrell copyright © 1990 by Lawrence Durrell. Reprinted by permission of Arcade Publishing.

Selection from "Sleepless in Aix" by Margaret McColley published with permission from the author. Copyright © 2003 by Margaret McColley.

Selection from "*Spécialité Provençal*" by Susan Tiberghien originally appeared in *Two Worlds Walking*, edited by Diane Glancy and C.W. Truesdale. Published with permission from the author. Copyright © 2003 by Susan Tiberghien.

Selection from "St.-Tropez" by Herbert Gold originally appeared in the June 1988 issue of *Travel & Leisure*. Copyright © 1988 by Herbert Gold. Reprinted by permission of the author.

Selection from *Travelers' Tales France* by James O'Reilly reprinted by permission of Travelers' Tales, Inc. Copyright © 1995 by Travelers' Tales, Inc.

Selection from *Travelers' Tales France* by Sean O'Reilly reprinted by permission of Travelers' Tales, Inc. Copyright © 1995 by Travelers' Tales, Inc.

Selection from *Travels with Lady Hester Stanhope* by Charles Lewis Meryon published in 1846.

Selections from *Van Gogh and Friends* by Wenda O'Reilly, Ph.D. reprinted by permission of Birdcage Books. Copyright © 2002 by Wenda O'Reilly.

Selection from "A Vegetarian in Provence" by Cassandra Dunn published with permission from the author. Copyright © 2003 by Cassandra Dunn.

About the Editors

James O'Reilly, president and co-publisher of Travelers' Tales, wrote mystery serials before becoming a travel writer in the early 1980s. He's visited more than forty countries, along the way meditating with monks in Tibet, participating in West African voodoo rituals, and hanging out the laundry with nuns in Florence. He travels extensively with his wife Wenda and their three daughters. They live in Palo Alto, California when they're not in Leavenworth, Washington.

Born to traveler parents, Tara Austen Weaver crossed her first international border at five weeks of age. She has since lived in London, San Francisco, Vienna, high in the mountains of central Japan, and on a small island off the coast of western Canada. When not dreaming of future travel, she works, plays, and writes near the beach, on the foggy side of San Francisco.

TRAVELERS' TALES

THE SOUL OF TRAVEL

Footsteps Series

THE FIRE NEVER DIES
**One Man's Raucous Romp
Down the Road of Food,
Passion, and Adventure**
By Richard Sterling
ISBN 1-885-211-70-8
$14.95

"Sterling's writing is like spit-
fire, foursquare and jazzy with crackle...."
—Kirkus Reviews

ONE YEAR OFF
**Leaving It All Behind for a
Round-the-World Journey
with Our Children**
By David Elliot Cohen
ISBN 1-885-211-65-1
$14.95

A once-in-a-lifetime
adventure generously shared.

TAKE ME
WITH YOU
**A Round-the-World
Journey to Invite a
Stranger Home**
By Brad Newsham
ISBN 1-885-211-51-1
$24.00 (cloth)

"Newsham is an ideal guide. His journey, at
heart, is into humanity." —Pico Iyer, author
of *Video Night in Kathmandu*

THE SWORD
OF HEAVEN
**A Five Continent Odyssey
to Save the World**
By Mikkel Aaland
ISBN 1-885-211-44-9
$24.00 (cloth)

"Few books capture the soul
of the road like *The Sword of Heaven*,
a sharp-edged, beautifully rendered memoir
that will inspire anyone." —Phil Cousineau,
author of *The Art of Pilgrimage*

LAST TROUT
IN VENICE
**The Far-Flung Escapades
of an Accidental
Adventurer**
By Doug Lansky
ISBN 1-885-211-63-5
$14.95

"Traveling with Doug Lansky might result in
a considerably shortened life expectancy...but
what a way to go." —Tony Wheeler,
Lonely Planet Publications

THE WAY OF
THE WANDERER
**Discover Your True Self
Through Travel**
By David Yeadon
ISBN 1-885-211-60-0
$14.95

Experience transformation through travel
with this delightful, illustrated collection by
award-winning author David Yeadon.

KITE STRINGS OF
THE SOUTHERN
CROSS
**A Woman's
Travel Odyssey**
By Laurie Gough
ISBN 1-885-211-54-6
$14.95 —★*★*★—

*ForeWord Silver Medal Winner
—Travel Book of the Year*

STORM
**A Motorcycle Journey
of Love, Endurance,
and Transformation**
By Allen Noren
ISBN 1-885-211-45-7
$24.00 (cloth) —★*★*★—

*ForeWord Gold Medal Winner
—Travel Book of the Year*

Women's Travel

A WOMAN'S PASSION FOR TRAVEL
More True Stories from A Woman's World
*Edited by Marybeth Bond
& Pamela Michael*
ISBN 1-885-211-36-8
$17.95

"A diverse and gripping series of stories!" —Arlene Blum, author of
Annapurna: A Woman's Place

A WOMAN'S WORLD
True Stories of Life on the Road
*Edited by Marybeth Bond
Introduction by
Dervla Murphy*
ISBN 1-885-211-06-6
$17.95

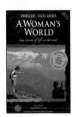

— ★ ★ ★ —

***Winner of the Lowell Thomas
Award for Best Travel Book—
Society of American Travel Writers***

WOMEN IN THE WILD
True Stories of Adventure and Connection
Edited by Lucy McCauley
ISBN 1-885-211-21-X
$17.95

"A spiritual, moving, and totally female book to take you
around the world and back." —*Mademoiselle*

A MOTHER'S WORLD
Journeys of the Heart
*Edited by Marybeth Bond
& Pamela Michael*
ISBN 1-885-211-26-0
$14.95

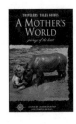

"These stories remind us that motherhood is one of the great unifying forces
in the world" —*San Francisco Examiner*

Food

ADVENTURES IN WINE
True Stories of Vineyards and Vintages around the World
Edited by Thom Elkjer
ISBN 1-885-211-80-5
$17.95

Humanity, community, and brotherhood comprise the marvelous virtues of
the wine world. This collection toasts the warmth and wonders of this large, extended
family in stories by travelers who are wine novices and experts alike.

FOOD (Updated)
A Taste of the Road
*Edited by Richard Sterling
Introduction by Margo True*
ISBN 1-885-211-77-5
$18.95

— ★ ★ ★ —

***Silver Medal Winner of the
Lowell Thomas Award for
Best Travel Book—Society
of American Travel Writers***

HER FORK IN THE ROAD
Women Celebrate Food and Travel
Edited by Lisa Bach
ISBN 1-885-211-71-6
$16.95

A savory sampling of stories by some of the best writers
in and out of the food and travel fields.

THE ADVENTURE OF FOOD
True Stories of Eating Everything
Edited by Richard Sterling
ISBN 1-885-211-37-6
$17.95

"These stories are bound to whet appetites for more
than food."

—*Publishers Weekly*

Spiritual Travel

THE SPIRITUAL GIFTS OF TRAVEL
The Best of Travelers' Tales
Edited by James O'Reilly and Sean O'Reilly
ISBN 1-885-211-69-4
$16.95
A collection of favorite

stories of transformation on the road from our award-winning Travelers' Tales series that shows the myriad ways travel indelibly alters our inner landscapes.

THE WAY OF THE WANDERER
Discover Your True Self Through Travel
By David Yeadon
ISBN 1-885-211-60-0
$14.95
Experience transformation through travel with this delightful, illustrated col-

lection by award-winning author David Yeadon.

PILGRIMAGE
Adventures of the Spirit
Edited by Sean O'Reilly & James O'Reilly
Introduction by Phil Cousineau
ISBN 1-885-211-56-2
$16.95

—★*★—

*ForeWord Silver Medal Winner
— Travel Book of the Year*

A WOMAN'S PATH
Women's Best Spiritual Travel Writing
Edited by Lucy McCauley, Amy G. Carlson & Jennifer Leo
ISBN 1-885-211-48-1
$16.95
"A sensitive exploration of

women's lives that have been unexpectedly and spiritually touched by travel experiences.... Highly recommended."
— *Library Journal*

THE ROAD WITHIN
True Stories of Transformation and the Soul
Edited by Sean O'Reilly, James O'Reilly & Tim O'Reilly
ISBN 1-885-211-19-8
$17.95

—★*★—

Best Spiritual Book — Independent Publisher's Book Award

THE ULTIMATE JOURNEY
Inspiring Stories of Living and Dying
James O'Reilly, Sean O'Reilly & Richard Sterling
ISBN 1-885-211-38-4
$17.95
"A glorious collection of

writings about the ultimate adventure. A book to keep by one's bedside—and close to one's heart." —Philip Zaleski, editor, *The Best Spiritual Writing series*

Adventure

TESTOSTERONE PLANET
True Stories from a Man's World
Edited by Sean O'Reilly, Larry Habegger & James O'Reilly
ISBN 1-885-211-43-0
$17.95

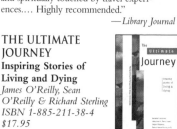

Thrills and laughter with some of today's best writers: Sebastian Junger, Tim Cahill, Bill Bryson, and Jon Krakauer.

DANGER!
True Stories of Trouble and Survival
Edited by James O'Reilly, Larry Habegger & Sean O'Reilly
ISBN 1-885-211-32-5
$17.95
"Exciting...for those who

enjoy living on the edge or prefer to read the survival stories of others, this is a good pick."
— *Library Journal*

Special Interest

365 TRAVEL
A Daily Book of Journeys, Meditations, and Adventures
Edited by Lisa Bach
ISBN 1-885-211-67-8
$14.95
An illuminating collection of travel wisdom and adventures that reminds us all of the lessons we learn while on the road.

THE GIFT OF RIVERS
True Stories of Life on the Water
Edited by Pamela Michael
Introduction by Robert Hass
ISBN 1-885-211-42-2
$14.95
"*The Gift of Rivers* is a soulful compendium of wonderful stories that illuminate, educate, inspire, and delight."
—David Brower, Chairman of Earth Island Institute

FAMILY TRAVEL
The Farther You Go, the Closer You Get
Edited by Laura Manske
ISBN 1-885-211-33-3
$17.95
"This is family travel at its finest." —*Working Mother*

LOVE & ROMANCE
True Stories of Passion on the Road
Edited by Judith Babcock Wylie
ISBN 1-885-211-18-X
$17.95
"A wonderful book to read by a crackling fire."
—*Romantic Traveling*

THE GIFT OF BIRDS
True Encounters with Avian Spirits
Edited by Larry Habegger & Amy G. Carlson
ISBN 1-885-211-41-4
$17.95
"These are all wonderful, entertaining stories offering a *bird's-eye view!* of our avian friends."
—*Booklist*

A DOG'S WORLD
True Stories of Man's Best Friend on the Road
Edited by Christine Hunsicker
ISBN 1-885-211-23-6
$12.95
This extraordinary collection includes stories by John Steinbeck, Helen Thayer, James Herriot, Pico Iyer, and many others.

THE GIFT OF TRAVEL
The Best of Travelers' Tales
Edited by Larry Habegger, James O'Reilly & Sean O'Reilly
ISBN 1-885-211-25-2
$14.95
"Like gourmet chefs in a French market, the editors of Travelers' Tales pick, sift, and prod their way through the weighty shelves of contemporary travel writing, creaming off the very best."
—William Dalrymple, author of *City of Djinns*

Travel Advice

SHITTING PRETTY
How to Stay Clean and Healthy While Traveling
By Dr. Jane Wilson-Howarth
ISBN 1-885-211-47-3
$12.95

A light-hearted book about a serious subject for millions of travelers— staying healthy on the road—written by international health expert, Dr. Jane Wilson-Howarth.

THE FEARLESS SHOPPER
How to Get the Best Deals on the Planet
By Kathy Borrus
ISBN 1-885-211-39-2
$14.95

"Anyone who reads *The Fearless Shopper* will come away a smarter, more responsible shopper and a more curious, culturally attuned traveler."
—Jo Mancuso, *The Shopologist*

GUTSY WOMEN
More Travel Tips and Wisdom for the Road
By Marybeth Bond
ISBN 1-885-211-61-9
$12.95

Second Edition—Packed with funny, instructive, and inspiring advice for women heading out to see the world.

SAFETY AND SECURITY FOR WOMEN WHO TRAVEL
By Sheila Swan & Peter Laufer
ISBN 1-885-211-29-5
$12.95

A must for every woman traveler!

THE FEARLESS DINER
Travel Tips and Wisdom for Eating around the World
By Richard Sterling
ISBN 1-885-211-22-8
$7.95

Combines practical advice on foodstuffs, habits, and etiquette, with hilarious accounts of others' eating adventures.

THE PENNY PINCHER'S PASSPORT TO LUXURY TRAVEL
The Art of Cultivating Preferred Customer Status
By Joel L. Widzer
ISBN 1-885-211-31-7
$12.95

Proven techniques on how to travel first class at discount prices, even if you're not a frequent flyer.

GUTSY MAMAS
Travel Tips and Wisdom for Mothers on the Road
By Marybeth Bond
ISBN 1-885-211-20-1
$7.95

A delightful guide for mothers traveling with their children— or without them!

Destination Titles:
True Stories of Life on the Road

AMERICA
Edited by Fred Setterberg
ISBN 1-885-211-28-7
$19.95

FRANCE (Updated)
Edited by James O'Reilly,
Larry Habegger &
Sean O'Reilly
ISBN 1-885-211-73-2
$18.95

AMERICAN SOUTHWEST
Edited by Sean O'Reilly
& James O'Reilly
ISBN 1-885-211-58-9
$17.95

GRAND CANYON
Edited by Sean O'Reilly,
James O'Reilly &
Larry Habegger
ISBN 1-885-211-34-1
$17.95

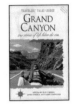

AUSTRALIA
Edited by Larry Habegger
ISBN 1-885-211-40-6
$17.95

GREECE
Edited by Larry Habegger,
Sean O'Reilly &
Brian Alexander
ISBN 1-885-211-52-X
$17.95

BRAZIL
Edited by Annette Haddad
& Scott Doggett
Introduction by Alex
Shoumatoff
ISBN 1-885-211-11-2
$17.95

HAWAI'I
Edited by Rick &
Marcie Carroll
ISBN 1-885-211-35-X
$17.95

CENTRAL AMERICA
Edited by Larry Habegger
& Natanya Pearlman
ISBN 1-885-211-74-0
$17.95

HONG KONG
Edited by James O'Reilly,
Larry Habegger &
Sean O'Reilly
ISBN 1-885-211-03-1
$17.95

CUBA
Edited by Tom Miller
ISBN 1-885-211-62-7
$17.95

INDIA
Edited by James O'Reilly
& Larry Habegger
ISBN 1-885-211-01-5
$17.95

IRELAND
Edited by James O'Reilly,
Larry Habegger &
Sean O'Reilly
ISBN 1-885-211-46-5
$17.95

SAN FRANCISCO
Edited by James O'Reilly,
Larry Habegger &
Sean O'Reilly
ISBN 1-885-211-08-2
$17.95

ITALY (Updated)
Edited by Anne Calcagno
Introduction by Jan Morris
ISBN 1-885-211-72-4
$18.95

SPAIN (Updated)
Edited by Lucy McCauley
ISBN 1-885-211-78-3
$19.95

JAPAN
Edited by Donald W. George
& Amy G. Carlson
ISBN 1-885-211-04-X
$17.95

THAILAND (Updated)
Edited by James O'Reilly
& Larry Habegger
ISBN 1-885-211-75-9
$18.95

MEXICO (Updated)
Edited by James O'Reilly
& Larry Habegger
ISBN 1-885-211-59-7
$17.95

TIBET
Edited by James O'Reilly,
Larry Habegger, & Kim
Morris
ISBN 1-885-211-76-7
$18.95

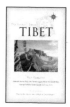

NEPAL
Edited by Rajendra
S. Khadka
ISBN 1-885-211-14-7
$17.95

TUSCANY
Edited by James O'Reilly, &
Tara Austen Weaver
ISBN 1-885-211-68-6
$16.95

PARIS
Edited by James O'Reilly,
Larry Habegger &
Sean O'Reilly
ISBN 1-885-211-10-4
$17.95